2000

ETHICS AND JUSTICE IN ORGANISATIONS

For My Parents

and

Alan and Alexander

Ethics and Justice in Organisations

A Normative-Empirical Dialogue

M. SINGER
Department of Psychology
University of Canterbury
New Zealand

Ashgate

Aldershot • Brookfield USA • Singapore • Sydney

Published by
Ashgate Publishing Limited,
Gower House,
Croft Road,
Aldershot,
Hants GU11 3HR,
England

Ashgate Publishing Company,
Old Post Road,
Brookfield,
Vermont 05036,
USA

Ashgate website:http://www.ashgate.com

Reprinted 1999

British Library Cataloguing in Publication Data
Singer, M.S.
      Ethics and justice in organisations : a normative-empirical
      dialogue. - (Avebury series in philosophy)
      1. Business ethics 2. Business enterprises - Moral and
      ethical aspects
      I. Title
      174.4

Library of Congress Catalog Card Number: 96-79370

ISBN 1 85972 609 7

Printed in Great Britain by Biddles Limited
Guildford and King's Lynn

Contents

Chapter 1   Introduction   1

Part 1   Normative, Empirical, and Applied Ethics and Justice:
                 Theories and Domains   7

Chapter 2   Philosophical literature on ethics and justice   9

                 Philosophy of ethics   9
                     Classical philosophy of ethics   11
                     Modern philosophy of ethics   14
                 Philosophy of justice   24
                     Classical philosophy of justice   25
                     Modern philosophy of justice   27
                 Postmodern philosophy of ethics and justice   30
                 Major issues of debate in the philosophy of ethics and
                 justice   32

Chapter 3   Psychological literature on ethics and justice   35

                 Moral psychology   35
                 Psychology of justice   43
                     Distributive or outcome justice theories   44
                     Process or procedural justice theories   52
                 Recent advances in the psychology of ethics and justice   57

Chapter 4   Ethics and justice applied to professional behaviour   63

                 Historical roots of the free-market ideology   64
                 On-Going Issues of debate in business ethics   67
                 Emerging themes of business ethics   71
                 Models of moral judgements, moral values and ethical
                 decision-making in business ethics   75
                     Ethical decision models in marketing   86
                 A postmodern approach to ethical decision-making in
                 business   90

Part 2	**A Normative-Empirical Dialogue**	93
Chapter 5	**Ethics and justice: The roles of philosophy and empirical sciences**	95
	Normative versus empirical approaches to ethics and justice	96
	Existing research attempting a normative-empirical dialogue	104
	The factual status of normative assumptions	104
	The interrelationship among standards of morality	108
Chapter 6	**Ethics and justice in organisational recruitment and selection**	121
	Dialogue concerning justifications for and empirical evidence on selection practices	123
	Justifications for diversity versus merit selection	123
	Empirical studies of people's reactions to justifications for merit versus diversity selection	127
	Dialogue concerning the "rightness or goodness" and the "perceived ethicality" of selection practices	132
	Empirical studies pertaining to the utility or consequences of diversity selection	132
	Empirical studies pertaining to the fairness or justice of diversity selection	137
	Empirical studies pertaining to individual rights of diversity selection	141
	A weakness in the empirical literature on the utility, rights and justice of selection practices	143
	Implications of findings	144
Chapter 7	**Ethics and justice in leadership**	147
	Personal ethics in leadership	148
	Good leadership skills guided by existing leadership theories and theories of organisational justice	149
	Personal ethics as foundation to good leadership skills	152
Chapter 8	**Epilogue**	155
Readings and references		157
Index		191

"Education without character, science without humanity, and commerce without morality are useless and dangerous pursuits."

----Sathya Sai----

Chapter 1 Introduction

This book deals with organisational ethics and justice from both a normative and an empirical perspective. To understand this topic requires a familiarity with subject areas which so far have remained in separate literatures. Therefore, one of the main aims of the book is to provide a comprehensive source reference on this interdisciplinary topic. To this end, the book brings together relevant literatures from moral philosophy, moral psychology, business ethics and organisational justice. Such a reference has three distinctive features. First, it presents a historical survey of philosophical thoughts on morality and justice. The survey traces back to ancient Greek masters who first painstakingly studied the all-embracing question of *how to live a good (happy, or moral) life*, and ends with the post-modern approaches to ethics and justice. Second, it constitutes an integration of the theoretical-normative discussions of what ethical and just behaviours in an organisation *ought to be,* with the descriptive-empirical findings of what people's understandings of such behaviours *actually are*. Third, it places the more recent organisational justice literature in the broader context of ethics. My specific rationales are three-fold:

First, the coverage of a historical survey of moral philosophical thoughts reflects my firm belief that one cannot achieve a basic understanding of organisational ethics by simply focusing on the current literature. This is not to be interpreted as a denial of the importance of contemporary thought. My point is that one simply must return first to the classical teachings on how to be *a good person,* to interpret and internalise these teachings, before moving on to synthesise the internalised values with lessons gained from modern-day literature. The theoretical basis of my argument here has its roots in early Platonic thoughts, eloquently expressed by Joseph Campbell, that while our outer world changes with time, our inner world remains constant. It is argued that the classical writings on how to be a good person so as to live a good life and to contribute to the good of the community represents a focus on the very essence of our constant inner world: the *fundamental* virtues and standards of

1

living a good and harmonious life do not change, even though their exact expressions would need to take account of the changing dynamics of the outer world.

A contemporary neglect of these very fundamental lessons from classical writings can, in my view, have dire consequences. These undesirable consequences range from the more concrete, i.e., frequent failures of ethics teaching in business schools (for reviews, see Glenn, 1992; Weber, 1990), to the more abstract in what Allan Bloom calls, "the closing of the...mind". In the context of teaching ethics, several scholars have argued for the practice to *live*, rather than *to learn,* ethics (e.g., Davis & Welton, 1991; Solberg et al., 1995). In a similar vein, Solomon (1992) asserts that ethics teaching should serve as a reminder that there are "*standards and virtues at issue...without which the enterprise will not and does not deserve to survive*" (p.224). This is precisely why we should return to the classical writings: After all, the old masters have taught us not only how to *live* ethics, but also what exactly these standards and virtues are. It is also through a return to classical writings that we can prevent our present-day tertiary educational institutions from degenerating into a kind of "trade schools for the bewildered", and equally importantly, prevent the "loss" of "paradigms" (in Casti's words) which are of paramount and fundamental significance to our existence.

The second rationale concerns the coverage of both the normative-philosophical and descriptive-empirical approaches to ethics and justice. This reflects my belief that both approaches together contribute to a greater understanding of the topic than either approach singularly is able to achieve. The call for such a combined effort in better understanding issues surrounding ethics is indeed a popular one in recent years. It has been voiced by researchers from different disciplines. For instance, in moral psychology, Waterman (1988) urges "*the development of dialogue between moral philosophers and moral psychologists*" (p.283); in moral philosophy, Etzioni (1989) pleads for a "deontological social science"; in business ethics, Donaldson (1994) advocates a symbiotic approach that "*credits the empirical and the normative with equal significance*" (p.167); and in the organisational justice literature, Greenberg and Bies (1992) argue for a "*desired goal...of integrating prescriptive and descriptive approaches to justice*" (p.433).

Although the question of how exactly such an integration can be achieved is still the subject of intense theoretical discussion (e.g., Victor & Stephens, 1994; Trevino & Weaver, 1994; Werhane, 1994), the task of integration, whatever mode it may take, requires a sound knowledge of individual component parts which are to be integrated. It is at this level that the present book is aimed: to provide a source which surveys relevant literatures in the component parts.

The third rationale places recent organisational justice literature within the broader context of ethics. In the philosophical tradition, justice has always been considered as an integral part of ethics. However, even in the classical tradition whereby both Plato and Aristotle regarded justice as the most fundamental of all Virtues (or morals), it is the "bigger picture" which embraces all Virtues in a harmonious fashion that entitles a person to the claim of "being moral". Similarly, while justice assumes a

2

paramount status in ethical theories in modernity (particularly in the deontological tradition) morality *per se* consists of considerations of not only justice, but also rights and duties. Other theories in modernity (e.g., those in the teleological tradition) focus morality primarily on utilitarian considerations. So, one cannot have a complete understanding of morality through a single-minded focus on justice, despite its pivotal status in the field of ethics.

Although recent empirical work on organisational justice has made an invaluable and scholarly contribution, its sole and singular focus on fairness leaves one with feelings of increasing uneasiness: that by focusing solely on being fair somehow allows the claim of being ethical or moral. This becomes an issue of concern when findings of justice research with a singular focus on perceptions of fairness are used, often as the only criterion, in the evaluation or justification of the overall "goodness" of important organisational decisions or social issues such as affirmative action and preferential hiring. What is to be achieved by placing justice back into its original broader context of ethics is exactly to inform this kind of decision exercise. I think that in the decision and evaluation processes, we should, where possible, appeal back to the bigger picture by asking the bigger question (i.e., "Is it right, ethical, or moral?") rather than stopping with the question of fairness. It is only by seeking answers to the overriding question can one commit oneself to a more thorough and comprehensive search for the "truth", which ultimately makes up for the best possible decision.

With these aims in mind, the book is divided into two parts: Part One (chapters two to four) provides a brief review of the literature of both the normative and applied ethics and justice. The review covers (1) the normative and empirical theories of ethics and justice in the philosophical and psychological literatures, and (2) theories and domains of business ethics. Part Two (chapters five to seven) focuses on the dialogue between the normative and the empirical approaches to organisational ethics and justice: the ways in which the empirical literature interacts with the normative endeavours of moral philosophy.

Since both moral philosophy and moral psychology contribute to ethical inquiry (Waterman, 1988), chapter two surveys the philosophical literature on ethics and justice, and chapter three deals with the psychological literature. In chapter two, the main themes of Plato and Aristotle's classical philosophy of ethics are described. Ethical theories in modernity are then briefly reviewed. These include (1) ethical egoism, act- and rule- utilitarianism, Sidgwick's dualism of rational benevolence and prudence in the teleological tradition, (2) Kant's categorical imperative, Rawls' contractarianism, Satre's existentialism in the deontological tradition, (3) Moore and Ross's intuitionism, as well as (4) emotive theories and theories of language of morality in the category of logical positivism.

The discussion of the philosophical theories of justice begins with a description of the three conceptions of justice: distributive justice, retributive justice and compensatory justice. In classicism, while justice was viewed in Homeric Greece as "meritocracy of might" and "vengeance", it was considered as "*the* personal virtue" by both Plato and Aristotle. Among teleological theories in modernity, while ethical egoists regard justice as "the result of social contract", utilitarians see it as involving the "consideration of community good". On the other hand, the deontologists define justice in terms of either "pure practical reason" (Kant) or "fairness of distribution" (Rawls).

The survey of the philosophical literature ends with a discussion of the key themes of contemporary schools of moral philosophy collectively referred to as the post-modern approach to morality. Following the survey, major issues of debate in philosophical theories of ethics are identified.

Chapter three focuses on the psychological literature. The review of moral psychology covers four major psychological approaches to moral behaviour: (1) Forsyth's personal ethics and Boyce and Jensen's moral reasoning theory, both take a taxonomic and individual difference approach to morality, (2) Hogan's ethics of social responsibility taking a multivariate and dialectical approach, (3) Kohlberg's justice-focused, and Gilligan's care-focused morality which is viewed from a cognitive-developmental perspective, and (4) Haan's ethics of social dialogue which adopts a postmodern interactional position.

Following the review of moral psychology, the chapter turns to the psychology of justice. The conceptual framework of the psychological research into justice stems from first, the philosophical tradition of distributive justice, and more recently, from the legal and judicial tradition of procedural justice. In this context, the chapter then surveys outcome (or distributive) justice theories separately from the procedural (or process) justice theories. Following the philosophical tradition, outcome justice theories are concerned primarily with the fairness of the outcome of resources allocation. Here the review includes Adam's equity theory, Leventhal's distributive justice judgement theory, Lerner's justice motive theory, Crosby's theory of relative deprivation, Folger's referent cognition theory, Lansberg's social categorisation theory of entitlement, and Skitka and Tetlock's contingency theory of distributive justice.

Inspired by the judicial tradition, procedural justice theories focus on the fairness of the procedures used in deriving final allocations. The survey of procedural theories includes Thibaut and Walker's theory of procedural justice, Leventhal, Laruza and Fry's allocation preference theory, as well as Lind and Tyler's models of procedural justice. Following the review, the chapter identifies recent advances in the psychology of ethics and justice. These include recent research on relational justice, the postmodern and feminist perspectives on justice, and the notion of evolutionary ethics.

Moral philosophy and moral psychology aside, there exists an independent literature of applied ethics which pertains to moral behaviour in specific social contexts including business and work organisations. Therefore, chapter four turns to a review of the business ethics literature. It begins with a survey of the historical roots of contemporary free-market ideology in business ethics. The views of Locke, Hobbes, Smith and Spencer are reviewed. The chapter also examines the traditional issues of debate in business ethics (i.e., the ethics and justice of the free-market system, corporate social responsibility and private versus public ethics). Emerging themes in business ethics are then identified. These include (1) the application of positive theories and empirical research to the debate over free-market efficiency, (2) social and business goals seen as in concert with each other, (3) personal and virtue ethics as foundation to business behaviour, (4) an increasing emphasis on the practice of "good ethics" (Baron and Mellema's work on supererogatory acts), (5) an increasing focus on the notion of justice in business ethics. The discussion covers these contemporary issues in the business ethics literature: social justice, environmental and ecological restoration, rights and protection, as well as the issue of corporate governance.

Chapter four also reviews the theoretical models of ethical decision making advanced in this applied ethics literature. These models include Fletcher's situational ethics, French's principle of responsive adjustment, Rest's four component model, Trevino's person-situation interactionist model, Jones' moral intensity model, Frederick's theory of business values, Solomon's ethical decision model, as well as Weber's multi-component model of institutionalising ethics. Ethical decision models with a specific focus on marketing behaviour are also included in the review: Ferrell and Gresham's contingency model, Hunt and Vitell's general theory of marketing ethics, Ferrell et al.'s synthesis model, and the reasoned action model of Dubinsky and Loken. Chapter four ends with a discussion of the postmodern approach to ethical decision making in a business context. Rossouw's rational model of moral sensitivity, which aims at the resolution of moral dissensus in a contemporary society, is used as an example.

After the review of relevant theories, Part Two of the book turns to the normative-empirical dialogue. Chapter five analyses the key issues pertaining to the interaction between the normative and the empirical approaches to ethics and justice. The potential contributions of each approach towards the other are outlined. The Chapter then describes existing research which has attempted such a normative-empirical dialogue. It is in this context that the Chapter addresses another main theme of this book: to place justice research within its original broader context of ethics. To justify this, one needs to carefully examine the justice-ethics relationship in terms of both the commonalities and differences between the two constructs. In exploring the commonalities, the theoretical justice-ethics link implicated in the philosophical literature is used as the epistemological framework in guiding empirical research. The research questions whether our moral considerations in the real world indeed consist of an evaluation of fairness. In other words, the research ascertains whether a parallel behavioural link also exists between people's judgements of ethicality and of fairness. Several studies designed to ascertain such a link are described in this chapter. Findings here are convergent in suggesting that people's judgements of ethicality and of fairness are rather closely related.

However, results of other studies, designed to explore the differences in judgements of ethicality and fairness, show that while fairness consideration is a *necessary* and pivotal criterion of moral judgements, it is by no means a *sufficient* one. The implication of these findings is clear: Significant decisions which satisfy the fairness criterion may or may not, taken in their entirety, be ethical and moral. Therefore, it is argued that where possible, organisational decisions need to be made on grounds of their overall ethicality rather than for reasons of fairness alone.

The following two chapters in Part Two further illustrate the normative-empirical dialogue with reference to two specific domains of organisational behaviour: affirmative action programmes in personnel selection and leadership processes in organisations. These two key organisational issues are chosen because they are overladen with ethical overtones. Chapter six shows the way in which affirmative action programmes can best be evaluated: the normative theories help to determine the criteria for the evaluation and the empirical evidence provides the factual data used in the evaluation. To this end, the chapter begins with a review of the philosophical, legal and social psychological literatures on the issue. The chapter then analyses existing empirical research pertaining to perceptions of justice (i.e., fairness) and of ethics (i.e., ethicality) of the selection practice. While empirical research on affirmative action focuses primarily on issues surrounding justice and fairness, it is argued that equal research emphasis should be placed on considerations of rights and utility. The evaluation of this social programme needs to address the all-embracing question of its overall "rightness" or "goodness", rather than its justice or perceived fairness alone.

With reference to leadership, it is argued in chapter seven that the concept of leadership should be firmly grounded in philosophical thoughts on ethics and that empirical theories and research on leadership serve to shed light on "technical leader skills". It is noted that since the 1990s, there has been a shift in the leadership literature from a traditional focus on the identification of behavioural and contextual determinants of "good leadership" to an emphasis on leaders' personal ethics and fairness. In an effort to integrate the literature, it is argued that good leadership consists of sound personal ethics as well as sound technical skills, and that personal ethics are to be foundational to formal technical skills by virtue of the fact that they are inalienable personal character traits which operate as an inbuilt check over the proper use of these skills. In this context, it is further argued that the existing empirical literature on leadership can best be deployed as providing practical guidance to sound formal leadership skills.

The epilogue provides a brief summary of the main themes of the book and clearly identifies the establishment of a normative-empirical dialogue as the key direction for future research in organisational ethics and justice.

Part One

Normative, Empirical, and Applied Ethics and Justice: Theories and Domains

Chapter 2 Philosophical Literature on Ethics and Justice

The philosophical literature on ethics and justice is vast and dates back to the ancient Greek period. From an historical point of view, it can be divided into at least three major categories: the Classicism of the Greek period, Modernism and Postmodernism. The main task of moral philosophy is to prescribe standards of moral behaviour (i.e., moral values or moral norms), by implication the task is a normative one. However, moral standards consist of a factual part (i.e., what these standards *actually are*) and an evaluative part (i.e., what these standards *ought to be*). The expertise of moral philosophy lies in the latter. Through reflective deliberations, moral philosophers identify the standards of behaviour which are judged as *good* and hence ought to be valued.

This chapter presents a brief survey of the moral philosophical literature. Although justice is considered as an integral part of ethics in this literature, the two notions have a differential influence on the empirical literature. As a result, distinctive domains have emerged under the separate headings of moral psychology and the psychology of justice. A similar separation is evident in applied ethics: specifically, that between business ethics and organisational justice. Because of these distinctions, the philosophical literatures on ethics and justice in Classicism and Modernity will be reviewed separately in this chapter. Following this review, the Postmodern perspectives to ethics and justice are outlined. Major issues of debate in the philosophy of ethics and justice are then identified.

PHILOSOPHY OF ETHICS

The basis of ethics in Western philosophical thought appears to be different in the three major schools of Classicism, Modernism and Postmodernism. The basis of the ethics of Classicism is grounded in "natural law", which presupposes the existence of

9

"the Idea of Good" (in Platonic ethics) or *"the Final Cause"* of human life and action (in Aristotelean ethics). What is "good" exists either as an eternal and immutable form or as the natural purpose (the final cause) of human existence. And in either case, the good can be objectively identified through the exercise of reason.

Philosophical theories of ethics in Modernity can be classified into four schools: teleology, deontology, intuitionism and logical positivism. The basis of both teleological and deontological ethics lies in that which is specified in various categorical moral rules. Teleological ethics are based on considerations of the results of action. Deontological ethics have their basis on moral obligations. What is "good" is no longer life's natural purpose; instead, it is defined by the objective absolute moral rules.

While these two schools in Modernity hold different views from Classicism about what constitute "good", they however subscribe to two similar positions of Classicism: First, "good" exists as a natural or objective entity like facts, hence can be analysed and defined. Second, the key to the identification of the content of "good" is through the intellectual faculty of pure reason.

Another school in Modernity, intuitionism, takes a non-naturalistic approach to ethics by rejecting both these propositions. Intuitionists argue that "good" has a subjective undefinable quality which cannot be analysed or defined through reason. What constitutes good can only be revealed by an individual's own intuition through the faculty of sensing.

In the early 1920s, the study of morality was revolutionalised by the prevailing scientific methods of positivism. According to August Comte, the evolution of human intellect begins with theology (i.e., explaining events in terms of acts of God), through metaphysics (i.e., explaining events by appealing to abstract concepts), to positivism (i.e., explaining events through scientific methods). Logical positivists contend that ethics, like all other knowledge, can only be studied by empirical methods of observation and verification. Any proposition about "good" is "factually meaningless" unless it can be empirically validated. According to logical positivists, before moral philosophers can engage in the normative task of prescribing moral rules through the use of moral language, it is necessary to understand the meaning and function of such language. Thus the main tasks of logical positivists concern a scientific analysis of moral statements. As a result of empirical investigation, statements about moral acts are found to serve the function of either expressing an individual's subjective emotions, feelings or attitudes towards such acts (i.e., emotivism), or recommending or evaluating a course of action (i.e., prescriptivism). Both emotivism and prescriptivism take an empiricist approach to ethics.

Despite many differences, ethics in both Classicism and Modernism presuppose the existence of a unifiable truth, be it life's final purpose, or that expressed in various moral rules, or that which can be identified through intuition or emotion. However, ethics in the Postmodern school deny the existence of a single unified truth.

Postmodern ethicists recognise that the truth about morality can only be discovered through social construction by taking account of diverse moral perspectives. The postmodern approach to ethics is primarily empiricist and relativistic (see further clarifications later in the chapter). What is "good" thus appears to constitute an acceptance of the co-existence of pluralistic moral perspectives and the multiplicity of truth. In the sections to follow, major theories of ethics from each of these philosophical schools are reviewed.

Classical Philosophy of Ethics

The writings of Plato which reflect Socrates' teachings, and the thoughts of Aristotle are still of relevance to contemporary life. While there are differences in the foci (i.e., reason vs. senses) of their theories of the physical world and human nature, the ethics of both Plato and Aristotle presuppose the existence of the "Soul" and the harmonious balance of various conflicting parts of the soul as the ideal state of an individual. Both stress the importance of the social context of individual existence and hence are group- or community-based. Therefore, according to these classical philosophers, ethics comprise not only a state of integrity of the soul of an individual, but also a state of equilibrium between the individual and his/her social environment. Such ideas of an integrated and balanced individual, and a cooperative and harmonious society still underlie the thinking of many modern-day moral philosophers.

Plato (427-347 B.C.)

Plato was a student of Socrates' in ancient Athens. His philosophy is documented in his writings of a number of Dialogues (conversations with Socrates) of which, the Republic is the most well known. The key ideas in Plato's philosophy which pertain to morality are summarised below:

(1) Plato presupposed that there exists two kinds of reality: the reality of the Senses which consists of things perceivable, ever-changing and mortal; and the reality of Ideas which is unchanging, immaterial and eternal. The reality of Ideas is not accessible by Senses, it can only be attained by pure intellect or reason.

(2) The *Moral Ideas* (e.g., *Good, Courage, Justice, Wisdom, Temperance*) are eternal and immutable forms of "good", which prescribe the absolute and ideal standards for the well-being of an individual as well as that of the larger society. These *Moral Ideas* have a permanent and independent reality hence can be observed and specified objectively.

(3) At the individual level, the dualistic reality of *Sense* and *Idea* is to be found respectively in the physical Body and the immortal Soul (Mind). The Soul's ultimate goal is to achieve the reality of the Moral Ideas. Education provides

the means for the Soul to attain the knowledge of these Moral Ideas and hence to achieve its goal.

(4)	The Soul contains three parts: *Appetite* (or Desire), *Will* (or Spirit) and *Reason*. Each part of the Soul has an ideal (i.e., the Virtue). The respective ideal or virtue of Appetite, Will and Reason is *Temperance, Courage* and *Wisdom*. Corresponding to the relative dominance of each part of the Soul, there are three types of individuals: those whose strongest desire is to seek material gains (*Appetite* dominates), those with the strongest desire for competition and success (*Will* dominates), and those whose predominant desire is to seek knowledge or truth (*Reason* dominates).

(5)	While there are these three types of individuals, the *perfect or ideal state* for an individual is a harmonious balance amongst the three parts of the Soul, with *Reason* having ultimate control over *Appetite* and *Will*. This balanced and harmonious state is what Plato refers to as "Justice" or "a good and happy life".

(6)	It is only natural that individuals are social beings. As society consists of individuals, there can also be three types of Nation States: the *timarchic* state (dominated by the competitive, ambitious and militaristic individuals), the *oligarchic* state (dominated by the money-makers or the rich). Plato regarded neither of these states as ideal. An ideal state (i.e., the *Utopian*), not unlike the ideal individual, is one which achieves a harmonious balance amongst the three classes of people (i.e., the philosophical *rulers*, the warrior *auxiliaries* and the traders or *labourers*). The balance in such a totalitarian society requires that people in each class perform their appropriate duties and recognize their own status in the society by not interfering with the duties of others.

(7)	There exists absolute truth and universal rules for what's right or wrong. The truth and the rules are only attainable through the exercise of *intellect* or *pure reason*.

(8)	Plato asserted that education is necessary for individuals to attain, through reason and intellect, knowledge of the eternal Moral Ideas. However, there are different levels of education, with the highest level being reserved only for the *elite* group of individuals (i.e., the *ruler* class). The key curriculum of this level of education concerns primarily with mathematics and philosophy—those fields of study which require the exercise of pure reason or intellect, and which Plato believed are necessary for the Soul to attain the truth or knowledge of the *Ideas*. Plato also regarded education as the means to achieve a harmonious society. Plato's emphasis on education has gained him the reputation as the *first* philosopher to advocate a state-supported schooling and educational system.

(9)	While Plato asserted that *Harmony* or *Justice* (i.e., a harmonious balance amongst component parts) characterises an ideal individual and an ideal society, he also regarded the *harmony* of the entire society as being of greater importance than that of the individuals. For instance, in a Utopia as prescribed in the *Republic,* the primary functions of the rulers and the *auxiliaries* were to serve the society: as such, they were not allowed to have a private family life or property. However, in Plato's later writings, a *Constitutional state* , described as a second best to a Utopian, would allow both private family life and property for those individuals serving the state. This preeminent status accorded the *society* or *community* in Plato's philosophy of ethics is clearly reflected by the Greek word *ethos,* which means the disposition or characteristic spirits and beliefs of a community.

While there have been various criticisms of Plato's philosophy, his insights into the role of reason in the acquisition of truth and knowledge (including truth about morality or *Moral Ideas)* and the role of such knowledge in the attainment of a balanced and fulfilled life are still very much upheld today. Plato's insights into the role of education in the achievement of Harmony (both at an individual and at a wider societal level) are still regarded by many as the key impetus of the present-day education system.

Aristotle (384-322 B.C.)

Born in Macedonia to a physician father, Aristotle went to Athens to study under Plato in the *Academy*. Having mastered Plato's philosophical thoughts, Aristotle refuted several key aspects and formulated his own philosophy. The key features of Aristotle's philosophy pertaining to morality are summarised below:

(1) Aristotle rejected Plato's idea of the two independent realities of an ever-changing reality of *Senses*, and a superior and eternal reality of *Ideas*. Instead, Aristotle argued for one unified reality, consisting of two inseparable dimensions: the *Substance* (i.e., the essence of what "a thing" is made of) and the *Form* (i.e., the actual manifestation or specific characteristics of "a thing"). The *Substance* of a thing contains all its "potentials", which can be transformed into its actual *Form.* The "human"*Form* consists of both a body and a soul (i.e., consciousness in the Aristotalian context).

(2) While still asserting that pure reason is the most essential characteristics of the human Form, Aristotle rejected Plato's idea of pure Reason being superior to Senses and that the higher level of reality (i.e., the *Ideas*) can only be attained through *thinking with pure reason*. Aristotle maintained that the reality can also be attained through *perceiving with senses*. Reason thus has to coexist with Sensing.

(3) Central to Aristotle's moral philosophy are the notions of Virtue and Happiness. Virtues are ideal traits that are necessary for an individual to attain a state of harmony within herself, and to attain such a state in relation to his/her social environment. In essence, Aristotle regarded Virtues as the very

13

fundamental ingredients of "happiness" (i.e., meaning *doing well , fitting-in well,* or *flourishing*).

(4)   Aristotle identified these traits as basic human Virtues: *Justice, Courage* (neither cowardice nor rashness), *Temperance* (moderation), *Liberality* (not miserliness), *Magnificence* (generosity), *Pride, Shame, Honour, Good Temper, Friendliness, Wittiness and Truthfulness.* While Virtues are fundamental to "a good life", they do not represent absolute rules and they need to be defined in terms of the *telos* (i.e., "purpose", "end", or "aim") of the context. In the context of an individual person, the *purpose* can be that of achieving happiness; in the context of a work group, the purpose can be that of fostering congeniality in relationship and excellence in performance.

(5)   Aristotle further identified three forms of happiness: to live an enjoyable life, to live as a responsible citizen, and to live as a rational thinker and philosopher. However, a harmonious balance among all three forms is necessary for a person to achieve happiness and fulfilment.

6)   Aristotle assumed that individuals possess innate and natural capabilities (i.e., "potentialities") and that an individual's main purpose in life is to actualise these potentialities. In the context of ethics, "good" or "evil" is defined in terms of whether the actualisation of these innate capabilities is facilitated or hindered: "good" is what fosters the fulfilment of one's natural potentialities; "bad" is what hinders such an attainment.

(7)   The Aristotelean ethics have a "natural law" basis. Aristotle believed that every living thing in nature has a general sense of purpose or "the final cause". And there is always "good" in this final purpose. This notion is clearly conveyed in his *Nicomachean Ethics: "...every action and pursuit, is thought to aim at some good; and for that reason the good has rightly been declared to be that at which all things aim."* The ultimate good that all human beings aim for is the state of "happiness".

Despite Aristotle's well-known distaste or even utter contempt for any business transaction involving profit-making, his notion of virtues and their role in the attainment of happiness is still widely regarded as being of paramount significance in today's modern society whereby business has assumed a much greater prominence than in the ancient times. This point will be returned to in later discussions of applied ethics in chapter four. It is also worth noting that, like Plato, Aristotle also stressed the importance of the larger, social context of human existence. In order to achieve "happiness", each person will need to attain a harmonious balance with his/her outer social community.

Modern Philosophy of Ethics

Four schools of ethics in modern philosophy are reviewed in this section: teleology, deontology, intuitionism and logical positivism. Both teleology and deontology theories of ethics involve the prescription of absolute or normative rules of morality. "Goodness" therefore is that which is explicit in these rules. Intuitionism however, maintains that "goodness" cannot be defined in terms of objective and factual rules; instead, goodness has a subjective quality which can only be revealed through each individual's own intuition, reflection and contemplation. The main task of logical positivism concerns a logical analysis of the function of the language of morality. Based on the results of the analysis, moral statements are said to be used either for expressing one's emotions or for making recommendations for moral actions.

Teleological Theories

Teleologists hold the belief that the key determinant of morality lies almost exclusively in the net results or consequences (the Greek word *telos* means *aim, end* or *purpose*). However, teleological ethicists differ in their point of reference regarding the target beneficiary (or victim) of such consequences. The reference target for ethical egoism is the self, and that for act- or rule-utilitarianism is the entire set of individuals affected by the consequences.

Ethical Egoism (Thomas Hobbes)

The only imperative of ethical egoism is that a person should act in such a way so as to maximise his/her own self-interest. Even though the emphasis of self-interest is evident in the Platonic philosophy, ethical egoism is primarily influenced by the writings of Thomas Hobbes. Hobbes wrote in his book, *Leviathan* (1926), that human nature is characterised by selfishness and that human behavior is primarily driven by self-interest. His assumption of human nature thus led him to propose the idea of *social contract* which functions as a kind of deterrent in preventing the potential brutal consequences of violent clashes when each individual seeks only to maximise his/her own self-interest in society.

Ethical egoists differ amongst themselves in their conception of the "goodness" of consequences. The extreme egoists (i.e., hedonism) define *goodness* exclusively in terms of *pleasure (*mere physical or materialist pursuits); others however emphasised less physical or materialistic forms in defining goodness.

Ethical egoists would also talk about *common good*, but the argument is that an individual would not be concerned about others' welfare simply for the sake of serving common good: he/she would be concerned about others only when such concerns serve as a means to achieve his/her own self-interest.

Act- and Rule-Utilitarianism (Jeremy Bentham and John Stuart Mill)

The traditional form of utilitarianism is typically referred to as act-utilitarianism, which is found in the writings of the English political philosopher Jeremy

Bentham (1748-1832). In a legal context, Bentham designed a *calculus* in weighing criminal behavior and corresponding punishment. This concept was extended to value judgements in the form of the *happiness calculus*. Simply stated, it's an "objective measure" of morality by using the principle of maximising happiness and minimising pain. This *calculus* thus forms the very basis of later utility calculations (i.e., cost-benefit analysis) in utilitarianism.

The moral principle of act-utilitarianism defines the morality of an action in terms of two criteria :

(1) The net utility of that action would outweigh the net utility of any other possible alternative action.
(2) The greatest net utility of the action is not defined in terms of the actor herself, but is defined in terms of all people (including the actor) affected by that action.

Traditional act-utilitarianism has since faced many criticisms towards its measurement of utility, including the concept of cost or gain, and the difficulty in quantifying certain intrinsic values in monetary terms. However, the most serious criticism, originating from deontologists, concerns its inability to assimilate the two fundamental moral values of *rights* and *justice.*

In an attempt to answer this latter criticism, rule-utilitarianism was proposed as a refined version of utilitarianism. John Stuart Mill is typically associated with this new version of utilitarianism. Mill has written about the status of rights and justice in the scheme of utilitarianism in his book *Utilitarianism* (Mill, 1957). In rule-utilitarianism, the utility-maximising principle is not applied directly to the action itself, but is only applied to an abstract or superordinate rule that is to govern that action. Specifically, rule-utilitarianism uses two criteria in making moral judgements:

(1) An action is moral if and only if it follows those rules which are considered morally correct.
(2) A rule is considered morally correct if and only if the net utility produced when everyone acts on that rule is greater than the net utility produced when everyone acts on any other alternative rule.

The manner by which rule-utilitarianism is able to accommodate the moral values of rights and duties is by treating these values as normative rules which are considered morally correct. This way, an act which fulfills both the criteria of act-utilitarianism may not necessarily be considered moral by rule-utilitarianism, unless the act also satisfies the criterion of obeying the normative rules of rights and duties.

Henry Sidgwick's Dualism of Rational Benevolence and Prudence

Sidgwick's dualism represents a compromise between the two extreme views of teleological morality based on either the individual's *own* self-interest (i.e. ethical egoism) or the interest of all parties concerned (i.e., act- or rule-utilitarianism). Sidgwick referred to the principle of the former as *prudence* and that of the latter as *rational benevolence*. However, he argued that, in reality, it would be irrational for a person to either completely sacrifice his/her own self-interest for the sake of all others, or to completely ignore others' interest for the sake of maximising his/her own. Sidgwick's dualism therefore is primarily concerned with the moral process which aims to achieve a "harmony" or "reconciliation" between self-interest and the interest of others.

Deontological Theories

Deontological theories accord the overriding status to *individual rights* and their reciprocal or correlative notion *duties* in ethical considerations. Utilitarian considerations are granted a minor role. The Greek word *Deon* (meaning "duty" or "obligation") hence reflects the pivotal role of rights and duties in these theories. To put in simplest terms, a deontological ethicist would argue that to be moral involves primarily a respect for each individual's rights (moral or contractual) by performing one's corresponding duties. Rights are a person's entitlements, they can be either moral or contractual in nature:

(1) *Moral rights (and Moral duties):* An individual's moral rights include his/her basic and unalienable rights as a human being. Such basic moral rights can be phrased either in positive terms (e.g., *the right to life , the right to privacy*) or in negative terms (e.g., *the right not to be killed, the right not to be intruded upon).* Typically, positive moral rights carry the explicit implication that others have the corresponding *duty* to allow the individual to freely pursue that right.

(2) *Contractual rights (and Contractual duties):* Contractual rights are results of mutual agreements or contracts. When a person enters an agreement or contract with another, the person then not only has the contractual duty to perform what the contract requires of him/her, but also the contractual right to what is promised of him/her.

Immanuel Kant's (1724-1804) Categorical Imperative

The 18th century German philosopher, Immanuel Kant, is generally regarded as the most influential deontologist. Central to his moral philosophy is the idea of "treating everyone as a free person equal to everyone else" (Velasquez, 1982). The key underlying implications are therefore (1) a person is a *rational* being with *free wills* , and (2) those free wills should be protected and promoted. But, how can one judge the right or wrong of such free wills? And, under what conditions should such free wills be protected and promoted? The answers can be found in Kant's well-known *categorical imperative* (i.e., "supreme principle", "absolute command" or "universal rules" which apply to all situations). Kant formulated his categorical imperative in at least two different versions in his book, *Groundwork of the Metaphysics of Morals.*:

> *Formulation 1: "I ought never to act except in such a way that I can also will that my maxim should become a universal law"*
>
> Kant used the word maxim to mean the reasons for a person to behave in certain way. This formulation thus contains two rules for the judgement of the rightness of a person's reasons (maxims):
>
> (a) the rule of reversibility: the person must be willing to have all others to use the same reason (maxim) for acting in a similar fashion towards her/himself.
>
> (b) the rule of universalisability: the person's reason (maxim) can be universalised in the sense that everyone else could use that as a reason to act in a similar fashion.
>
> *Formulation 2: "Act in such a way that you always treat humanity, whether in your own person or in the person of any other, never simply as a means, but always at the same time as an end"*
>
> This formulation thus suggests that the criterion to judge the morality of an action is by asking the question of whether that action, in the course of serving one's own self-interests, involves a denial of another's free will to choose. Or, simply the question of whether anyone has been unwillingly exploited to satisfy the interests of another.

There have been several criticisms of Kant's theory, in particular, his rules of universalisability and reversibility of maxims. His notion of respecting each person's free wills (within the constraints specified by the categorical imperative) is still widely regarded as the fundamental rule in guiding our social behavior.

John Rawls' Contractarianism and the Theory of Justice (1971)

While the focus of the Kantian theory is on moral rights and duties at the individual or interpersonal level, John Rawls approached such notions from a collective or societal level by addressing the issue of how such rights (entitlements to benefits) or duties (burdens of responsibility) can best be distributed in a society. Central to the Rawlsian view is the concept of justice, which he equates with fairness. According to Rawls, the distribution of benefits and burdens should follow the universal principle of justice. Rawls' theory therefore concerns two issues, (1) how can such universal principles be worked out? and (2) what exactly are these rules?

In addressing the first issue, Rawls argued that any universal principle of distribution, which is fair for all concerned, can only be worked out hypothetically by placing imaginary people in a hypothetical "original position". These procedures are detailed in his principle of "veil of ignorance". Specifically, a group of rational persons, unaware of their own future position in a future society, are asked to choose the rules of allocating benefits and burdens in that society in which they themselves are going to live. Rawls argued that it is only by having people make rules this way, as if behind a "veil of ignorance", that principles which are universally fair can be attained. This is because every decision maker would be mindful of his/her possible future position in that society. Each person would want to have maximum provision for him/herself should he/she turn out to occupy the worst possible position in that future society; the person would also want to attain maximum benefits for him/herself should he/she turn out to occupy a privileged position. It is therefore the uncertainty of one's own future position that motivates the person to act in an utmost fair fashion in designing the rules of allocation.

So, what are the rules these "people in original position" would come up with? Rawls argued that they would come up with three basic universal principles of justice:

(1) *Principle of equal liberty—each person has an equal right to the most extensive basic liberties compatible with similar liberties for all.*
Rawls identified a person's basic liberties as including basic human rights and other civil liberties. This principle thus stipulated the role of equality in the allocation of rights and duties.

(2) *Principle of difference—Social and economic inequalities are arranged so that they are to the greatest benefit of the least advantaged persons.*
This principle requires that just allocations of rights and duties would involve compensatory means to improve the position of the worse-off or the most needy in society.

(3) *Principle of fair equality of opportunity—Social and economic inequalities are arranged so that they are attached to offices and positions open to all under conditions of fair equality of opportunity.*
This principle ensures that just allocations of rights and duties would involve equal opportunity for everyone in not only qualifying for, but also in competing for, the most privileged position in society.

It is generally agreed that, as a theory of distributive justice, one of the most significant contributions of Rawls' theory lies in its taking into account not only individual needs and wants, but also individual talents and efforts in the allocation of societal resources. It is perhaps worth noting here that the recent empirical research in organisational justice has been very much guided by Rawls' definitive writing on *justice as fairness*, in the sense that the construct justice is repeatedly operationalized in terms of fairness.

Jean-Paul Satre's Existentialism

The main concern of existentialism is with *the individual*, the meaning or purpose of his/her existence and with his/her most distinctive property, *freedom*. Satre's existentialism thus stresses the pivotal role of one's own free will in morality. Existentialism rejects rule-following in ethical decisions. Instead, it argues for the internalisation of basic virtues and for making them *authentically* one's own. The key features of morality are therefore the *authenticity* of individual decisions and the *purity of the person's motives*. Satre's idea of authenticity of personal virtues reflects explicitly the classical philosophical thoughts whereby the key to morality concerns an individual's own endeavour in integrating various virtues into a harmonious or equilibrium state. Because the focus of morality for existentialism is on the self and the will or motives, this school of thoughts has been criticised for not adequately providing specific guidance or concrete rules of morality.

Intuitionism

So far moral philosophers have treated morality as an "object" which exists in moral words such as "good", hence morality can be defined by analysing and breaking down the word good into identifiable "qualities" or "properties". Such theories of ethics are typically referred to as naturalistic theories. However, a new category of moral philosophy, intuitionism, rejects these presumptions and argues that morality consists of a subjective quality which can only be revealed through one's own intuition.

G.E. Moore

G.E. Moore has been regarded as one of the most prominent proponents of intuitionism. His criticism of the naturalistic position is summarised in his well-known proposal of the naturalistic fallacy. Moore's views are that morality does not constitute an objective property or quality which can be identified or defined like other natural sciences such as physics. Instead, morality consists of moral values or moral standards which have not only a *factual* part (e.g., possible consequences of moral behavior) as well as a *non-factual* part (e.g., those possible consequences are good or bad for each individual). It is the existence of this latter non-factual part that distinguishes morality from other naturalistic sciences. Moore argued that the non-factual aspect of moral values involves subjective evaluation, therefore it can only be revealed through each individual's own "intuition" or "reflection" (the faculty of senses). Because of this, Moore insists that previous naturalists have committed the *naturalistic fallacy*, in that they ignored the subjective evaluative aspect of morality and equate the factual-part of morality to the entire morality itself. In other words, naturalistic ethicists equate *fact* to *values*; or they equate *is* (i.e., what can be observed by sciences of observation) to *ought to be* (i.e., what can only be evaluated, intuited or reflected upon subjectively).

Moore's views thus led him to question the definability of moral words such as *good*. Moore's position also raises the practical questions of how then can one evaluate the *goodness* or morality of an act and what rules ought to guide behavior.

Despite his view that the "good" can not be objectively defined as earlier normative ethicists have done, Moore still recommended the practice of traditional and commonly-held moral standards. Moore (1903) however maintained that individuals could, through thoughtful introspection and by appeal to intuition, identify those which are "intrinsically good" for themselves (i.e., Moore's ideal utilitarianism). The question of ethical practice was also addressed by a later intuitionist, W.D. Ross in his idea of *prima facie duties*.

W. D. Ross

While teleological and deontological ethicists emphasise the overall utility or rights and duties respectively as the key ethical consideration, an intuitionist speaks of both in the all-embracing notion of prima *facie obligations*. The 20th century British philosopher W.D. Ross sought to combine the fundamental moral themes from both the teleological school (ethical egoism and rule utilitarianism) as well as the deontological school (contractarianism and existentialism). Hence his approach to morality is typically referred to as pluralism. He identified seven principles of *prima facie obligations or duties*. These *prima facie duties* are results of our social relationships with one another, hence are morally correct in particular situations at a particular time. Because *prima facie duties* are situationally and contextually specific, they are different from the absolute duties in earlier theories of ethics. Ross (1939) suggested that the word *responsibility* captures the essence of the terms *prima facie duties*. These duties are therefore seen as the responsibilities of a person conditional upon specific given contexts. The prima facie duties are expressed in terms of these moral principles:

Principle of fidelity—a person should keep explicit and implicit (truth-telling in contracts) promises.
Principle of reparation—a person should make reparation for wrongful acts.
Principle of gratitude—a person should express gratitude for other's services.
Principle of justice—a person should use just rules in the distribution of resources.

Principle of beneficence—a person should do his/her best to improve others' situation.

Principle of self-improvement—a person should improve his/her own virtues and intelligence.

Principle of noninjury—a person should not cause injury to others.

Through these prima facie duties, Ross thus provided practial guidance on moral behaviour. Ross further asserted that when these obligations conflict, a person would need to appeal to his/her intuition.

Logical Positivism

As mentioned earlier, the rapid development of positivism in science at the beginning of the twentieth century had a profound influence on the philosophical study of ethics. Moral philosophy taking the positivist approach can be further divided into two categories: Emotivism (or noncognitivism) and Prescriptivism.

Noncognitivism (Emotive Theories of A.J. Ayer and C. Stevenson)

Introducing the scientific method of analysis of logic into the study of morality, some logical positivists, notably Ayer, argued that morality, like any other kind of knowledge, can only be understood by the empirical method of observation and verification. Any proposition of morality is rendered meaningless unless it can be empirically tested for its truth (or falsity). Because early propositions of normative ethics were not formulated by following the methodology of scientific positivism, they are therefore considered "factually meaningless". Ayer further asserted that the only function of moral philosophy is the logical analysis of the statements (or sentences, utterances) of morality. As a result of such analyses, logical positivists concluded that these statements do not function in asserting a fact or moral rule, they simply represent the expressions of a person's feelings or emotions. Hence such theories came to be known as emotive theories of morality.

Ayer's view of rejecting moral philosophy as a study of metaphysical and normative ethics was often misinterpreted by critics as to mean that *ethics* itself is being rejected. A later emotivist, Stevenson, countered such a criticism by pointing out that emotivists are interested in logical analysis not as an end in itself, but as a means to an end; the primary objective of emotivism is to seek clarity of normative ethical statements by focusing on the analysis of what functions these statements serve. It is only after the real functions of moral statements have been identified that moral philosophers can embark on the task of using such statements to prescribe normative moral rules.

Prescriptivism (Theories of the language of Morality: Hare, Urmson, Braithwaite)

Inspired by logical positivism and the approach of emotive ethicists, a group of Oxbridge philosophers, in 1950s and 1960s, focused their study of morality exclusively on comprehensive analyses of the usage of moral words such as *good, ought* or *right* in daily language. Their main premise was that "ethics is a logical study of the language of morals", and as such, it is of primary importance to understand how moral words are used in normative prescriptions of moral rules. To this end, one needs to first understand how exactly these words are used by people in both a moral and non-moral context in daily conversations. For instance, Hare's analysis focused on the use of key moral words in sentences like *"The design of this furniture is good"*, or *"You ought to use a pen which writes"*. His analysis led him to the claim that the key function of moral words is in *commending* and in prescribing or *providing guidance* to behavior. For instance, consider the use of the words *good* and *ought* in these sentences: *To keep one's promises is good* and *One ought to keep one's promises.* Hare argued that both words are primarily used in commending and recommending the act of keeping promises. Having identified "the recommendation of an act" as one function served by normative moral statements, Hare went on to argue that the choice of whether or not to accept the recommendation ultimately lies with each individual.

Other theorists of this morality-as-language school adopted similar method of analysis but came to somewhat different conclusions about the primary function of moral words used in normative moral statements. While Urmson argued that the key function of these words is in the *grading*, (i.e., appraising, evaluating, or assessing) of moral acts, Braithwaite asserted that their primary function is in the declaration or the proclamation of moral policies.

The primary concern of logical positivists focuses on the linguistic functions of moral utterances or expressions, rather than on the provision of guidance and wisdom on how to behave morally. In this regard, logical positivists are concerned with issues of meta-ethics (e.g., the nature and functions of ethical language) rather than the task of normative ethics (e.g., prescribing ethical norms). However, because of the generally-held belief of what moral philosophers should be doing (and indeed had been doing) is to provide moral guidance, this school of moral philosophy has frequently been criticised for the failure of doing so (e.g., Gellner, 1959; Russell,1959; Trevino & Weaver, 1994). Despite these criticisms, it should be noted that Urmson's views on morality can be characterised by a "minimalist approach": to behave morally involves performing what is minimally necessary for a cooperative and harmonious co-existence of people in a society. This involves performing one's moral duties by respecting others' moral rights. This minimal moralist position has also had various criticisms (see Mellema, 1991).

PHILOSOPHY OF JUSTICE

In philosophical discussions of justice, three conceptions of justice are identified and distinguished:

(1) *Distributive Justice*

This concerns the allocation or distribution of resources that are scarce and are in short supply relative to their demand. Issues of distributive justice arise only when the demand for particular resources exceeds the supply. By implication then, the term distributive justice would be meaningless if there were no shortage of supply of desired resources, or if the supply were to always match the demand. Because of the limited supply of many valued resources in a modern-day society (e.g., employment opportunities), the issue of distributive justice in resource allocation has assumed supreme importance. Contemporary philosophical discussions of distributive justice have identified several rules of fair allocation of resources. These rules will be discussed later in the chapter in relation to Rawls' theory of justice.

However, it needs to be pointed out that the formal contemporary conception of a just allocation of resources is grounded in early Aristotelean thoughts and in normative theories in classicism. This formal notion of justice entails (1) equal treatment of equal cases and (2) unequal treatment of unequal cases, proportional to the similarities and differences relevant to that treatment (e.g., Feinberg, 1973; Perelman, 1963). While this represents the formal principle of distributive justice, it fails to specify the exact meaning of relevant similarities or differences which need to be taken into account in the unequal treatment of unequal cases.

(2) *Retributive Justice*

This concerns the punishment for wrongdoings. Philosophical discussions and debates of retributive justice have focused on three major topics:

(a) the justifications for and against *vengeance* (i.e., revenge, getting even) and the role of emotion versus reason in acts of vengeance

(b) the objectives of punishment: objectives either in terms of the deterrence and prevention of future wrongdoing (i.e., the *utilitarian* view of punishment), or in terms of redressing justice (i.e., the *retributivist's* view of punishment).

(c) the criteria for punishment: philosophical discussions have identified several prerequisites for punishment, including

   (i) *unintentionality*
   The wrongdoing is either unintentional or is due to the ignorance of relevant moral rules on the part of the wrongdoer.

   (ii) *inability*
   The wrongdoer is unable to be in control of the act of wrongdoing (e.g., soldiers obeying killing orders at war).

   (iii) *certainty*

The person punished is the one responsible for the wrongdoing.
(iv) *consistency*
The same punishment is applied consistently to identical wrongdoings.
(v) *proportionality*
The severity or magnitude of punishment is proportional to that of the damage the wrongdoing has caused.

(3) *Compensatory Justice*
This concerns the restitution or reparation made to the victim of a wrongdoing. Philosophical discussions have focused on these issues:
(a) the rules of determining the type and magnitude of restitution for victims of wrongdoings.
(b) the criteria for making reparation: Several prerequisites for making reparations to victims of wrongdoings have been identified, including
 (i) *intentionality*
 The wrongdoer has the moral obligation to make restitution when the wrongdoing is an act of intention.
 (ii) *wrongfulness or negligence*
 The wrongdoer has the moral obligation to make restitution when the act is wrongful or is due to negligence.
 (iii) *certainty*
 The wrongdoing is the very cause of the victim's injury or suffering.

Moral philosophers have so far explored the notion of justice from all these three conceptual perspectives. However, during certain periods in history (notably the Plato and Aristotle era), distributive issues were not a justice consideration by virtue of the fact that resource allocations in those times took on a distinctively different meaning from today. This point will become clear in the following historical survey of the meanings of justice.

Classical Philosophy of Justice

Several twentieth century philosophers such as Popper, Rescher, and Sidgwick, have argued that the concept of justice in ancient Greece can be characterised by two key principles: (1) to treat equally all those who are equals, and (2) to give each individual his/her due. Although it seems that the former may translate into the present-day distributive rule of equality, and the latter, the rule of equity, the social-political and economic conditions of ancient Greece would make such a direct translation somewhat unjustifiable.

Homer's Greece (800 B.C.): Justice as "Meritocracy of Might" and "Vengeance"

Robert Solomon in his 1990 book, *A passion for justice*, gave an insightful account for the differential conceptions of justice from Homer (800 B.C.) to Plato and Aristotle (400 B.C.) in ancient Greece. Solomon argued that the Homeric Greece was very much a "tribal" or "warrior" society. Two features characterised *justice* in such a society: "might makes right" and "those who won the wars deserve the spoils". Given today's commonly-accepted definition of merit which consists of *ability, effort and results,* it can be said that might was considered the all-embracing "merit" in Homer's Greece (i.e., the *ability* and skill as a warrior, the *effort* that was demonstrated in winning a war, as well as the *results* of having won a war). The fact that the mighty were automatically allowed all the privileges and possessions thus qualifies Homer's Greece as a "meritocratic" society by today's standards. Cast in this context, justice at that time thus pertained to the "meritocracy of might".

Another conception of the then justice notion, which was embedded in the idea of might, concerned the notion of *vengeance*. As mentioned earlier, vengeance involves the act of revenge or getting even. Although vengeance is very much frowned upon nowadays, it was only through such an act that *might* was demonstrated and that justice was believed to prevail.

Plato and Aristotle (400 B.C.) : Justice as *"the* Personal Virtue", "Harmony", and "the Good Life"

The fact that Plato's Greece inherited the Homeric view of justice was seen by Solomon as "Plato's problem" with the notion of justice. Plato's notion of justice can be summarised as follows:

(1) Justice is not concerned with vengeance. Plato rejected the idea of vengeance on two grounds:
   (a) that "two wrongs do not make a right", and
   (b) that it is *pure reason*, and not at all *emotion* that should guide behaviour.
(2) Justice is not "meritocracy of might". Plato rejected both the ideas of "might makes right" and "the mighty deserves all the privileges". Plato interpreted the pursuit of self-interest as including a concern for others in the society, rather than as sheer selfishness in excluding such a concern.
(3) Justice is the most essential of all the absolute, unchanging and eternal *Moral Ideas*. In other words, justice is the most essential of all the personal Virtues.

(4) Justice is the ideal state of an individual. In this context, it refers to a state of harmonious balance amongst the three parts of the Soul. Such a harmonious state is the key constituent of a "good and happy life".

(5) Justice is the ideal state of a society. In this context, it refers to a state of harmonious co-existence among the three classes of people in the society (i.e., the *rulers*, the *auxiliaries* and the *labourers*). As mentioned previously, such a harmonious state is characterised by each individual performing his/her appropriate duties and being content with his/her assigned lot. Justice so defined also constitutes the core of a good and happy life.

Aristotle's views on justice were essentially the same as those of Plato. Aristotle considered justice as "the sum of all Virtues". It should be remembered that, for Aristotle, Virtues were not absolute moral rules hence their definition needs to take account of the *telos* (purpose) and the context. In the context of either an individual or the larger society, justice constituted a state of harmony within each person as well as amongst all persons in the society.

Modern Philosophy of Justice

Teleological Theories

Moral philosophers adopting a teleological or consequentialistic view of morality tend to view justice differently according to the specific branch of teleological ethics they subscribe to.

Ethical Egoism: Justice as "Result of Social Contract"

Egoism defines morality in terms of maximisation of personal good. Based on the Hobbesian view of human nature, social contracts become a necessity to gain control over potential conflicts in society where each person pursues to maximise his/her own self-interest. Justice in this context can only be achieved through each adhering to such socially-agreed-upon contracts.

Utilitarianism: Justice as "Consideration of Community Good"

Proponents of either act- or rule-utilitarianism define morality in terms of the greatest amount of net good for the greatest number of people concerned. Individual's own self-interest therefore is balanced out against that of all relevant others in society. Justice in this context involves the consideration of others' interest in the net-utility calculation.

Deontological Theories

Deontological ethicists view rights, duties as well as justice as the key constituents of morality. There were two major conceptualizations of justice among these theorists.

Immanuel Kant: Justice as "Pure Practical Reason"

Kant's morality involves the exercise of pure practical reason in the formulation of absolute moral rules which obey both the principles of reversibility and universalisability. Kant's views on justice were consistent with his overall excessive emphasis on rationalism, and they can be summarised as follows:

(1) Justice relies exclusively on pure intellect and reason. Subjective emotions, inclinations, or intuitions do not play any part in the conceptualisation of justice.

(2) Kant's views on distributive justice rest on his idea that people have not only positive moral rights such as the right to a decent life and freedom of choice, but also moral duties such as the duty not to coerce others against their free will. Justice in resource allocation involves a balance between people's entitlements and their moral duties. In other words, the exercise of one's rights would need to be constrained by one's duties to others. As the right to a decent life entails the sustaining of human dignity, when individuals cannot provide for themselves to meet basic physiological needs (e.g., hunger), society or government would have the duty to make such provisions (e.g., social welfare). In that context, the government can then impose taxes on individuals for social welfare purposes.

(3) Kant rejected the idea of vengeance as a constituent of justice on the grounds that it involves emotions and hence is not the work of pure reason or intellect.

(4) To Kant, there is a clear distinction between vengeance and retribution (i.e., punishment for wrongdoing). Kant upheld that retribution is a rational form of maintaining justice. He further argued that the exact form and the magnitude of punishment for a wrongdoing should be determined by following the principle of *proportionality* (i.e., making retribution fit the crime) and that they can only be rationally determined by the court of justice.

(5) Kant emphasised the notion of proportionality in retribution and referred to it as a means of achieving equality in punishment. Kant maintained that it is this feature of fittingness or equality that makes retribution a rational means of justice.

John Rawls: Justice as "Fairness of Distribution"

Rawls' theory of justice, as reviewed earlier, is regarded as the most comprehensive account of the concept of justice in modernity. Rawls' justice deals primarily with the distribution of limited societal resources. A thorough understanding of this all-embracing theory of distributive justice would require some knowledge of the various criteria of "just allocation" in modern philosophical thoughts:

(1) *Just Allocation by Merit: Individualism*
The principles of equity and meritocracy govern all fair allocations of resources. The key features of meritocracy include:
   (i) Resources or rewards are allocated in open competitions according to relative merit.
   (ii) Merit is typically defined in terms of relevant talents (i.e., special capabilities), effort (i.e., contributions towards the objectives of the community) and result (i.e., evidence of productivity). The main problem with allocation by merit concerns the measurement of these three qualifications of merit.
   (iii) Equality of opportunity (i.e., equal life chances) in open competition for resources.

(2) *Just Allocation by Equality: Egalitarianism*
This notion of distributive justice involves the division of resources available to a community equally among its members. This practice is justified by the notion that "all men are created equal". However, critics argued that the egalitarian approach to resource allocation neglects important individual differences in ability, effort and productivity.
   To counter this criticism, some egalitarians (e.g., Bowie) replied by making the distinction between the allocation of political opportunities (e.g., controlling or participating in the political process) and the allocation of economic opportunities (e.g., employment, wealth). By virtue of the fact that equality in political opportunities is considered by most people as a basic right, the criticism only applies to the allocation of economic resources.

(3) *Just Allocation by Ability and Need: Socialism*
In the socialistic ideology of Karl Marx and Nikolai Lenin, societal resources and tasks are to be allocated according to the ability and the need of each individual. Specifically, distributive justice in this context involves the following arrangements:
   (i) Tasks or work burdens of the society are allocated by ability. This practice is justified on the grounds that individuals place high intrinsic value on being able to fully realise their own potentials. To be given

29

the tasks proportional to one's ability provides the opportunity of such self-realisation.

(ii) Rewards or resources of the society are allocated by need. This practice is justified on the grounds that individuals' basic needs would have to be catered for before the welfare of the society can be fostered. Societal resources should therefore be allocated so as to meet the basic needs of each individual.

The most serious attack on the socialistic principle of allocation concerns the distribution of work and burdens in society. Critics argued that ability-based work allocation (being carried out by the political power or authority) negates the fundamental human right of freedom of choice.

(4) *Just Allocation by Freedom of Choice: Libertarianism*

This notion of distributive justice reflects the libertarian's exclusive emphasis on one fundamental moral right, that is, freedom from coercion. Libertarians such as Robert Nozick, took the Kantian categorical imperative (i.e., one should not use others only as means to achieve one's own interest) to the extreme, and interpreted it as meaning that society or government should not impose any restrictions on the individual so as to satisfy its own purposes. The key features of the libertarian justice in resource allocation are as follows:

(i) Individuals should be given the freedom to choose the type of tasks or societal burdens in utilising their abilities.

(ii) Individuals should be given the freedom to choose the share of rewards or societal resources for their effort.

(iii) People should have the right to own property and the right to the free use of their property.

(iv) People should also be free from any restrictions imposed by the government on making contracts, exchanging goods, making profits or paying taxes for social welfare purposes.

Among other issues, critics of libertarianism have pointed out that its interpretation of the Kantian imperative was biased so that its conclusions are in conflict with many of Kant's ideas about justice in resource allocation. For instance, Kant would argue in favour of the idea of governmental imposition of social welfare taxes on its members, on the grounds that justice in allocation involves considerations of both rights and duties.

POSTMODERN PHILOSOPHY OF ETHICS AND JUSTICE

The term postmodernism was originally a description of a contemporary style of art and architecture. When the term is applied to moral philosophy, it refers to a contemporary school of philosophical thoughts which consist of first, a rejection of the "unifying" moral norms explicit in modern philosophy of ethics, and second, an acceptance of the co-existence of pluralistic moral perspectives. Such key themes of postmodern morality can be found in the writings of Nietzsche (1969), Habermas (1983), Derrida (1978), Lyotard (1984), and Rorty (1979, 1982). According to how these theorists deal with the differences and commonalities existing in pluralistic moral perspectives, Nielsen (1993) classified the theories into three categories of postmodernism:

(1) *Unfriendly deconstruction postmodernism* (e.g., Nietzsche, Heidegger, Derrida)—This approach focuses on preserving differences in perspectives. No attempt is made to synthesise the diverse perspectives. As a result, different perspectives co-exist in a "minimal peaceful" or "unstable" state.

(2) *Friendly reconstruction postmodernism* (e.g., Gadamer)—This approach focuses on a respect for differences and a search for commonalities amongst diverse perspectives. This thus results in "temporary progress" towards peaceful co-existence.

(3) *Experimental pragmatism* (e.g., Rorty)—This approach goes a step further than a friendly reconstructivist by continuously exploring and experimenting on ways of satisfying the needs of people holding different moral perspectives.

Despite the difference in the manner of accommodating pluralistic perspectives, all postmodern approaches to morality share these main themes:

(1) A rejection of the "grand narratives" (in Lyotard's terms) which reflects postmodernists' denial of the existence of an absolute, unifiable or totalisable truth. The belief of the existence of a truth is the basic presumption of modern ethicists such as Kant or Mill, whose main contribution was in the identification of such truth in the form of grand narratives.

(2) An insistence on the view that the moral reality can only be discovered by a pluralistic approach which takes account of diverse perspectives.

(3) A rejection of the scientific empirical approach to morality adopted by the logical positivists. Even though some postmodernists (i.e., the pragmatists) subscribe to an "experimental" approach to resolving moral conflicts, that approach does not follow the positivist principle of empirical verification or falsification. Instead, the experiment involves a continuous and on-going social dialogue which focuses on formulating consensus and finding common grounds.

(4) An emphasis on tolerance of the differences in moral perspectives. This emphasis has led some writers to claim that postmodernism has revived an emphasis on virtue ethics in the study of morality (e.g., Walton, 1993).

(5) An emphasis on the attempt of "resolving" systemic or social issues of morality. By giving equal consideration to the perspectives of both the

mainstream majority and the marginalised minorities, Postmodernism has a primary concern with contemporary macro-social issues of morality.

MAJOR ISSUES OF DEBATE IN THE PHILOSOPHY OF ETHICS AND JUSTICE

Each school of moral thoughts reviewed above has made a contribution to the overall understanding of ethics and justice. However, there are some major issues about morality which are the source of disagreement in philosophical theories of ethics and justice. Despite intensive debates, there has been no general consensus amongst moral philosophers. These issues are briefly identified as follows:

(1) *The issue of objectivity vs. subjectivity*
     A contemporary philosopher, Luther Binkley, has identified the exact issues involved in the rather confusing debate over objectivity v. subjectivity. Binkley (1961) argued that this debate has been carried out at least in the context of three different questions:
     (a) *"Is morality an objective property or quality that can be defined or identified?"*
          This question is at the heart of the naturalistic versus non-naturalist debate. While the Greek philosophers asserted that there exists factual Ideas or Forms which are both real and immutable, other theories of ethics (i.e., intuitionism) deny that morality is an definable or identifiable objective property and assert that it can only be "intuited", "reflected upon" and "discovered" by each individual self. The former represents the objective-naturalistic position of ethics, whereas the latter captures the subjective-non-naturalistic view of morality.
     (b) *"Are standards of morality objective in the sense that they are universalisable across all times and all situations?"*
          In this context, the issue of objectivity v. subjectivity is at the core of the debate of relativism versus absolutism.
          While both the teleological and deontological theories in modernity take the affirmative position to this question, postmodernists firmly take the opposite stance. Binkley argued that the answer to this question depends entirely on the type of justifications one provides for the answer: either moral standards are the results of the cumulative experience of human race and civilisation (hence the objectivists' justification for universality), or these standards are the products of a specific culture at a given period in history (the subjectivists' justification for non-universality). Binkley concluded that no "clear cut choice can be made", as both are "calling attention to certain features of moral judgement" (p.192). Binkley also seemed to think it pointless to carry on with this circular debate and suggested that "it is now time to recognise the truth in the claims of both

the absolutist and the relativist. To force an exclusive choice here might well blind us to important aspects of moral judgements" (p.196).

(c) *"Are moral judgements objective in the sense that moral disputes can be settled by rational means rather than by personal preferences?"* Binkley argued that the answer would depend on the stage of the "dispute process" one refers to. Up to the stage when all reasons for dealing with the dispute have been carefully examined, this phase of the resolution can be said to be a rational one. So objectivists are correct in insisting that moral disputes can only be settled by rational considerations of all reasons for the conflict. However, in the event that an individual has to choose one of the reasons to follow or to act upon, then this choice is ultimately the responsibility of that individual. The subjectivist's view that disputes can only be resolved by personal preference or choice would be correct when it is applied to this stage of the moral dispute-resolution process.

(2) *The issue of priority of moral imperatives or rules*

Different normative theories of ethics prescribe different rules or sets of rules in guiding moral acts. One logical question concerns the priority of these various rules. Although there is no general consensus among moral philosophers, many hold the view that the "priority" would depend on the particular context of the moral judgement or moral act hence there is no overriding priority of any one set of rules over the other (e.g., Binkley, 1961; Velasquez, 1982).

(3) *The faculty of reason and the notion of rationality*

Plato not only accorded Reason (intellect) the highest status in the human Soul, but also its ideal Wisdom, the highest status of human Virtues. To Plato, the ideal state for an individual is one in which reason is ultimately in control. It is only through pure reason that a person can attain knowledge and the eternal truth. Aristotle also considered pure reason as the most essential characteristics of the eternal Form , but it is inseparable from the reality of perception or Senses.

However, the status of reason in Scholasticism changed: it was equated with the moral convictions of the church in the Medieval period (i.e., the Middle Ages or the Dark Ages); but was redefined in terms of both *subjectivism* (as individual free will) and *universalisation* (as a general rule) during the Renaissance period. This latter status of *reason* was maintained in both the Kantian and the Utilitarian ethics in modernity. However, the prevailing influence of Comte's positivism in modernity has led many to subscribe to the view that there ought to be one single unified faculty of reason which is identifiable by methods of empirical verification. The very existence of vastly different moral imperatives was therefore suspicious and they were rejected as meaningless by logical positivists. As a result, Rossouw (1994) pointed out that the study of morality in modernity is much restricted in scope.

Postmodernists aim to redress this problem by broadening the scope of reason so as to include diverse moral perspectives in rational interactions or dialogues. The philosophical treatment of reason has developed into an independent academic discipline under the general topic of rationality. Postmodernist and feminist critiques of rationality-based ethical theories in modernity are briefly discussed in chapter three.

(4) *The status of self-interest (and the issue of innateness of morality)*

In classicism, self-interest, in its purest form as selfish personal wants, was seen as an antithesis of virtues. However, in modernity, it was considered by ethical egoism as the motivating force in moral behaviour. Both act- and rule-utilitarianism have since toned down the role of pure self-interest in morality by including the interest of all affected parties in the net-utility calculation. For the deontologists, self-interest plays a minor role in morality. The discussion of the role of self-interest and the issue of whether morality is "innate" is embedded in the debate of human nature. To gain an understanding of the topic, one would need to study not only the philosophical position on human nature held by the classical masters as well as Hobbes, Rousseau, Smith, but also the biological (Darwin) and sociobiological (e.g., Dawkins, Wilson) positions on human nature. The sociobiological perspective on the origins of morality is discussed briefly in chapter three under the heading of evolutionary ethics.

Chapter 3   Psychological Literature on Ethics and Justice

From an historical point of view, while moral philosophy dates back to ancient Greece, moral psychology is a far more recent development in the social sciences. In terms of expertise, moral philosophy prescribes what ought to be norms of moral behaviour. However, twentieth century mainstream psychology is very much influenced by scientific positivism, hence its main task is to identify, describe and analyse typical patterns of behaviour. In the context of ethical inquiry, psychologists' expertise lies with the descriptive task of how people typically act and what they typically judge as being right or wrong.

Given that moral standards consist of both a factual component (i.e., what these standards actually are) and a value component (i.e., what these standards ought to be), it becomes evident that the input from both moral philosophy and moral psychology is of necessity for ethical enquiry. While philosophers engage in the evaluation of moral behaviour through reflective consideration, psychologists provide factual descriptions of people's understandings of ethics and justice through empirical investigation.

The contribution of psychologists towards ethical enquiry is briefly reviewed in this chapter. As psychological theories and research pertaining to ethics and morality in general appear to exist independently from those pertaining to justice, these two literatures will be reviewed separately. Following the review, recent advances in the psychology of ethics and justice are briefly discussed.

MORAL   PSYCHOLOGY

This section reviews the four theoretical and empirical approaches to morality in the psychological literature. The four approaches are identified by Waterman (1988) as the taxonomy approach (e.g., Forsyth's personal ethics), the dialectical approach (e.g., Hogan's ethics of social responsibility), the cognitive-developmental approach (e.g., Kohlberg's justice-focused morality), and the interactional approach (e.g., Haan's ethics of social dialogue).

The Taxonomy Approach

Forsyth's (1980) Personal or Individual Ethics

Forsyth takes an individual differences approach to morality. His theory of personal moral philosophy focuses on the classification of a person's predominant philosophical orientation into a 2 x 2 taxonomy. Two conceptual dimensions are used in the classification which then result in *four* categories of philosophical orientation. The two conceptual dimensions are:

(1) *Relativism*: defined in terms of the extent to which an individual believes in the feasibility of a universal set of moral rules. On the extremely low end of this continuum, individuals typically operate on universal ethical principles irrespective of the context. On the other high end of the continuum, individuals typically give primary consideration to the particularities of the circumstance in their moral functioning.

(2) *Idealism*: defined in terms of the degree to which an individual is concerned with the welfare of others. Individuals high on this dimension typically subscribe to the teleological principle of maximising good consequences for *all* people, and this way they also obey a basic moral ideal of never harm others. However, those low on this dimension typically operate on the egoists' principle of maximising the utility of one's own consequences even when that involves violating others' rights or harming others in some way.

The combination of these two criterial dimensions results in four types of philosophical orientation:

(1) *Situationists* (high on both relativism and idealism):
those who reject universal moral rules but insist on never harming others and on maximising good consequences for all. This orientation parallels the situation ethics of Fletcher.

(2) *Subjectivists* (high on relativism but low on idealism):
those who reject universal moral rules but insist on maximising consequences only for oneself. This orientation parallels the ethics of ethical egoism.

(3) *Absolutists* (low on relativism but high on idealism):
those who follow universal moral principles and insist on never harming others and on maximising good consequences for all. This orientation parallels to the ethics of Kantian deontology.

(4) *Exceptionists* (low on both relativism and idealism):
those who follow universal ethical principles but insist on maximising consequences only for oneself. This orientation parallels the ethics of rule-utilitarianism.

These individual differences in moral orientation can be assessed by the Ethics Position Questionnaire (Forsyth, 1980). Empirical research using the EPQ has shown that individual moral orientation can have a significant influence on

(1) *moral attitudes*—among all four types, absolutists tend to take a most conservative position in contemporary controversial moral issues (e.g., Forsyth, 1980; Leary, Knight, & Barnes, 1986; Singh & Forsyth, 1989).

(2) *moral judgement*—among all four types, absolutists tend to make the most harsh and negative moral judgments by focusing primarily on potential harm to others (e.g., Forsyth & Pope, 1984). However, situational and cognitive factors such as perceived personal responsibility can sometimes moderate the above relationship between personal moral orientation and moral judgements (e.g., Forsyth, 1981; 1985). More recently, Barnett et al. (1994) found that personal moral ideology affected moral judgements about business-related ethical issues.

(3) *moral behavior*—several studies found no significant relationship between personal moral orientation and actual behavior or the propensity to act immorally (e.g., Forsyth & Berger, 1982). However, individuals high on idealism (situationists and absolutists) were more likely to be persuaded to act immorally (e.g., Nye & Forsyth, 1984). Based on other similar findings (e.g., Forsyth & Nye, 1990), it was concluded that *"people who espouse lofty moral values may tend to behave the most immorally"* (Forsyth, 1992, p.466).

(4) *emotive reactions*—personal orientations have a differential effect on self-esteem (e.g., Forsyth & Matney, 1990) as well as on subjective feelings or emotions about immoral behavior (e.g., Forsyth & Berger, 1982).

(5) *ethical decision making in a business context*—personal ethics have a significant effect on business ethical decisions and the suggested punishment for ethical infractions (e.g., Barnett et al., 1994; Giacalone et al., 1995).

Boyce and Jensen's Theory of Moral Reasoning

Boyce and Jensen's (1978) taxonomy used three conceptual dimensions which resulted in eight categories to classify moral thought and reasoning. The three conceptual dimensions are:

(1) *teleology*— either egoistic or utilitarian concerns

(2) *definition of good*—either the hedonistic definition of good as pleasure and pain; or the deontological definition of good as duty and justice

(3) *rule- versus act-perspective*—either the moral principle is applicable to an act, or it is applicable to a overriding rule that governs the act

The eight resulting categories are: (1) hedonistic egoism (2) nonhedonistic egoism (3) hedonistic rule-utilitarianism (4) nonhedonistic rule-utilitarianism (5) hedonistic act-utilitarianism (6) nonhedonistic act-utilitarianism (7) rule deontology (8) act deontology.

These styles of moral reasoning can be assessed by the Moral Contents Components Test (Boyce & Jensen, 1978). Empirical research using the MCCT has been limited; however, it has been shown that different types of criminals on probation had different moral reasoning styles. Those with more frequent arrests and convictions used the hedonistic act-utilitarianism style; whereas those with less frequent arrests used the act-deontology style in their moral reasoning (e.g., Wolff & Smith, 1983).

The Dialectical Approach

Hogan's (1973; 1974) Ethics of Social Responsibility

From a developmental perspective, Hogan criticised early approaches to morality (i.e., Piagetian and Freudian models) of focusing only on a singular psychological construct in interpreting moral development. Instead of providing another such "univariate" interpretation, Hogan proposed a "multivariate" theory of morality which focuses on the "dialectical aspects" of moral development. Hogan's (1974) dialectical analysis of the emergence of morality is primarily concerned with the identification of *"critical paradoxes, polarities or discontinuities in nature"* and the attempt to *"reconcile them in terms of more fundamental principles"* (p.109).

Hogan's theory of morality is grounded in two philosophical schools of thoughts: *existentialism* (i.e., morality is a result of individual free will hence there can be no absolute or universalised moral rules), and the Hobbesian notion of *egocentrism* (i.e., people are naturally selfish and can't be trusted to behave morally; hence the need for social contracts to ensure mutual protection of self-interest). Based on these presumptions, Hogan identified five dimensions of morality:

(1) *moral knowledge*—defined in terms of the learning of social contracts or social rules pertaining to moral behavior.

(2) *socialisation*—defined in terms of the extent to which an individual considers social contracts or rules to be "personally binding". Individuals high on this dimension of *socialisation* tend to internalise the existence of such contracts hence their behavior is more likely to be so constrained.

38

(3) *empathy*—defined in terms of the degree of sensitivity to others' perspectives and reactions to a moral act. Individuals high on this dimension tend to follow the utilitarian rule of "greatest good for all"; those low on this dimension are inclined to follow the egoistic rule of "greatest good for self".

(4) *autonomy*—defined in terms of the degree to which an individual is autonomous or non-conforming in moral decision making.

(5) *the basis for moral judgments*—defined in terms of either following the principle of natural law (i.e., a natural-law-orientation to morality) or the principle of positive law (i.e., a positive-law-orientation). Individuals with a predominant natural-law-orientation believe in the existence of universal moral standards, hence their behaviors are guided by such absolute moral rules. However, those with a predominant positive-law-orientation reject the existence of absolute moral standards; instead, they are guided by the positive laws of the society (i.e., legal laws and legislations). In Hogan's theory, the morality of individuals taking the natural-law-orientation is referred to as *"the ethics of personal conscience"*; and that of those with a positive-law-orientation is referred to as *"the ethics of social responsibility"*.

Despite Hogan's efforts in using the dialectical analysis to resolve the many paradoxes apparent in his theory, critics have argued that these efforts are only partially successful (for a review, see Waterman, 1988). However, from an empirical point of view, Hogan's theory has been shown to have external validity in predicting moral actions. Using Hogan's (1970) Survey of Ethical Attitudes in assessing individual differences in ethical orientations, it has been shown that a differential use of the two ethics was evident (a) between samples of criminals and college students (Hartnett & Shumate, 1980), and (b) between samples of criminals who had committed either alcohol-related or drug-related offences (Williams, Vaugan, & Savia, 1976).

The Cognitive-Developmental Approach

The cognitive-developmental approach to morality follows the Piagetian tradition (Piaget, 1932, 1965) which deals with the development of cognition and intellect in general. Central to this approach is the premise that intellectual and cognitive functioning develops in several hierachically structured stages of invariant sequence. These stages of intellectual development were said to be universal across different cultures. Within the Piagetian framework, the development of morality is a by-product of an individual's general intellectual development. As an individual's general intellectual and cognitive functioning becomes increasingly complex, as the result of on-going processes of *accommodation* and *assimilation*, the individual's moral reasoning also acquires greater sophistication. The development of moral reasoning in Piagetian theory is characterised by a gradual differentiation in the emphasis on either the *severity of the consequences of the moral act,* or the *intentionality* of the moral agent. Kohlberg followed the Piagetian tradition and the structural framework in developing his theory of moral development.

Kohlberg's (1969, 1976) Justice-focused Morality

Kohlberg's theory of moral development consists of six invariant stages within three levels:

Level 1: *Preconventional Level*
Morality involves the consideration of the hedonistic rule of maximising pleasure and minimising pain. The main criteria of morality therefore are seeking reward and avoiding punishment. The right or wrong of an act is therefore judged in terms of its consequences.

    Stage 1: *Punishment and obedience orientation*
    The key criterion of morality is avoiding punishment by obedience.

    Stage 2: *Instrumental relativist orientation*
    The key criterion of morality is being instrumental in gaining reward.

Level 2: *Conventional Level*
Morality involves the consideration of consequences for others in society, and of social rules and contracts. Morality is defined in terms of conformity to the rules of the authorities (e.g., parents, or law-makers).

    Stage 3: *"Good boy-good girl" orientation*
    The key criterion of morality is gaining social approval.

    Stage 4: *Law and order orientation*
    The key criterion of morality is a rigid adherence to social rules and laws of society for the sake of conformity.

Level 3: *Postconventional Level*
Morality involves the exercise of internalised principles of ethics or personal conscience.

    Stage 5: *Social-contract legalistic orientation*
    The key criterion of morality is respecting the rights of others by following social contracts. However, respect for others' rights and consequences take precedence over rigid social-rule-following.

    Stage 6: *Universal ethical principle orientation*
    The key criterion of morality is respecting the rights of others by following one's internalised ethical principles.

Kohlberg's theory of morality is based on the deontological notion of *justice*. The justice of an act is defined in terms of both the principle of *reversibility* (i.e., an act is considered just if it can still be considered just after reversing the roles of the actor and the recipient) and the principle of *universalisability* (i.e., an act is considered just if it can still be considered just when everyone in society acts in that way). The notion of justice is the core of Kohlberg's theory. The six different stages are defined in terms of the extent to which the principals of justice are applied in typical moral reasoning. In lower stages of moral reasoning, there is little evidence of the application of justice principles. However, moral reasoning in the postconventional level is characterised by the exclusive use of justice principles.

Empirically, Kohlberg's theory has been repeatedly put to test by the use of either the instrument Moral Judgement Interview (Colby & Kohlberg, 1987), or the Defining Issues Test (Rest, 1979). These studies have been rather consistent in demonstrating the external validity of the theory in predicting individual differences in moral judgments and moral acts. There have been several reviews of these empirical research (i.e., Blasi, 1980; Derry, 1987; Elm & Weber, 1994; Higgins, Power, & Kohlberg, 1984; Rest et al., 1986; Trevino, 1992).

Gilligan's (1982, 1986) Care-focused Morality

As a result of her empirical work on moral reasoning which was carried out within Kohlberg's stage framework, Carol Gilligan pointed out the inadequacy of that theory in its conceptualisation of morality solely in terms of the principals of justice. Guided by her data on obvious gender differences in moral reasoning, Gilligan proposed an alternative *affective* perspective to morality which focuses on care for, and relationship with, others. This "care" perspective to morality is in sharp contrast with the traditional justice-perspective which emphasises individual rights and autonomy. The care orientation to morality appears consistent with Kagan's (1984) notion of the feeling-based processes of morality.

It is worth noting that Gilligan did not completely reject the Kohlbergan notion that morality is justice-based. She only rejected the singular and pivotal role of justice that Kohlberg attached to the highest postconventional level of moral reasoning. Because females' care-focused morality only characterises the conventional level of moral thoughts in Kohlberg's theory (a lower-level of development), Gilligan argued that equal emphasis should be given to the care-based ethics at the highest level of moral development, as empirical studies have shown that individuals' moral reasoning can readily be categorised along the care-justice distinction (for a review, see Gilligan & Wiggins, 1988).

Conceptually, Gilligan's notion of the two-voices of morality has been applied to a variety of disciplines of ethical decision making (e.g., law, depth psychology, medicine and business). The notion is used primarily in explicating gender differences in decision making style (e.g., Dugan, 1987; Gilligan & Pollak, 1988;

41

Hasse, 1987; Jack & Jack, 1988; Kitwood, 1990; Martin & Shaw, 1993; White, 1992; Wood, 1986). At the practical level, recent educational programs on the training of prosocial or moral behavior have also been designed on the basis of a moral system which integrates the principles of care and justice (e.g., Battistich, Waston, Solomon, Schaps, & Soloman, 1991; Lickona, 1991).

A great deal of recent research generated from the cognitive-developmental approach to morality has centred around the care-justice debate. While some research focuses on the incompatability and differences between the two moral persepectives (e.g., Pratt, Diessner, Hunsberger, Pancer, & Savoy, 1991; Skoe & Diessner, 1994), other research however suggests that justice considerations naturally include an affective component, hence the care-justice connection needs to be emphasised (e.g., Blasi, 1990; Puka, 1991).

The Interactional Approach

The interactional approach rejects the existence of normative or natural principles of ethics. Instead, morality is defined in terms of social constructions. That is, morality is the result of a dynamic process of on-going social interactions which aim to achieve a "moral balance" or a consensus agreed-upon by all parties concerned. Considering that these features are what define postmodernism in the philosophy of ethics, the interactional models in moral psychology could be seen as taking a distinctive postmodern approach to morality. Specifically, these models appear to resemble the position of experimental pragmatism in the postmodern school of philosophy described in the previous chapter.

Haan's (1982, 1983) Ethics of Social Dialogue

Haan argued that in order for people to live harmoniously together in society, situations which call for ethical decisions occur continuously. Morality therefore is characterised by the on-going process of social dialogues between parties holding different perspectives. In this context, the success of the social dialogues requires that (a) each party has the motivation to partake in the dialogues, (b) that each party possesses the necessary social skills for successful interactions, and (c) that each party adheres to the principle of equality or equity in the interaction. The last requirement means that all perspectives are given equal consideration in the process, and that the interests and needs of all parties are taken into account in reaching the consensus. Haan further pointed out that to the extent that these principles are not used by all parties in the dialogue, the consensus reached may not be an *authentically balanced* one. However, this can be redressed at a later point of the on-going dialogue process.

Central to Haan's ethics of social dialogue is the idea that individuals interact with one another with the intention to achieve new moral balances through

42

mutual understanding and compromises. Based on Kohlberg's definitions of moral developmental stages, Haan identified five levels of "interpersonal morality", which characterise an individual's level of social skills of engaging in such moral dialogue. The progression in the level of interpersonal dialogue skills is characterised by an increasing awareness of the self-other differentiation, and an increasing sensitivity to the requirements of achieving moral balances.

Empirical research has been limited. (e.g., Haan, 1977, 1983). Studies of the model have employed Haan's manual for the analysis of interactional morality. Haan's 1978 study showed that when participants of social dialogues were under stress and when their status was unequal, the achievement of moral balance was less likely.

Rossouw's (1994) Rational Interaction Approach to Moral Dissensus

The framework of Rossouw's approach is described in detail in Chapter 4 which deals with applied ethics. The focus of this approach to morality is on the resolution of moral dissensus. Rossouw has identified the situations to which the proposed resolution processes apply, "...*When a moral dispute develops and when moral dissensus is accepted as a permanent feature of our culture*" (p.17). Rossouw also pointed out that moral dissensus is a distinct feature of the post-modern culture in general. The proposed resolution processes, like Haan's ethics, involve an ongoing dialogue between disputing parties. The dialogue aims to enhance the moral sensitivity of each party and to develop empathy with the other party. Therefore, both Haan and Rossouw take a postmodern interactive approach to the resolution of moral dissensus and morality in general.

PSYCHOLOGY OF JUSTICE

The dominant conceptual frameworks in the psychological literature of justice stem from two distinctively different traditions:

(1) *The philosophical tradition of distributive justice*
These psychological theories focused mainly on issues pertaining to distributive justice by following the tradition of philosophical enquiries of justice. Examples are the justice motive theory, relative deprivation theory or equity theory. Their main concerns are the fairness of the final decision of an allocation and the social psychological consequences of that decision. Because of the focus on allocation outcome, these theories are generally referred to as outcome or *content* theories (Greenberg, 1987).

(2) *The legal and judicial tradition of procedural justice*
Roughly parallel to the development of outcome theories, psychological conceptualization of justice in the 1970s was influenced greatly by the

research on judicial procedures. John Thibaut and Laurens Walker first applied the justice concept in court-room legal proceedings to social psychological research on conflict resolution. Inspired by their work, justice researchers began to explore the notion from a procedural perspective and to formulate various theories of procedural justice which prescribe fair allocation rules. Thibaut and Walker's pioneer work thus marks an important turning point in psychological research on justice. Because the focus of procedural justice theories is on the process leading to the final allocation decision, these theories are typically known as *process* theories

The following sections present a brief review of the key justice theories developed within each of these two traditions.

Distributive or Outcome Justice Theories

Adam's (1965) Equity Theory

The conceptual basis of equity theory stems from the principle of social comparisons and balance theory (Heider 1958). The main propositions of equity theory are:

(1)   Individuals have the tendency to compare their own outcome of an allocation with a *referent other*. The unit of comparison is defined in terms of the *input/outcome ratio*.

(2)   The criteria for choosing the referent other for a comparison are: the relevance of the comparison, and the availability of information for comparison.

(3)   When one's own "input/outcome ratio" is perceived as smaller than that of the referent other (e.g., own: 10/20; other: 15/17), the person is likely to see him/herself as being under-rewarded. Conversely (e.g., own: 20/25; other: 15/25), the person is likely to perceive him/herself as being over-rewarded.

(4)   The threshold for perceiving oneself as being over-rewarded is typically higher than that for perceiving oneself as being under-rewarded. In other words, people are more ready to perceive injustice in terms of under-rewardedness.

(5)   Perceived inequity causes tension. The amount of tension felt is proportional to the level of perceived inequity. Tension motivates the person to take action to reduce it so as to achieve equilibrium. This proposition was also emphasised by other equity theorists including Walster, Walster, and Berscheid (1978).

(6)   When faced with inequity, people may react differently by taking one of these alternative courses of action to redress equity: they may change their own input, change their own outcome, act on the referent other to make changes, rationalise or reinterpret their own input/outcome ratio so that it can be seen

in a more favourable light, choose another referent person for comparison, or they may opt to leave the field to escape inequity altogether (e.g., quitting work).

Adam's equity theory has dominated psychological research in justice for more than two decades since its conception. Empirical research has been largely supportive of the predictions generated by theory (for reviews, see Folger, 1986a; Greenberg, 1982; 1987; 1990; 1993; Greenberg, 1993). The main criticism concerns the theory's conceptualisation of the social comparison process solely in terms of a "local comparison" which involves one specific referent other. Later equity theorists have addressed this criticism by conceptualising the comparison process in terms of a "referential comparison" involving a non-specific generalised other (i.e., Berger, Zeiditch, Anderson, & Cohen, 1972). Yet another conceptualization of the comparison process involves an intra-personal cognitive process, rather than a social or inter-personal process. One such example is Folger's referent cognitive theory to be discussed later.

Leventhal's (1976, 1980) Distributive Justice Judgement Theory

This theory concerns judgements of distributive justice. The theory posits that individuals make distributive justice judgements according to whether actual outcomes correspond to perceptions of *deserved outcomes*. Several allocation rules are used to determine the deserved outcome (e.g., a need-based rule, a contribution-based rule, an equality rule). Individuals assign relative weights to each of the allocation rules according to the specific situation. For instance, in situations whereby social harmony is most emphasised, a greater weight will be given to the equality rule. However, an equity-based distributive rule is most likely to be adopted for situations emphasising competition or productivity. Relevant research has been supportive of this theory (for review, see Deutsch, 1985).

Lerner's (1977, 1982) Justice Motive Theory

Lerner noted that most traditional theories of justice carry the assumption that people are predominantly concerned with maximising their own outcome. Lerner argued that the self-interest notion does not capture the unique qualities of justice. The key features of the justice motive theory are:

(1) Justice is a fundamental concern of human beings and it is inadequate to conceptualise the notion as a means to an end (maximising self-interest). Rather, it should be conceptualised as an end in itself.

(2) People have a basic need to "believe in a just world". This belief is formed as a result of universal childhood experiences with delayed gratifications. During the delayed waiting period, children learn the association between expectation

and desired outcome, and hence the meaning of the notions of deservingness and entitlement. Such an understanding forms the basis for a belief in a just world where people always receive what they deserve.

(3) This need to believe in a just world is pre-eminent and more powerful than other motives of maximising own interest.

(4) The model identified four rules of resource allocation: (i) competition: allocation based on results of performance, (ii) equity: allocation based on relative contribution, (iii) parity: allocation based on equality, and (iv) Marxian justice: allocation based on need. The choice of the allocation rules depends on the personal relationship (e.g., intimacy) among the parties concerned, and the interdependence (e.g., cooperation) required to attain the outcome.

Empirical research has been supportive of the just-world hypothesis (e.g., Lerner, 1980; Lerner & Lerner, 1981). Research evidence has also been consistent with the theory's predictions concerning the choice of the allocation rules (e.g. Charles & Carver, 1979; Deutsch, 1985; Greenberg & Cohen, 1982; Lerner, 1980).

Crosby's (1976, 1982) Relative Deprivation Theory

The conceptual basis of this theory stems from earlier relative deprivation models dealing with sociological, political and economic problems (e.g., Davies, 1959; Gurr, 1970; Pettigrew, 1967; Runciman, 1966). The term relative deprivation, coined by Stouffer, Suchman, DeVinney, Star, and Williams in 1949, was used to account for an unexpected empirical finding that Black American military personnel stationed in northern military bases were less satisfied than their counterparts stationed in southern bases, despite the fact that economic and social conditions were overall more favourable for the former. Stouffer et al. interpreted the results in terms of the differential referent used by the two groups of soldiers in the comparison process: minority soldiers in the north tend to compare themselves with their civilian counterparts in the north and as a result, they felt relatively less privileged. However, the southern soldiers compared themselves with the civilians in the south and perceived themselves as being in a more favourable position. The observed feelings of discontent or deprivation hence are the result of the social comparison process involving different referent others. The key propositions of the relative deprivation theory are:

(1) In resources or reward allocations, an individual has the tendency to compare his/her outcome with a referent other. As a result, the person may feel that he/she has been deprived of a more deserving outcome.

(2) The preconditions of feelings of deprivation consist of the subjective perception of *entitlement* or *deservingness* (i.e., seeing oneself as deserving a

better outcome), *desire* or *wanting* (i.e., seeing an outcome as desirable to have), *referent other* (i.e., seeing a referent other possessing the desired outcome), as well as *feasibility* or *future expectations* (i.e., perceived likelihood of getting the desired outcome in the future). The level of felt deprivation is positively related to the level of felt entitlement, desire and the presence of referent other possessing the desired outcome. However, it is negatively related to the level of future expectations.

(3) Feelings of deprivation serve to motivate the person to take actions to redress equity hence they have behavioural consequences. The behavioural consequences of feelings of deprivation can be either individual-oriented (e.g., resentment or depression) or system-oriented, which may be either constructive (e.g., forming a union, peaceful demonstration) or destructive (e.g., riot or social unrest).

(4) Following the earlier relative deprivation models, the theory makes the distinction between *egoistic deprivation* and *fraternal or group deprivation*. The former refers to an individual's feelings of discontent resulting from a comparison involving one referent other. The latter refers to the discontent stemming from the status of the entire group, to which the person belongs, as compared to another referent group (e.g., gender group or ethnic groups).

(5) Fraternal or group deprivation has a broader definition in this theory than in its predecessors. In its broadest sense, group deprivation can refer to feelings of grievance about any group, regardless of whether the person feels part of the group. This more general conceptualisation of group deprivation is similar to an earlier notion, "relative deprivation on behalf of others" (Runciman, 1966).

The theory of relative deprivation has been applied to several contemporary issues of resources allocation, including pay satisfaction and inequity (e.g, Clayton & Crosby, 1992; deCarufel, 1986; Dornstein, 1989; Jackson, 1989; Moore, 1991a, 1991b; Sweeney, McFarlin & Inderrieden, 1990), employment and career opportunities (e.g., Barnes Nacoste, 1993; Singer, 1992b; 1993; Tougas & Veilleux, 1989; Veilleux & Tougas, 1989), and advance notice of outcome (e.g., Cropanzano & Randall, 1995). However, Wegener (1990) found that people's perceptions about social economical allocations were distorted as a result of the levelling vs. sharpening process in social hierarchy perceptions. These observed misperceptions about resource distribution may create illusory justice evaluations. As a result, Wegener warned that relative deprivation research would have to take account of this phenomenon of perceptual distortion.

Folger's (1986a, 1986b) Referent Cognition Theory

Folger noted the major inadequacies with equity theory: the definition of the social comparison process in terms of a specific referent person; the unit of comparison

47

in terms of input/outcome ratio; the neglect of the notion of procedural justice; and the lack of specificity in the prediction of individuals' reactions to perceived injustice. In an attempt to address these inadequacies, Folger proposed the theory of referent cognition. The key propositions of the theory are:

(1) Perceptions of inequity as well as feelings of deprivation stem from a hypothetical intrapersonal, rather than an interpersonal, comparison process. The intrapersonal process involves a comparison between a state of reality (i.e., the actual allocation outcome) and a state of imaginable mental referent (i.e., a referent cognition of outcome of *what could have been instead* or *what might have been instead*). While the *actual outcome* refers to what in reality the individual gets from the allocation, the *referent outcome* refers to what the individual imagines that he/she could have got. *Referent outcomes* may vary according to the *degree of favourability* of the specific imaginable outcome:

  (i) *high-referent outcome (high degree of favourability)*
      An imaginable outcome that is more favourable than the actual outcome in reality.

  (ii) *low-referent outcome (low degree of favourability)*
      An imaginable outcome that is "not any better than" the actual outcome in reality.

(2) The unit of comparison no longer includes the input factor; the evaluation of the outcome takes account of "all possible circumstances that are instrumental in producing the outcome" (i.e., the *instrumentalities*). The *instrumentalities* thus include

  (i) *actual instrumentalities*
      The actual input or other actual events that are responsible for the actual outcomes.

  (ii) *referent instrumentalities*
      All other imaginable events, policies, procedures or factors that might have operated instead, and that might have produced other more desirable referent outcomes.

  Conceptualised this way, the notion of instrumentality thus includes the original equity notion of input (as one of the *actual instrumentalities*). Further, the notion also includes considerations of procedural justice factors as one of the *referent instrumentalities*. (i.e., imaginable procedures that may have been instrumental in producing another, more desired referent outcome).

(3) The felt level of deprivation is determined by three factors:

  (i) *level of referent outcome*
      The level of referent outcome interacts with the next factor in determining the level of felt deprivation.

48

(ii) *likelihood of amelioration*
This refers to the perceived likelihood of attaining the outcome in the future, a notion akin to the future expectation concept in the relative deprivation theory. The theory posits that high likelihood of amelioration results in less resentment or feelings of deprivation. Empirical evidence further suggests that the highest level of resentment or feeling of deprivation was associated with the combined condition of high likelihood of amelioration and high referent outcome.

(iii) *level of justifiability*
This refers to the extent to which referent instrumentalities are perceived as more reasonable or justifiable than the actual instrumentalities. The theory posits that the level of felt deprivation is determined by the result of the comparison between actual and referent instrumentalities; the more that the referent instrumentalities are perceived as justifiable, the greater the level of felt deprivation.

The main predictions of referent cognition theory have been well supported by several empirical studies (e.g., Brockner et al., 1994; Cropanzano & Folger, 1989; Folger & Konovsky, 1989; Folger, Rosenfield, & Robinson, 1983). However, a recent study found only partial support (Syroit, Lodewijkx, Franssen, & Gerstel, 1993). When the theory was applied to employees who had to go through an outplacement programme due to their organisation's retrenchment strategy, the theory correctly predicted job commitment and satisfaction for those employees who were successful with the transfer program and found new employment. The theory failed to predict such job attitudes for employees who were unsuccessful with the transfer programme.

Lansberg's (1989) Social Categorisation Theory of Entitlement

Drawing upon the conceptual notions of justice in classical philosophy as well as the empirical findings of justice research, Lansberg proposed a three-step model of entitlement in an organisational context. Central to the model is the dynamic process of social categorisation. The key propositions of the theory are:

(1) *Step-one: "Segmenting the social environment into discontinuous group categories"*
An individual member of an organisation categorises all members of that organisation into two broad categories:
  (i) *inclusive group or referent similars*
  Members in this group are considered as similar or "equals" to the individual. The theory posits that several contextual factors can have an influence on this categorisation process: organisational size, its social composition, and the structure of the organisation. Members in this

group are entitled to the same treatment in the allocation of organisational resources.

(ii) *differentiated group or referent dissimilars*
Members in this group are considered as dissimilar to, or as "unequals" of, oneself. Members in this group may legitimately claim different entitlement from the individual.

(2) *Step-two: "Locating the self in the social categories"*
The individual places him/herself into the appropriate social group (i.e., the equals or similars) by identifying with that group.

(3) *Step-three: "Engaging in two different comparison processes"*
The individual makes two social comparisons:

(i) *Social comparison with similar others in the same category*
The person asks him/herself the question, "Am I being treated equally as my similars?" The answer to this question determines the person's reactions. However, individuals' reactions typically aim to preserve a sense of equality within the referent similar group.

(a) If the answer is affirmative, the person sees him/herself as getting just entitlement. The person may offer help to other referent similars to achieve a better outcome. The person may also "downplay the significance of the advantage". Both reactions aim to maintain a sense of equality within the group.

(b) If the person perceives him/herself as being treated less well than others, the person may seek help from other referent similars, or to appeal to the allocator for a better outcome. The aim is to preserve a sense of equality within the group.

(ii) *Social contrast with dissimilar others in the differentiated category*
The individual first determines what differential entitlements for the dissimilars are regarded as legitimate. The person then asks the question, "Am I treated in accordance to the legitimate criteria vis-a-vis my referent dissimilars?"Again, the person may react differently according to the answer to this question:

(a) If a person unduly receives more favourable entitlements (with reference to a legitimate entitlement), the person may rationalise this, or try to increase input to match the outcome, or simply ignore the over-reward.

(b) If a person feels unduly disadvantaged vis-a-vis referent dissimilars, the person would react in a similar fashion as predicted by relative deprivation theory (i.e., *social unrest, resentment, forming a union*).

Skitka and Tetlock's (1992) Contingency Model of Distributive Justice

This model applies to the allocation of societal resources such as social welfare and health care. Its focus is on the appraisal of the deservingness of the claimants for such resources. The model posits four kinds of evaluations in the appraisal process:

(i) *evaluation of the availability of the resources*
In the absence of resource constraints on the capacity of the allocators to provide aid, the decision process ends and all claimants receive the resouces claimed. If the resources are insufficient to meet all claims, the decision maker will engage in further kinds of evaluation described below.

(ii) *attributional analysis of claimant responsibility in relation to their need*
Claimants' reasons for their claims are analysed. Attributions are made in terms of an "internal" or "external" locus of responsibility. The former includes claims based on such reasons as laziness, greed or self-interest which are under the control of the claimant; the latter includes claims based on personally uncontrollable reasons such as accidents. Claimants are classified into the categories of "internal controls" (IC) and "external controls".

(iii) *evaluation of the claimant deservingness*
The deservingness of the claimant is evaluated in terms of need and efficiency. Claimants with high need and efficiency are considered most deserving, followed by those with high need but low efficiency, and those with low need but high efficiency. Claimants low on both criteria are considered as the least deserving.

(iv) *setting priorities among claimants*
When the amount of resources exceeds the claims from all IC claimants, allocation will be made to all except those classified as the least deserving (low need/low efficiency). However, under higher resource constraint situations, aids are given only to the most deserving.

In addition to the three factors (i.e., resource constraint, claimant responsibility, and deservingness), the model further posits that the personal attributes of the allocations would exert an influence on the evaluation hence the allocation decisions. These predictions have received some empirical support (Skitka et al., 1992).

Process or Procedural Justice Theories

Thibaut and Walker's (1978) Theory of Procedural Justice

Thibaut and Walker analysed the effects of judicial procedures in the resolution of legal disputes, on people's reactions to the final verdict. The key points of their theory are:

(1) The procedures used in resolving legal disputes involve two stages: the process stage during which relevant information is presented, and the decision stage during which the information is used in reaching a verdict. In this context, two types of *controls* over the entire legal process are distinguished:
   (i) *process control*
   This refers to the ability to have control over the procedures during the process stage (e.g., control over the collection of information, the presentation of information, the selection of attorneys).
   (ii) *decision control*
   This refers to the ability to have control over the procedures during the decision stage (e.g., influence over how the information is used, how the final verdict is reached).

(2) Using the two major types of controls, several types of *procedures* can be distinguished according to the degree and type of control interested parties (i.e., disputants) may have:
   (i) *autocratic procedures*
   Parties to the dispute have neither process control nor decision control over the legal procedures. Both types of controls are in the hands of the decision maker (i.e., the judge). The European inquisitorial system involves the application of the autocratic procedures.
   (ii) *arbitration procedures*
   Parties to the dispute have only process control but not decision control. Disputants may have control over the selection or presentation of information, or the selection of own attorneys. Decision control is however in the hands of the judge. The adversary system, used in both America and Britain involves the application of these arbitration procedures.
   (iii) *In addition, there are other types of procedures:* mediation procedures (i.e., the decision maker has only process control), bargaining procedures (i.e., the decision maker has neither types of control), and moot procedures (i.e., the decision maker and the disputants share both types of controls).

(3) The *adversary system*, which allows disputants process controls, can best ensure that all information concerning the individual disputants is taken into account in reaching the verdict. This system thus maximises *fairness* of the decision. On the other hand, the *inquisitorial system*, which allows interested parties no control over the entire legal process, can better ensure the objective accuracy of information gathering and utilisation. This system thus maximises the *accuracy* of the decision.

(4) Two types of legal disputes are distinguished, the theory also identifies the best procedure for the resolution of each type of conflict:

(i) *cognitive conflicts (i.e., conflicting opinions about "truth")*
Parties to cognitive conflicts are concerned with the validity of facts and not with self-interest. As such, these conflicts can only be resolved by objectively finding out or ascertaining the truth. Procedures which maximise accuracy of decision (i.e., the inquisitorial system) should be used for resolving these cognitive conflicts.

(ii) *conflicts of interest (i.e., disputes over an allocation outcome)*
Parties to this type of conflict are concerned primarily with the fairness of the allocation rather than the objective accuracy of information. These conflicts can therefore best be resolved by the adversary system.

(5) The theory further predicts that people (interested parties, the decision maker, or disinterested observers) typically are more satisfied with the adversary system which allows for process controls, than with the inquisitorial system. Final decisions based on the former procedures are also perceived as fairer.

Thibaut and Walker's pioneer work on extending legal procedures to the social psychology of conflict resolution has redirected justice research from a traditional focus on outcome justice to a new emphasis on procedural justice. Such research covers a variety of topics including legal dispute resolutions (for a review, see Lind & Tyler, 1988), organisational conflict management (e.g., Chusmir & Mills, 1989; Karambayya & Brett, 1989), grievance procedures (e.g., Klaas, 1989; Pavlak, Clark, & Gallagher, 1992), resource allocation (e.g., Bies & Shapiro, 1988), organisational commitment and satisfaction (e.g., Sweeney & McFarlin, 1993), performance evaluation (e.g., Konovsky & Cropanzano, 1991), pay and compensation (e.g., Folger & Konovsky, 1989), satisfaction with union and management (e.g., Fryxell & Gordon, 1989), promotion system (e.g., McEnrue, 1989), organisational lay-off decisions (e.g., Brockner, 1990, 1994; Brockner, DeWitt, Grover, & Reed, 1990; Konovsky & Folger, 1991), drug-testing procedures at workplace (e.g., Kulik & Campbell Clark, 1993), and self-esteem (e.g., Koper, Van Knippenberg, Bouhuijs, Vermunt, & Wilke, 1993).

Leventhal, Karuza and Fry's (1980) Allocation Preference Theory

Conceptually, this procedural justice theory represents an extension of Leventhal's distributive justice judgement theory. The focus is on prescribing procedural rules that would result in a fair allocation. Leventhal et al. prescribed six procedural justice rules which consist of both process control and decision control procedures:

(1) Consistency of rules:
Fair allocations involve the application of the same rule consistently to anyone at anytime. Consistency in application across individuals means equal treatment of everyone concerned. Consistency over time requires that the same allocation rules be used every time a similar allocation is made.

(2) Accuracy of information:
Fair allocations are based on accurate information about all the people concerned (e.g., the needs, contributions, or any other relevant information used in making the allocation decision).

(3) Opportunity to select the decision makers:
Fair allocation procedures would allow people the opportunity to have a voice in the composition of the decision making panel and to identify the structure of the decision making power.

(4) Correctability of procedures and final decisions:
Fair allocation procedures would not only allow people the opportunity to make appropriate changes in procedures used in the allocation, but also the opportunity to appeal against the final decision perceived as unfair.

(5) Safeguards against bias:
Fair allocation procedures would have safeguards against possible biases associated with either the decision maker's own vested interest in the allocation, or the decision maker's inability to objectively consider all points of view in making the decision.

(6) Following universal ethical standards:
Fair allocation procedures would adhere to commonly accepted ethical rules (e.g., avoid intrusion to privacy, bribery, deception or spying). Fair allocations involve making moral and ethical decisions.

Empirical research generated by allocation preference theory has been supportive of the theory. The research has been carried out in a variety of organisational behaviour contexts including performance appraisal (e.g., Greenberg, 1986a, 1986b; Kanfer, Sawyer, Earley, & Lind, 1987; Landy, Barnes, & Murphy, 1978), resource allocation (e.g., Barrett-Howard & Tyler, 1986; Fry & Cheney, 1981), employee motivating and planning (e.g., Sheppard & Lewicki, 1987). The theory has been useful in an analysis of justice perception in divorce settlements (Rettig & Dahl, 1991, 1993).

Lind and Tyler's (1988) Two Explanatory Models of Procedural Justice

In their 1988 book *The social psychology of procedural justice,* Allen Lind and Tom Tyler reviewed existing theories and research on procedural justice from the legal, political, and social-organisational psychology literatures. Based on their comprehensive review, they argued for the generality of procedural justice effects on attitudes, judgements and behaviour: these effects are generalisable beyond the legal and conflict resolution contexts as well as beyond the American culture. Lind and Tyler then drew several conclusions about the generality of the procedural justice effects. In an attempt to account for these effects, they proposed two models of procedural justice: the *informed self-interest model* and *the group value model.*

(1) *Conclusions of procedural justice effects*
  (i)   In terms of the validity of procedural justice effects, these effects are robust across methodologies.
  (ii)   Procedures which allow individuals to have process control or voice are perceived as fairer than procedures which do not make such allowances.
  (iii)   Judgements of procedural justice have a satisfaction-enhancing effect; especially when outcomes are unfavourable.
  (iv)   Judgements of procedural justice are one of the most important predictors of people's preference for certain type of procedures.
  (v)   Judgements of procedural justice have consequences for attitudes and beliefs: they enhance individuals' attitudes towards the authorities (e.g., judges, police officers, political leaders) or institutions (e.g., the court system) which mandate the procedure; they also enhance individuals' commitment and loyalty to these groups or institutions.
  (vi)   Judgements of procedural justice have behavioural consequences: they affect behavior in disputes, task performance, compliance with decisions, protest behavior, and participation in institutional activities.
  (vii)   Procedural justice effects operate beyond the legal context of dispute resolution: they are observed in political and organisational contexts as well as in other allocation issues.
  (viii) Procedural justice involves not only issues of allocation decisions, but also issues of how people are treated by authorities or institutions in the allocation process.
  (ix)   Process control effects are not simply due to the desire for fair outcomes. The opportunity to voice one's views per se can enhance procedural justice judgements.

(2) *The informed self-interest model: the first explanatory model of procedural justice effects*

This model represents an extension of traditional self-interest models: it contends that concerns for procedural justice are explicable by a long-term or delayed view of self-interest. As members of social groups, individuals realise that their own pure self-interest gains are often incompatible with the interests of other group members, the gratification of the former at the expense of the latter can threaten group harmony or cohesiveness. As a result, individuals make tradeoffs by delaying their immediate gratification in favour of maintaining group harmony, and with a view to seeking long-term gains from their group membership. The model makes several specific predictions:

(i) Several variables are expected to affect judgements of procedural justice: the subjective favorability of the procedure to the individual, the amount of control over outcomes, the outcome fairness provided by the procedure, the consistency of the procedure.

(ii) The importance accorded to procedural justice is a joint function of (a) the subjective importance accorded to the outcome decision, and (b) the subjective importance of the harmony of the group in question. As either the importance of outcome decision or group harmony increases, the fairness of the procedure becomes more important.

(iii) Judgements of procedural justice have consequences for individuals' attitudes, beliefs and behaviours.

(3) *The group value model: the second explanatory model of procedural justice effects*

This model accounts for procedural justice effects by appeal to the notion of group identification. The model rests on three premises (a) individuals are social beings hence they place great importance on identifying with social groups or group membership, (b) procedures adopted by a group are manifestations of the values of the group, and (c) as a result of socialisation, individuals hold fundamental values (e.g., harmony in social relationships, opportunity to participate in group activities).

Given these, the group value model contends that when group procedures correspond with a person's fundamental values, the person identifies more strongly with the group. The sense of group membership thus accounts for most procedural justice effects. The model also makes several specific predictions:

(i) *Judgements of procedural justice are affected by these factors:*

(a) factors covered by Leventhal et al.'s six procedural justice rules (e.g., consistency, ethicality, correctability)

(b) factors pertaining to the socialisation process: more traditional procedures are seen as more just

(c)   factors such as the extent to which the procedure provides for value expres*sion, and the extent to which people are treated with dignity.*
(ii) *The importance accorded to procedural justice is a function of*
(a)   the importance of the group to the individual.
(b)   the importance of traditional values to the individual: Group members who hold more traditional values are more likely to place greater importance on the justice of group procedures.
(c)   the degree of certainty an individual has about his/her group status: Group members who are uncertain about their status within the group are more likely to place greater importance on the justice of group procedures.
(iii) *Judgements of procedural justice have consequences for attitudes, beliefs and behaviour pertaining to the group which adopts the procedure.*

Empirical research pertaining to the self-interest and group value models, although limited in its extent, has provided general support for the models (for a review, see Lind & Tyler, 1988, Tyler & Lind, 1990). More recent research has applied the theoretical frameworks to various issues including attitudes towards affirmative action programmes (e.g., Ayers, 1992), behavioural consequences of procedural justice judgements in managerial selection (e.g., Singer, 1990), as well as performance appraisals (e.g., Reiley & Singer, 1996). However, Bora (1995) evaluated the group value model from a sociological perspective and pointed out some conceptual and methodological limitations of the procedural justice notion implicit in the model. It was suggested that the notion be reformulated at a general social system level so that the model could also account for procedural outcomes based on rational considerations other than justice (e.g., utility considerations).

RECENT ADVANCES IN THE PSYCHOLOGY OF ETHICS AND JUSTICE

Three recent and independent advances are noted: First, in the psychology of justice, advances have been made in the integration of both distributive and procedural justice notions for a comprehensive understanding of people's attitudes and reactions to perceived justice and injustice (e.g., Folger, 1994; Rutte & Messick, 1995; Sheppard, Lewicki, & Minton, 1992). Advances have also been made with reference to interactional, relational and intergroup justice. Second, the concept of justice itself has been reconsidered in the light of feminist theories and postmodern philosophies. Third, there has been a recent revival of the notion of evolutionary ethics, which concerns the very origin of ethics and justice. These advances are briefly discussed in the following sections.

Interactional, Relational and Intergroup Justice

In the early literature on procedural justice, the notion of interactional justice was proposed and defined in terms of the quality of interpersonal treatment an individual receives in resource allocations (e.g., Bies, 1987; Bies & Moag, 1986; Karambayya & Brett, 1989; Koper & Vermunt, 1988; Lind & Tyler, 1988). Interactional justice has been found to be a key criterion in people's justice evaluation (e.g., Lipkus, 1992). The criteria of interactional justice have been distinguished from those of procedural justice (e.g., Vermunt, Van der Kloot, & Van der Meer, 1993). However, both forms of justice were found to better account for organisational citizenship behaviour than work satisfaction (e.g., Organ & Moorman, 1993).

As a special case of interactional justice, the relational model of authority (Tyler & Lind, 1992) describes the effect of the procedures adopted by an authority on superior-subordinate relations. The model proposes that the procedures adopted by a leader of a group (authority) would influence subordinates' perceptions of (i) their own standing in the group, (ii) the leader's neutrality, and (iii) the leader's trustworthiness. Such perceptions then determine the subordinates' judgements of the justice of the procedures. This, in turn, would finally lead to subordinates' reactions towards the leader.

The interactional justice notion and the relational model concern primarily justice issues occurring between individuals. This form of justice has been referred to as interpersonal justice, which is distinguished from social justice concerning relations between larger groups (Syroit, 1991). In an effort to extend the justice notion from a personal to a group level, the relational model of authority has recently been integrated with the social identity theory (Tajfel & Turner, 1979) in accounting for various distributive and procedural justice issues at the intergroup level (Bruins, Platow, & Ng, 1995). Other research has considered the cross-cultural implications of the relational model for justice judgements and dispute resolution (e.g., Sugawara & Huo, 1994).

Justice in a Postmodern and Feminist Context

The principles of justice in modernity are grounded in the notion of rationality. Under utilitarianism, justice is achieved through either adhering to social contract (egoism) or the consideration of others' interest in the calculation of the net or aggregate utility (act- or rule- utilitarianism). Both forms of utilitarianism require the exercise of reason to contain self-interest. In the deontological tradition, Kantian justice firmly rests on the assumption that individuals have the capacity of free will and pure reason to act on the universal moral principles. For the libertarians such as Rawls, justice is to be achieved through the rationality of a set of specific decision procedures, with the decision maker taking a detached, neutral "original position". The notion of rationality also underlies other libertarian theories of justice, including that of Nozick (1974) and more recently, Lehning (1990). In these theories, justice is based on the principle that the state takes a minimal or neutral stance which then allows its citizens the freedom to pursue their national rights or interest.

Justice theories in modernity are based on the two related notions of rationality and neutrality. In this context, justice is construed as the result of the exercise of a purely objective and rational mind, totally detached from and disinterested in its surrounding social realities.

Postmodern and feminist critics speak with one voice in rejecting the rationality-based definition of justice, although for different reasons. For postmodernists, justice so defined carries the presumption that there exists only one single unifying and dominant standard by which justice is evaluated and achieved. Their rejection of a rationality-based justice notion is consistent with the objection by postmodernism to the existence of any "grand narratives" or universal norms of morality (e.g.,Derrida, 1978; Gadamer, 1976; Lyotard, 1984; Putnam, 1990; Rorty, 1979, 1989).

For feminism, the objection stems from its perspectives on gender differences. When justice is defined solely by the operation of rationality, it precludes the exercise of other socially relevant human capabilities including compassion, empathy, care and other subjective feelings. By focusing solely on rationality, the conceptulisation of justice affirms the pervasive male-domination form of thinking. This has the negative consequence of blocking the development of the typically "feminine" traits of subjective feelings, which are also necessary for the effective functioning of justice (e.g., Flax, 1993; Gatens, 1991; Sampson, 1994; Sandel, 1982).

Apart from rationality, the libertarian notion of justice rests also on the notion of neutrality, which postmodernism and feminism reject on similar grounds: that it conceals both a singular and a masculinist bias. Recently, Rawls (1993) and Lehning (1994) addressed this criticism by arguing that the ideals of neutrality apply to the aims of the state with respect to its policies and conceptions of the good. Neutrality of aim thus disallows policies that are designed to favour any particular doctrine with its special conception of good. Following this interpretation of the term neutrality, the term should not be interpreted to mean "indifference to differences", because, as Lehning put it, the notion should "*guarantee that differences will be taken care of in such a way that each citizen, male or female, hetero- or homosexual, will be treated with equal concern and respect*" (p.164).

Given their similar criticisms towards the theoretical approach to justice in modernity, postmodernism and feminism both conceptualise justice in terms of an ongoing dialogue or a process of interaction between all parties concerned. When justice is defined as a dynamic process rather than a set of preconceived standards, it requires four kinds of operations, as identified by Flax (1993): (i) the reconciliation of diversities into a new unity of differences, which is to be preserved, (ii) the reciprocity of authority and domination through a continuous process of sharing with, and mutual respect for, each other's perspectives, (iii) the recognition and acceptance of the separateness and differences of others' perspectives from one's own, and (iv) a judgemental process characterised by balancing seemingly opposing criteria (e.g., evidence and reflection, ration and feelings, particularity and collectivity).

In a recent analysis of the notion of social justice from the perspective of the modern sociological theory of functionism, which lies outside the realm of feminism, Boudon (1992) reached a similar conclusion: justice can be understood only from the knowledge of social interactions. Considering that differences of opinion inevitably exist, questions of social justice can only be resolved by "the method of regulated political debate", and "in no way be resolved *a priori*" (p.113). Boudon's view of social justice is therefore consistent with the feminist and postmodern perspectives on justice.

Evolutionary Ethics

The term evolutionary ethics has its origin in Herbert Spencer's Social Darwinism, in which Darwin's idea of natural selection in the biological evolution of species was applied to the progression of social behaviours and ethics. Evolutionary ethics aim to address the origins of human morality, a topic untouched by any other approaches to ethics and justice. Despite the stigmas associated with the evolutionary approach to morality (for a review, see Nitecki & Nitecki, 1993), the topic has been gaining currency in recent years (e.g., Alexander, 1987, 1993; Dawkins, 1976; Mackie, 1978; Ruse, 1979, 1989; Wilson, 1975; 1978). The key theme of evolutionary ethics is that moral thoughts and actions are believed to come into being because they have been selectively advantageous from an evolutionary perspective: they enhance the "inclusive fitness" (Hamilton, 1964) of a person in a social context. A person's inclusive fitness, calculated in quantitative terms, refers to the total genetic success through either direct kin reproduction or non-kin reproduction. Therefore, the argument is that, like biological and genetic evolution by natural selection, moral beliefs are also the result of an adaptational progression which aims to further our biological or reproductive ends (e.g., Ruse & Wilson, 1985; Ruse, 1993). The view has come under attack for several reasons including the commitment of the naturalistic fallacy and the neglect of cultural influences in human behaviours (e.g., Dennett, 1995; Rottschaefer & Martinsen, 1990). Among critics emphasising the role of the human culture, Ayala (1987) drew the distinction between the evolution of the *capacity* for humans to exhibit ethical behaviour and that of the *moral norms;* while the former follows the biological selection process, the latter involves a cultural rather than a biological evolutionary process. Gould (1991) has argued that the evolutionary process of behavioural traits may not involve directed adaptation through natural genetic selection, rather, the process may involve a non-biological cause. Gould referred to such a process as "extraptation". Through extraptation, coopted traits can also acquire the advantageous effect of selective fitness.

Empirically, certain types of moral values such as cooperation and altruism have been examined from an evolutionary perspective. Using the Prisoner's Dilemma game to roughly simulate the evolutionary competition process, it has been shown that the "tit-for-tat" strategy, beginning with cooperation with one's opponent, was a superior strategy than most other strategies including those based on self-interest (e.g., Axelrod & Hamilton, 1981; Axelrod, 1984). This finding has been generally regarded as an evidence for the selective or evolutionary advantage of "cooperative and reciprocal behaviour". Using a similar method, Nowak and Simund (1993) recently discovered that under certain conditions, the "win-stay lose-shift" strategy resulted in a greater selective advantage than tit-for-tat cooperation. Other studies also showed that cooperation helped to enhance one's genetic success in the next generation (e.g., Maynard Smith, 1978). In addition to cooperation and altruism, researchers have sought to delineate the conditions under which the act of forgiving also results in a greater selective advantage, as compared with other not-so-charitable acts (Kitcher, 1993).

Adopting Gould's (1991) perspective, Petrinovich, O'Neill, and Jorgensen (1993) recently explored the question of whether there exists a set of biologically-based moral rules (biological moral universals) people typically deploy in moral considerations. Their results revealed several significant decision rules which respondents used across various moral dilemmas. These include (i) *Speciesism*: the rule that favours the protection of the lives of the human species over those of other living species, and (ii) *Inclusive Fitness*: the rule that favours the protection of the respondent (and his/her kin or friend) over a stranger (and the stranger's kin or friends). The findings thus suggest the existence of biologically-based moral rules. The authors argued that the study helps to reveal the nature of moral intuitions and moral thoughts and if the universality of the findings can be demonstrated across different human cultures, a case could then be made for evolutionary ethics. However, caution still needs to be exercised in making inferences from the existence of moral universals to genetic adaptation. Dennett (1995) considered this problem as a *"fundamental obstacle to inference in human sociobiology: showing that there is a particular type of human behaviour is ubiquitous or near ubiquitous in widely separated human cultures goes no way at all towards showing that there is a genetic predisposition for that particular behaviour"*, although he did point out that the problem is not "insuperable" (p.486).

Cast in the context of the eternity of time, what is right or wrong may not be understood in terms of a set of *a priori* ethical norms; its understanding may require a never ending vigilance to each action and a foresight of far-reaching consequences of the action for humanity. Again, Dennett (1995) has summarised it succinctly, *"Ethical decision making, examined from the perspective of Darwin's dangerous idea, holds out scant hope of our ever discovering a formula or an algorithm for doing right. But that is not an occasion for despair; we have the mind-tools we need to design and redesign ourselves, ever searching for better solutions to the problems we create for ourselves and others"* (p.510). Thus, the evolutionary framework may also point to the need for conceptualising ethics in terms of a dynamic and ongoing process, a theoretical position not unlike that of postmodern and feminist perspectives to morality.

Chapter 4 Ethics and Justice Applied to Professional Behaviour

Quite independently of the philosophical and psychological literatures of ethics and justice, there exists an applied ethics literature which focuses on the application of moral principles to specific social and professional contexts. In the social context, ethical enquiries into these issues have been well documented:

(1) *Behavioural medicine, bioethics, and health psychology*
   This literature addresses ethical issues associated with the promotion of individuals' physical or mental well-being. Issues include the ethics of specific medical intervention program (e.g., behaviour modification, abortion, euthanasia, genetic engineering), the ethics of medical research (e.g., intelligence testing, use of human or animal in experimentation, the role of scientific research and positivist science), and the ethics of related political, economic and societal activities.

(2) *Clinical psychology*
   Ethical issues pertaining to clinical psychology include aspects of those mentioned above, as well as interpersonal issues arising from therapist-client interactions.

(3) *Law enforcement, community and social work*
   The literature deals with ethical issues pertaining to the underlying ideologies of policing and law enforcement, as well as community and social work in general.

(4) *Business and organisational behaviour*
   This literature concerns the application of moral standards to business practices, policies and strategies, as well as institutional and individual behaviour pertaining to the conduct of business.

In the professional context, existing literature deals primarily with the ethics of professional conduct. Explicit rules or guide-lines of conduct in various professions have been well documented in each of the above areas.

The present chapter focuses on only one of these applied ethics literatures: business and organisational behaviour. The justification is straightforward: Behaviours in business and organisations embrace a vast spectrum of human relationships. While these relationships pertain primarily to economic behaviours, such behaviours however are assuming an increasingly central and foundational role in modern living. Ever since the eighteenth century, scholars have been referring to their own time as "the age of the economist". Among the latest in making such a claim is Kenneth Lux (1990), who further argues that this expression is "even more appropriate" for the present time. In a similar vein, business has also been referred to as a "fully human activity" (Solomon, 1992, p.16). The centrality and pivotal role of business or economic relationships thus ensures that these relationships are all-embracing and have significant political, economic and societal consequences.

Formal interpersonal and institutional relationships in business include those among employees, stockholders, directors and managers as well as those between competing and cooperating organisations, between business organisations and other political institutions, and society at large. These relationships are constrained by legal and contractual rules. In addition to their legal aspects, business relationships also take on a moral dimension. The ethics of these relationships have received increasing attention from scholars and practitioners alike. The application of ethical standards and moral principles to these relationships forms the very core of the study of business ethics.

The study of business ethics as a distinctive academic discipline has only had a short history dating from the 1970s. The remaining sections of this chapter will review the key topics in the business ethics literature. The first topic concerns the historical roots of the free-market ideology. The second section reviews the on-going issues of debate which have constituted much of the business ethics literature. Several new and significant themes have emerged in recent years. These emerging themes are then reviewed. Following this, the chapter turns to another core topic of business ethics: ethical decision making in a business context. Existing models of ethical decision making, together with relevant empirical studies, are described. The chapter ends with a brief discussion of the postmodern approach to ethical decision making in business. Rossouw's (1994) model of rational interaction and moral sensitivity is used to illustrate this approach.

HISTORICAL ROOTS OF FREE-MARKET IDEOLOGY

The ideology of the free-market system prevalent in the developed world is characterised by two key features: (1) private ownership of properties (goods, firms, commodities) by self-interested parties, and (2) voluntary exchange of such properties in competitive free markets (Friedman, 1962). This prevailing capitalistic ideology has been associated with several moral philosophical thoughts:

(1) *John Locke' (1632-1704) theory of natural rights*
Locke contended that individuals possess two natural rights in a "state of nature" (i.e., without the constraints imposed by governmental or political bodies). The two inalienable rights are the right to liberty and the right to private property. In the natural state, individuals would have "perfect freedom" and "perfect equality". Locke's notion of natural rights and natural states has been cited as a justification for the free-market system. Individuals have a natural right to private ownership of their properties (i.e., own "labour" and the "work" of their own "hands"), they also have a natural right to the free and voluntary exchange of these properties with others through mutually-agreed-upon social contracts. These social contracts thus serve the purpose of protecting individuals' natural rights. Locke's views have been criticised however for the assumption of the existence of natural rights and its implications for justice (for review, see Velasquez, 1982).

(2) *Thomas Hobbes' (1588-1679) egoistic self-interest*
In Leviathan, Hobbes proposed that people have "natural passions" in the form of self-interest and these passions are the primary driving force behind all human action. Each individual acts to maximise his/her own good ("pleasure of senses" or "pleasure of the mind") and to minimise pain (displeasure or harm). Hobbes wrote,"...in the nature of man, we find three principal causes of quarrel. First, competition; secondly, diffidence; thirdly, glory. The first maketh man invade fr gain; the second, for safety; and the third, for reputation". To prevent such "natural" human tendencies as invasion and war (in the pursuit of each person's natural passions) social agreements or contracts become necessary. These contracts result in the conferring of power on a sovereign person or a governing "political commonwealth". Hobbesian notions of "natural" self-interest, competition and social contracts are reflected in the underlying free-market ideology.

(3) *Adam Smith's (1723-1790) "free market" and "invisible-hand"*
Adam Smith is widely recognised as the "father of modern economics", "father of capitalism" or "father of modern business". Smith advocated a free-market system of competitive markets and private property. Central to this argument is the idea of self-interest. Individuals, intending only to maximise own gain, freely compete with others in producing and selling commodities demanded by the society. According to Smith, the entire self-interest-seeking process is aided by an "invisible hand" (free or fair competition and utility-maximising), and as an inevitable but unintended consequence, will result in promoting the welfare of the society. Fair competition in the free market involves self-interested economic agents engaging in utility-maximisation and mutually-beneficial exchanges. With each individual seeking to maximise own gain through fair competition, the

natural and unintentional consequence is that the entire economic system improves gradually and moves steadily towards the ideal state of economic efficiency (i.e., the Pareto optimal state). In Smith's own words, "...(a person) intends only his own gain, and he is in this ...led by invisible hand to promote an end that was no part of his intention...By pursuing his own intent he frequently promotes that of society more effectively than when he really intends to promote it" (Smith, 1976).

The philosophical sentiment expressed in his Wealth of Nations has generated a great deal of debate in the literature. Many critics, holding the "prevailing view" (a term used by Werhane, 1991) on Adam Smith, believe that Smith equated self-interest to the antisocial pursuit of sheer personal greed, and as such, self-interest inevitably leads to "social strife, ecological damage and the abuse of power" (Lux, 1990). Other critics however defend Smith's position on self-interest by pointing out that Smith himself emphasised ethics and social agreements in the pursuit of self-interest (Coker, 1990). In a similar voice, Solomon (1992) also notes that Smith's self-interest notion should be seen "first of all, in terms of social solidarity and cooperation" and "a desire for approval and the respect of our fellows", rather than solely in terms of selfish "personal want" (p.89). More recently, Bishop has analysed Smith's original writings and made clear two specific points: First, Smith thought that economic agents' (i.e., merchants and manufacturers) pursuit of their personal interests often led them "to deceive and even oppress" the public. Second, it was Smith who warned that the generally-held belief that self-interested materialistic pursuits would bring personal happiness was an illusion and a deception, yet according to Smith, it was this deception that formed the driving force behind the "industry of mankind" (cf, Bishop, 1995, p. 178).

(4) *Herbert Spencer's (1820-1903) Social Darwinism and "the survival of the fittest"*
Charles Darwin's concept of natural selection (i.e., the preservation of the fittest in the evolution of living species) has been applied by Social Darwinists to the progression of economy. One of the most prominent advocates of this school of thought, Herbert Spencer, argued that the principle of "the survival of the fittest" also characterises economic competition. Social Darwinists argue that fair competition, by having the "best" competitors survive in the jungle of the market, ensure that the entire economic system would steadily improve in its overall efficiency. This argument has been cited as the justification for the modern free-market economy. However, the main criticism against Social Darwinism is directed at the presumption which equates "the fittest" to "the best". In this context, critics have argued that actions that prove to be conducive to survival in business may not necessarily be the best or right actions that foster the survival of human good and humanity (e.g., Fleming, 1970; Wilson, 1967).

ON-GOING ISSUES OF DEBATE IN BUSINESS ETHICS

Three major issues pertaining to ethics and justice have been the focus of debate in the literature of business ethics. The first issue concerns the ethics and justice of the prevailing free-market system in the allocation of societal resources. The second is whether business corporations should have social responsibilities. The third issue addresses the ethics and justice of the behaviour of individuals in business; the question is whether individuals should follow a distinctively different set of moral rules in their roles as a private citizen and as a business person.

(1) *The ethics and justice of the free-market system in resource allocation*
Given that the prevailing system in contemporary societies is shaped around a free market economy, the obvious question of ethics is then whether that system does indeed result in a just and fair allocation of existing societal resources. The debate thus concerns distributive or economic justice. This debate has been carried out in the literatures of politics and economics. The justifications for the rights and wrongs of the free market system in resource allocation have been drawn from philosophical theories of ethics (e.g., teleological, deontological, contractarian, and libertarian views), game theory (e.g., decision theoretic models applied to competitive or cooperative economic behaviour, social choice theory), and the general theory of rationality including multiple forms of rationality (e.g., utility-maximisation, Rawlsian deliberative rationality). The application of normative theories to economic justice and fairness typically carries the presumption that the "economic agents" are both self-interested and rational. Constrained by such a presumption, normative theories when so applied, can only indirectly address the issue of economic fairness or justice (Zajac, 1995).

As pointed out earlier, the ideology of the free-market economy is characterised by self-interested economic agents seeking utility-maximisation through voluntary exchange. When all mutually-beneficial exchanges have taken place, the entire economic system achieves an equilibrium state (i.e., a state of Pareto optimality). Within such a system however, the "lot" for particular individuals may not necessarily be fair or just (under various common usages of fairness). In other words, while Pareto optimality guarantees the "efficiency" of resource allocation by balancing the supply and demand, it by no means ensures fairness in allocation. This is due to the fact that there exists several important limitations of the free-market system, which can be identified as sources of unfairness:
(i) *the level of "initial endowment"*
The free market system focuses mainly on the mutually-beneficial exchange process, it does not take into account the level of "initial endowment" of each individual economic agent at the start of the exchange process. Fairness typically requires some attention to this.

(ii) *rewarding "individual effort"*
While the free market system rewards individual effort or production in an entrepreneurial sense, it by no means ensures that each and every individual's effort is proportionally rewarded.

(iii) *availability of relevant market information*
For a free market system to achieve Pareto optimality, a necessary condition entails full access to relevant market information. In reality this is far from the case (e.g., insider trading, consumers purchasing decisions under inadequately-informed conditions).

(iv) *the problem with "alienation of workers"*
The Marxist criticisms towards the free market system focus primarily on the issue of worker alienation and exploitation. According to these critics, lower class workers in free markets are denied not only the opportunity to fully realise their potential for production, but also their control over their own products; the system further alienates its workers by not taking into account their individual needs and wants.

However, among theoretical developments in the normative approach to economic justice, Varian's (1975) Envy-Free or Superfairness theory appears to have addressed the first two limitations or sources of unfairness in the free-market system (i.e., initial endowment and individual effort). Varian's theory incorporates features of earlier normative notions from Nozick's libertarianism and Rawls' contractarianism. The theory proposes that each individual be given an equal share of societal resources at birth. With this equal initial endowment, individuals then engage in mutually-beneficial exchanges with others through their lifetime. Upon death their properties then go back to the state for future allocations to its new members. The free exchanges aim at an equilibrium state which involves the comparisons of the "complete position" of each individual in the economic system. Each person's complete position consists of the entire lot of his/her consumption (demand for societal resources) as well as his/her effort or production (supply to the resource pool). As a result of the exchange process, a superfair state is achieved if each person prefers his/her own complete position to that of any other person. Despite that the theory shares other weaknesses of a normative model and is virtually impossible to be put to practice in its present form, the theory is nonetheless considered by some as having provided "*...a framework of analysis for a whole class of economic fairness issues, and has laid the groundwork for further applications*" (Zajac, 1995, p.99).

(2) *The ethics and justice of corporate behaviour: Corporate responsibilities*
The traditional debate over corporate responsibility centres around the moral status of a business corporation. The key question has been phrased as either "Is a corporation a moral agent?" or "Can a corporation have a conscience?". At one extreme, scholars argue that a business corporation is an economic agent with a

single-minded pursuit of excellence in economic performance (e.g., Sherwin, 1989) and of making profit within legal constraints (e.g., Friedman, 1962). As such, a corporation is not considered a moral agent, therefore it has no conscience or special moral obligations. However, it should be noted that among scholars espousing this position, some further argued that in order to excel in economic performance, corporations would need to consider the needs of three constituencies (employees, shareholders and customers), even though such a consideration is not an end in itself, but solely a means to achieve optimal economic performance.

At the other extreme, philosophers have argued for the case that a business corporation is a moral agent with a conscience and hence has full moral responsibilities (e.g., French, 1979; Goodpaster & Mathews, 1982; Singer, 1994).

More recently, Solomon (1992, p.149) argues that the question of whether a corporation has moral responsibilities is a *"non-starter"*. This is because the question carries the assumption that a corporation is an independent entity in society and as a result, it needs to define its responsibilities for the society. By rejecting this assumption, Solomon asserts that corporations should be viewed as *"part and parcel of the community that creates them"*, and as such, *"the responsibilities they bear are not the products of argument or implicit contracts but intrinsic to their very existence as social entities"* (p.149).

(3) *The ethics and justice of individual behaviour in business*
The key question in this debate has been framed in different ways:
(i) *The "game-ethics" analogy*
The question is whether the role of a businessperson requires a set of ethical rules which is distinctively different from that required by his/her role as a private citizen in society. The poker-game analogy of business ethics made infamous by Carr represents the most extreme position on this issue. Carr argues that competitive pressures in business often demand the skills of a shrewd game player, which involves deception, lying, bluffing or other devious and antisocial behaviour deemed unethical under the rules of everyday morality. While there have been overwhelming attacks on Carr's view, scholars to this day have been ambivalent and have left open the specific question as to *"whether business virtues might indeed be more like those of the poker player than the family minister"* (Solomon, 1992, p.197).
Other scholars adopt a similar but much less extreme view to Carr. Their sentiment is captured by a consideration of "social consensus among referent group members". This view stems from the legal position of morality advocated by Lord Devlin (Wasserstrom, 1971) which defines the morality of an act in terms of the majority consensus among members of the reference group. Applying this view to a business group context and suggesting a business ethics based on a consensus among members of the business community, Grace and Cohen recently (1995) write, "...*While not endorsing*

Lord Devlin's view wholeheartedly, neither do we want to dismiss it altogether as inappropriate or inapplicable in the context of morality in business. Recognition of the legitimacy of a view like Lord Devlin's, however, certainly does not require acceptance of a Laissez-faire of the type advocated by Carr."(p.50).

(ii) *The dichotomy of "private vs. public ethics"*

With primary reference to political life, Thomas Nagel (1978) writes about the ruthlessness in public life where he argues that the role of a public office-holder may entail different moral obligations from those required of the role of a private citizen. Moreover, in the public role, the primary consideration of the morality of an act should be given to the moral consequences of that act, whereas such a consideration of consequence may carry a significantly less weight in private morality. Similarly, in the context of business ethics, Ladd (1970) draws the distinction between "personal" versus "social" actions and goals. The former actions and goals are relevant to personal pursuits whereas the latter, the pursuits of the organisation. Ladd claims that it is inappropriate for a businessperson in his/her organisational role to pursue own personal goals; social actions that are necessary for achieving organisational goals may then not be deemed moral by the normal standards of personal actions. As such, the dichotomy can be seen as having provided yet another justification for the position of the existence of separate personal vs. business ethics.

(iii) *The necessity of "dirty hands"*

The key ethical debate here concerns the necessity of dirty hands (i.e., doing wrong in order to do good) in business. The moral philosopher Niccolo Machiavelli first argued for the necessity of such actions in politics. Machiavelli wrote about the ethics of political rulers in *The Prince*. While there have been severe attacks on the Machiavellian ethics, it is widely recognised that life inevitably presents situations that require the impossible decision of having to choose between "two evils". Again in the context of politics, moral philosophers including Nagel (1978) have taken a consequentialist perspective to dirty hands: when the consequences of doing wrong are the attainment of the overall good of the state, then doing wrong could override morality.

In the context of business behaviour, Solomon similarly delineates the boundaries of dirty hands by defining the goals ("the good") of "doing wrong" solely in terms of the ultimate survival of the organisation or the perseverance in achieving the long-term vision of the organisation. As such, the goals (the good) cannot be sheer greed or gain in profits and they must be *"insulated against greed as well as weakness"*. When the "good" achieved through dirty hands is so specified, Solomon further claims that "doing wrong" through dirty hands would require personal virtues such as toughmindedness, integrity and moral courage. When the goals are so circumscribed, the necessity of dirty hands in business thus takes on a totally positive meaning.

EMERGING THEMES OF BUSINESS ETHICS

(1) *The application of positive theories and empirical research to the debate over the ethics and justice of the free market system*

As mentioned earlier, the traditional debate over the ethics and justice of the free market system is grounded in normative theories. Given the prescriptive nature of normative theories, the debate has been more of a theoretical and intellectual endeavour than an exercise capable of providing guide-lines for practice. The main reason for this limitation is that normative theories focus on the prescription of formal ethical and just principles. However, in actual practice, social policy decisions need to take into account not only these formal rules, but also people's typical beliefs of ethical and just actions. The information about the latter can only be found in the empirical literatures in psychology (as reviewed in chapter three), in applied ethics (to be reviewed later in this chapter) and in economics (positive theories of economic efficiency or fairness). These literatures describe what people actually perceive and judge as being ethical and just in various contexts of resource allocation. Policy decisions which take account of such information are likely to be perceived by the public as more ethical and just. Using the affirmative action programmes as an example of social justice policies, chapter six describes how empirical findings concerning the utility, rights and justice of the programme can aid the policy implementation decisions.

In the context of positive theories in economics, Zajac (1995) recently writes"...*in my view, the research on positive theories holds the most short-run promise of giving policy makers tools to cope with (economic) fairness issues.*" (p.104). These positive theories have been applied to many ethics and justice issues of the free market system. These include government regulation and intervention in pricing, taxation, market failures, and regulation of public utilities.

(2) *Social goals and business goals are not antagonistic but in concert with each other*

Implicit to the traditional debate over the social responsibilities of business is the assumption that the goals of business are distinctively different from those of the society. Business, as a collective of economic agents, seeks to optimise economic gains; the society, as a collective of individual citizens, aims to maximise social justice. In recent years, there has been an increasing awareness of the interdependence of society and business. As a result of rapid changes in technology, legislation and the environment, business has taken on both a social and an economic role not only as a means to an end (i.e., survival) but also as an end in itself. Social justice issues are taking on an increasingly central role in business ethics. These issues include the following:

(i) *the distribution of limited employment opportunities*

In this context of the allocation of limited societal resources, issues surrounding affirmative action in organisational recruitment have been the subject of intense research efforts and public debate over the last 30 years. Traditionally, the debate rests on the assumption that the organisation goal (profit-maximising) is incompatible with the social goal (equality of life chances). However, there has been an increasing awareness that a diversity of human resources may result in a net advantage for the competitiveness of today's organisations. Affirmative action, seen in this light, can then achieve both the business goal and the societal goal. This issue of affirmative action will be discussed in detail in Chapter six.

(ii) *environmental ethics and ecological restoration*

In the context of social policies on environmental and ecological protection, Sagoff (1988) argues that these issues are primarily moral, aesthetic and cultural in nature hence they must be evaluated in those terms, rather than solely in terms of the goal of economic efficiency. Environmental and ecological restoration should be based on reasons of efficiency, but also on social and ethical grounds. Westra (1994) also stressed the ethics in the environmental cause by claiming the ethical principle of "integrity" as the key to environmental protection and restoration. There has been many recent discussions of contemporary environmental issues confronting the business, from the perspective of ethics and morality (for a review, see the Special Issue of Business Ethics Quarterly, 1995). In the recent social justice literature, results of the Montada and Kals (1995) study affirmed that social, ethical and justice considerations are key determinants of people's affective, cognitive and behavioural reactions towards ecological and environmental policy decisions.

(iii) *protection of stakeholder rights and the issue of governance*

In recent years, there has been an increasing public concern over the fairness and the accountability of business activities. As a result of concerns about fairness, a substantial number of laws have been introduced to ensure the legal protection of the rights of consumers as well as employees. Issues about the accountability of business firms include the proper monitoring, assessment and control of business activities to ensure the protection of the rights of all parties concerned (i.e., the stakeholders and the shareholders). This concern over the accountability of business firms has been the driving force behind the many reforms relating to corporate governance. The legislative changes and business reforms have significant implications for the debate over organisational versus social goals: the increasing attention given to the fairness and accountability of business activities suggests a greater emphasis on the role of business in achieving a greater social good. Thus, social goals and corporate goals are seen as being in concert with each other. For a more detailed discussion on the issues of rights and governance, see Cannon (1994), and Starkey (1995, the Special Issue on corporate governance and control). Among other recent advances, a theory of pluralism in corporate governance was proposed which predicted that pluralistic control of a firm would lead to its improved social performance. However, an empirical test failed to provide support for the proposition (Molz, 1995).

(3) *Personal and virtue ethics as foundation to all business behaviours*
In the recent business ethics literature, an increasing emphasis has been placed on personal virtues of individuals. This literature comes under the generic term of virtue ethics. This notion of virtue ethics places a person's moral traits or moral character at the core of morality. Instead of defining morality in terms of moral rules, the morality of an act is judged by reference to the typical moral character of its actor. The logic here is that a person's moral judgements, moral intent and moral actions are all manifestations of his/her natural moral disposition. A person of good virtues is naturally inclined to act morally. Moral behaviour therefore is a natural product of a moral character. The increasing emphasis on virtue-based ethics has led some theorists to argue for a "paradigm shift" for business ethics (e.g., MacIntyre, 1984; for discussion, see Horvath, 1995).

The most recent development in virtue ethics is Solomon's Aristotelean virtue ethics. Solomon distinguishes his version of the virtue ethics from others along three dimensions: (1) In the Aristotelean sense, virtues are not instances of the type of rational abstract principles of morality in the philosophical theories of ethics (e.g., deontological principle of "do not lie"), rather, they are internalised values and an integral and inalienable part of a person's character. (2) Solomon's version of virtue ethics shares one essential assumption with other versions: Individuals are social beings who derive their identity and worth from their communities. However, Solomon rejects the frequent definition of a community in terms of religion or other forms of communal contracts or consensus. Instead, his definition is derived from the original Aristotelean notion of a community. (3) The focus of morality has shifted from one on justice, as in philosophical theories of ethics, to one on compassion and caring, as in virtue ethics. Many scholars characterise this shift in "gender" terms, that is, in terms of a shift from a "masculine" to a "feminine" ethics. While acknowledging the argument, Solomon stresses the non-gender-related nature of Aristotelean virtues by pointing out that *"...Aristotle...has much to say about the virtues that has little or nothing to do with the fact that one is a male or a female."*(p.116). Solomon's theory of virtue ethics will be discussed later in the chapter under models of ethical decision making.

It is worth noting that the emergence of virtue ethics has a significant implication for the practical issue of the "teaching" of business ethics. The underlying justification for current business ethics courses is grounded in

73

traditional philosophical notions of ethics, that is, morality entails moral-rule-abiding. Therefore the teaching and learning of these rules become central to moral behaviour in business. However, virtue ethics conceptualise virtues as an integral part of a person's character, which form the very foundation of his/her cognition, reasoning and behaviour across all roles of life including that of a businessperson; business ethics then become an inseparable part of living. Cast in this light, one would need to rethink the teaching of business ethics, bearing in mind that the most logical stance is perhaps "to *live*" rather than "to *learn*" ethics (e.g., Davis & Welton, 1991; Solberg, Strong, & McGuire, 1995).

(4) *"Practising good ethics": The emerging case for "supererogatory" and "non-obligatory but blameworthy-if-omitted" behaviours*
Theories of virtue ethics aside, there has been an increasing attention to the identification of the sorts of behaviour that contribute to the actual practice of good ethics. Traditional philosophical theories of ethics stipulate that the practice of ethics entails the enactment of at least two types of moral acts:
(i) *"obligatory-to-perform acts"*
    The acts which one has a moral duty to carry out. If they are not performed, one is then morally blameworthy.
(ii) *"obligatory-to-omit acts"*
    The acts which one has a moral duty to omit. If they are performed, one is then morally blameworthy.

Practising ethics as defined solely by the enactment of these two types of acts would mean "simply doing one's duties". This duty-bound approach to ethics has been referred to as duty ethics. However, inspired by the writings of Urmson and Ewing, moral philosophers (e.g., Baron, 1987; Kolnai, 1973; Mellema, 1991, 1994) have since identified two more types of moral acts which are "non-obligatory" in that there is no moral duty or obligation for their enactments. Despite being non-obligatory hence *"beyond the call of duty"*, they are nonetheless deemed necessary for the practice of "good" ethics.
(iii) *"supererogatory acts"*
    The acts which one has no moral duty to perform, however is morally praiseworthy for their performance.
(iv) *"non-obligatory but blameworthy-if-omited acts"*
    The acts which one has no moral duty to perform, however is morally blameworthy for their omission.

Practising "good ethics" thus entails the enactment of all these four categories of acts: those which are obligatory and necessary for the fulfilment of duties, and those which are non-obligatory but are either praiseworthy in their performance, or blameworthy in their omission. The practice of good ethics thus includes not only responding to the call of moral duty but also "doing what one ought to do" (Mellema, 1994).

(5) *An increasing emphasis on the notion of "justice" in business ethics*

One general trend in business ethics concerns the increasing emphasis on the notion of justice. One of the key issues of business ethics as identified earlier is the ethics and justice of the prevailing free market system in the distribution of societal resources. This issue has traditionally been addressed from the perspective of economic efficiency. However, economists themselves have become increasingly aware of the inadequacy of such a singular perspective and have called for a greater emphasis on the notion of fairness (e.g., Zajac, 1995). Business ethicists have also criticised economists for ignoring the fairness side of issues in their discussions of market behaviours (e.g., Kuhn, 1992).

In the general literature of organisational behaviour, the most rapid recent development in theory and research focuses on organisational justice. Justice concerns, from both a distributive and a procedural perspective, are assuming a central status in many research areas of organisational behaviour including employee motivation, conflict resolution, staff selection, performance appraisal, resource allocation, leadership, quality of organisational life and organisational decision making (for reviews, see Gilliland, 1993; Singer, 1993).

An increasing emphasis on the notion of justice is also evident in the literature of business ethics pertaining to the social responsibilities of business: the stakeholder here refers to the society at large. As discussed earlier, business is expected to assume a significant role in redressing social justice by implementing affirmative action programmes in personnel recruitment and selection. Business is also expected to "do justice" to the natural environment by attending to environmental issues including ecological restoration. The notion of justice is therefore receiving an increasing attention in the economic, organisational and business ethics literatures. The contributions of the psychological research on justice to business ethics have been the subject of the recent Special Issue of Social Justice Research (1996).

MODELS OF MORAL JUDGEMENTS, MORAL VALUES AND ETHICAL DECISION-MAKING IN BUSINESS ETHICS

In the business ethics literature, several models of ethical decision-making and moral values have been proposed. These models are briefly reviewed in this section. However, empirical studies generated from these models have been extremely limited. For this reason, the review focuses primarily on theoretical frameworks.

Fletcher's (1966) situational ethics

Central to the notion of situational ethics is the idea that ethical decisions are made on a case by case basis by taking into account particularities of each situation calling for an ethical decision. However, Fletcher prescribes a set of

75

procedures for the deliberation of situational particularities. The decision maker needs to include four factors in the deliberation:

(i)   *identifying organisational goals*
      In analysing the goal structure of the organisation, considerations should be given to "goal multiplicity" (e.g., profit-maximisation, environmental restoration, redressing social justice, consumer protection, employee rights), "goal priority" (i.e., the ranking of each goal in terms of its priority in the overall goal structure of the organisation), and "goal compatibility" (i.e., checking for the compatibility of the multiple goals; when incompatibility arises, the decision maker would need to make a choice)

(ii) *selecting the most appropriate method to achieve goals*
      Several factors need to be considered before a method is chosen: "constituent acceptability" (i.e., whether the constituencies accept a specific method), "what a method can achieve" (i.e., whether a method can serve to simply satisfy the goals or to maximise the goals?), "the degree of method necessity" (i.e., is the method absolutely essential, incidental or simply extraneous for the purpose of achieving the goals?)

(iii) *examining the motives*
      The decision maker would need to examine the individual motives behind goal identification and method selection. In this regard, several questions need to be asked: "are the motives hidden or known?", "should the motives be made public?", "are the motives shared by many?" and "what are the value orientations underlying or reflected by the motives?"

(iv) *considering potential consequences of decision*
      The decision maker would also need to think about potential consequences of each likely decision or alternative course of action. The questions are: "constituency impact" (i.e., potential consequences for each individual constituency from its own perspective", "time frames" (i.e., consequences of decision over different time periods), "exogenous effects" (e.g., potential consequences of competitors' behaviour, changing technology or political climates).

Fletcher's model represents the traditional approach to ethical decision making, which concerns the effects of situational factors on ethical decisions. More recent approaches have shifted the emphasis from the moral environment to the moral agent or the decision maker. This trend is evident in the upsurge in research into virtue ethics and personal values. The relationship between virtue ethics and ethical decision making is discussed later in this section under the Solomon (1992) model. The effect of personal values on ethical behaviour in organisations has been the subject of several recent empirical investigations (e.g., Akaah & Lund, 1994; Finegan, 1994; Fritzsche, 1995; Jones, 1995; Singhapakdi & Vitell, 1993).

French's (1984) principle of responsive adjustment

The principle of responsive adjustment (PRA) focuses on the judgement of accountability of a moral agent's action which although unintentional, has nonetheless caused harm. The PRA was developed with reference to the event of an Air New Zealand DC-10 crash at Mt Erebus in Antarctica. The PRA was used as a framework in the analysis of the accountability of Air New Zealand for the crash. The theoretical basis of the PRA is grounded in Aristotelean notions of "intentionality of act" and "moral expectations". In his *Nicomachean Ethics*, Aristotle argued that a person should not be held morally accountable for an act which he/she unintentionally performed. In other words, one is not to be blamed for unintentionally causing harm to others. However, Aristotle also argued that people typically hold expectations that a moral agent, with the knowledge that his/her unintentional act has caused harm to others, will make appropriate corrections henceforth so as to prevent any future repetitions of the previous moral act. Extending these Aristotelean notions, French's principle of responsive adjustment contends that "...*a person can be held morally accountable for previous non-intentional behaviour that has harmful effects if the person does not take corrective measures to adjust his ways of behaviour so as to produce repetitions*".

Regarding the intentionality of the early act, French argues that once the early act has been judged on evidence as being unintentional, the issue of intentionality of that act is then "settled" regardless of the agent's subsequent behaviour. Therefore, the fact that the moral agent subsequently refuses to make corrective adjustment to the earlier harmful act, would not change the "unintentionality settlement" regarding that act. The subsequent failure of readjustment only makes the agent morally accountable for his/her unintentional yet harmful past act.

Rest's (1979, 1983) four-component model

This model extends Kolhberg's stage notion of cognitive development to ethical decision making. However, Rest (1979) argued that the stage progression may not follow an invariant sequence as suggested by Kohlberg. Rather, the progression allows for regression to an earlier stage or vacillation between stages. Specifically, the four-component model contends that a moral agent would go through four stages of processing in making an ethical decision:

(i) *recognising the moral issue*
   This stage involves the analysis of the situation and the identification of the problem as having moral implications.
(ii) *making a moral judgement*
   This stage involves moral reasoning and hence the stage notion of moral reasoning is most relevant here.

(iii) *establishing moral intent*
    This stage involves the moral agent making the resolution to give moral concerns a greater weight than any other concerns.
(iv) *implementing moral action*
    The moral agent puts into action his/her moral intent and moral concerns.

These four stages are assumed to be conceptually independent and operationally distinct from each other. Empirical research has provided general support for the model (e.g., Elm & Weber, 1994; Rest, 1986; Rest et al., 1986). More recent studies have explored the roles of education and work on the process of moral judgement development (e.g., Rest, 1989; Wilson et al., 1992).

Trevino's (1986) person-situation interactionist model

The model proposes that when faced with an ethical dilemma, an individual would react with a set of cognitions which are characterised by his/her cognitive moral developmental stage. These cognitions, together with several other personal and situational factors, form the basis of the individual's moral reasoning and moral judgements about the ethical dilemma. The set of personal factors include:

(i) *ego strength*
    ego strength refers to the strength of conviction and determination in carrying out a decision. Therefore, individuals with high ego-strength are hypothesised in the model to show more consistency between moral judgement and moral action.
(ii) *field dependence v. field independence*
    This refers to the extent to which an individual's functioning is dependent on the external cues provided by the field. Field-independent people tend to function more autonomously and rely to a less extent on the external cues. The model hypothesises that external social influences will play a less influential role in both the moral reasoning and moral action of people who are more field-independent.
(iii) *locus of control*
    This refers to the extent to which an individual perceives that he/she has the control over life events. The model hypothesises that internals, who believe that events are under their control and prefer taking responsibilities themselves, would be less likely to be influenced by external cues in their moral reasoning and moral action.

The set of situational factors include:

(i) *immediate job context*

The immediate job context pertains to reinforcement contingencies and external pressures (e.g., time constraint, lack of resources). The model hypothesises that these factors will have an effect on individuals' moral behaviour.

(ii) *organisational culture*
The cultural factors include the formal organisational structure, the employee's significant referent others, the culture's definition of an authority relationship, and the culture's "ascription of responsibility for consequences of action". These factors all exert an effect on individuals' moral behaviour.

(iii) *characteristics of work:*
When the work itself provides the opportunities for role-taking and for being responsible for conflict resolution, the work then would have an effect on individuals' continuing moral development and hence his/her moral behaviour.

Empirical research testing the Trevino model has in general provided supportive evidence (e.g., Trevino, 1986; 1992; Trevino & Youngblood, 1990). Both the Rest (1979; 1983) and Trevino (1986) models rest on the the assumptions made in Kohlberg's theory of cognitive development. The applicability of the cognitive moral development construct to business ethics has recently been reassessed (e.g., Fraedrich et al., 1994).

Jones' (1991) moral intensity model

In a review of existing organisational ethical decision making models, Jones argued that these models focus primarily on either the moral agent (the decision maker) or the moral environment. As a result, the characteristics of the moral issue itself have not been given due attention. Jones' moral intensity model thus places "the issue" at the core of the ethical decision process. Specifically, Jones contends that in making an ethical decision, the moral agent would systematically evaluate each of several key dimensions of the moral issue and make intensity judgements with reference to each issue dimension. The perceived overall intensity of the issue then determines the recognition of the moral issue, moral judgements, moral intent and subsequent moral action. Specifically, Jones has identified these issue characteristics as the key dimensions to be evaluated in the judgement of the moral intensity of the issue:

(i) *magnitude of consequence*
This refers to the total sum of harm or benefit done to the target person of the moral decision or moral act. The notion is akin to "severity of consequence" in Piagetian theory of moral development.

(ii) *social consensus*

This refers to the degree of perceived social agreement that the decision or action is ethical or unethical. The inclusion of this factor as an intensity dimension points to the generally recognised importance of social influence on people's ethical judgements.

(iii) *probability of effect*

This issue dimension consists of two components: (a) likelihood of act (i.e., how likely the moral act in question will actually be carried out) and (b) likelihood of consequence (i.e., when the act is carried out, how likely would it bring about the expected consequences)

(iv) *temporal immediacy*

This refers to how soon the expected consequences of the moral act will be felt after it has been carried out.

(v) *proximity:*

Proximity refers to the closeness or nearness of the moral agent to the target person(s) of the moral act in question; the concept applies to physical, psychological or social closeness.

(vi) *concentration of effect*

This is defined in terms of the inverse function of the total number of target persons affected by an act of a given magnitude.

Jones contends that the moral decision process is contingent upon the perceived intensity of a moral issue. Compared to issues perceived as having low moral intensity, high-intensity issues (a) will be recognised more frequently as moral issues, (b) will elicit moral reasoning characterised at higher levels of cognitive development, (c) will have a greater effect on the establishment of moral intent, and (d) will result more frequently in moral action. Recent empirical studies have provided support for the model. The studies found that some moral intensity dimensions (i.e., magnitude of consequences and social consensus) are more important in ethical decision making than other dimensions (e.g., Morris & McDonald, 1995; Singer, 1996; Singer & Singer, in press; Singer, Mitchell, & Turner, in press).

Solomon's (1992) ethical decision-making model

Solomon's ethical decision-making model is embedded in an integrative framework of virtue ethics based on the Aristotelean conception of virtues. Therefore to understand the model would require some knowledge of the entire ethics framework (for reviews of that framework, see Boatright, 1995; Ewin, 1995; Nesteruk, 1995). Solomon identifies six dimensions as the defining features of business ethics:

(i) *a business corporation as a "community"*

A community is one entire moral unit. Solomon argues that the fundamental flaw in the current thinking about business ethics lies in its treating the individual as a moral unit. The Aristotelean view however holds that "...(individuals) are all first of all members of a community and ...self-interest is for the most part identical to the larger interests of the group". Individuals are viewed not from an atomistic but rather a collective perspective. The collective, or the business corporation, then becomes the basic unit of morality.

(ii) *excellence as the purpose of business*

Solomon uses the word excellence in the Aristotelean sense of "arete", which can be interpreted as meaning either "excellence" or "virtue". The purpose of business, when defined as the search for excellence, would involve the pursuit of both "doing well" in terms of profit-maximising as well as "doing good" in the sense of moral virtues. Solomon further argues that when the word excellence is used in this sense, it carries a significant implication for "justice": for excellence to have its due reward, business must "defend the ideal of a meritocracy". Business ethics thus mean the practice of business virtues for the purpose of achieving both an economic and an ethical goal of the corporation.

(iii) *individual role identity and personal virtues*

The Aristotelean approach to ethics places the individual firmly within his/her community. Each individual's identity and worth are derived from the roles he/she plays in that community. Each role has a set of duties or metaduties (e.g., loyalty to the community) attached to it. Given that each individual may take on several roles within the community, the duties and metaduties associated with these different roles may well be in conflict with one another. Personal virtues thus are "context-bound" and involve the recognition of the multiplicity of duties and the potential "disunity of the virtues". The key point is that role identity defines the contexts within which virtues are exercised. In other words, the practice of personal virtues are relative to the specific situations circumscribed by specific roles.

(iv) *integrity as personal integration of all roles and virtues*

Given the multiplicity of roles an individual has to play in a community and the frequent conflicting demands of these roles, the ability to harmoniously balance these demands without compromising one's basic moral stance then inevitably becomes a most essential personal quality. Because of this, Solomon considers integrity as a "supervirtue" and equates its meaning to "wholeness", and to "getting it all together, not being torn by conflicts and doubts such that one cannot enjoy...life", and as such, integrity is then essentially "moral courage" or "the will and willingness to do what one knows one ought to do".

(v) *good judgement and the Solomon model of ethical decision-making*

In Aristotelean ethics, the ability to make "good" ethical judgement is regarded as most important. Good ethical judgement consists of three key ingredients: (a) it is based on the "perception of the individual" rather than on some external abstract moral principles, (b) it is a "product of good up-bringing, a proper education", and (c) it is situation-specific and involves careful consideration of the particular circumstances of each individual ethical issue.

It is in the context of this parameter of good judgement, Solomon proposes his ethical decision-making model as a practical guide. The model prescribes five steps for making an ethical decision:

(step i) Identify the problem by asking questions about rights, obligations, justice, or integrity. In other words, identify the reasons as to why it is an ethical problem.

(step ii) Identify the constituents by asking questions such as, "Who has been hurt?", "Who could be hurt?", "Who could be helped?", "Are they willing players or are they victims?" or "Can you negotiate with them?"

(step iii) Diagnose the situation by asking questions such as, "Is it going to get worse or better?", "Who is to blame?", "Who can do something now?", "Can the damage now be undone?"

(step iv) Analyse the options by thinking through "the range of possibilities", "limiting oneself to the two or three most manageable", and by asking questions like, "What are the likely outcomes or cost of each option?", "How can each option be achieved?", or "Which option is most desirable, given the circumstances?"

(step v) Act on the decision by "doing what one has to do", "not being afraid to admit errors", and by having moral courage to carry the act through.

(vi) *holism*

The traditional debates over the social responsibilities of business and over the necessity of dirty hands tend to presume the separateness of an individual's role as a businessperson from the rest of the roles he/she plays as a person. Aristotelean virtue ethics rejects this presumption and argues for the integration of all life's roles for each and every individual. The notion of holism thus rejects the many traditional antagonistic dichotomies in business ethics such as "competition versus cooperation", "self-interest versus duties", "selfishness versus community good". Instead, business roles are considered an integral part of a businessperson's entire life. Business virtues are then not to be differentiated from personal virtues.

According to Solomon, the first two parameters (community and excellence) are concerned with the basic conceptual framework of the Aristotelean perspective on ethics, the remaining four are more concerned with process issues pertaining to *"...the navigation of virtue throughout the...passages of community, corporate purpose, and personal virtue"* (p.161). These six parameters as a whole *"...form an integrative structure in which the individual, the corporation, and the community, self-interest and the public good, the personal and the professional, business and virtues all work together instead of against one another"* (p.145).

Although the Solomon model is more philosophical than practical in nature, its emphasis on Aristotelean virtues in ethical decisions has received a great deal of discussion in recent business ethics literature (e.g., Boatright, 1995; Ewin, 1995; Koehn, 1992; McCracken & Shaw, 1995; Nesteruk, 1995; Newton, 1992; Olson, 1995; Shaw, 1995). In line with the recent revival of virtue ethics, the Aristotelean theory of causation (material, formal, efficient and final causes) was also used as a foundational framework for organisational behavioural analysis (Malloy & Lang, 1993).

Frederick's (1992) Nature-based business value theory

The term value as used in the model is defined as *"the outcome of life's important processes"*, and embraces such forms of experiences as "beliefs", "standards of worth" or "judgements and appraisals". Values, gained through life-affecting experiences, then become an integral part of our existence.

Frederick argues that a theory of business values *"must be able to account for—that is, to describe—the core values that give life and continuity to business activities"*. However, Frederick notes that the most dominant theme of existing theories of business ethics concerns the analysis of the "X-factor values". The X-factor values are defined as the totality of personal beliefs, commitments and values held privately by individual managers and employees in a given organisation. These idiosyncratic personal values are the products of both nature (i.e., having a biological or a genetic origin) and nurture (i.e., having a sociocultural or an organisational origin). Frederick points out that the predominant emphasis on this specific type of values in business ethics is very much at the expense of three other nature-based values of any business system. The model contends that because the *"central normative problem facing business and society is posed by nature"*, business ethics needs to place primary emphasis on such values anchored in nature. The three categories of nature-based values are:

(i) *economising values*
   Frederick defines the word "economising" in terms of "prudent actions that produce a net excess of outputs from a given amount of resources. An economical action is one in which this net excess has been produced...A benefit-cost calculus is the typical way of knowing whether or to what extent

economising has occurred". The sets of values identified as serving the economising function of an organisation include sustained input-out balance, growth and productivity increase, systemic integrity or organisational bonding. Frederick likens the process of economising to that of energy transformation governed by the natural law of thermodynamics. Economising viewed in this context thus serves the function of generating energy for the purpose of achieving a net excess of outputs over inputs. The model contends that this process of economising is "the central, indispensable, defining characteristic of business. It emerges as the main normative principle of business activity."

(ii) *power-aggrandising values*

These values pertain to the organisation's power hierarchy and include status hierarchy, status-based decision power, power-system dynamic equilibrium and power aggrandisement. Frederick argues that aggrandisement is "proentropic" in the sense that it diverts vital inputs from economising to power seeking, and it should not be confused with the "antientropic" process of economising and growth.

(iii) *ecologising values*

Frederick considers this set of values as outside the main part of business operations, and defines it in terms of the interconnectedness between the business organisation and its "ecological environment". Business is thus part of an ecological network or an ecosystem. The set of ecological values of business include functional symbiosis , collaboration and mutual life-support, group defence and integrity, and community sustenance equilibrium.

Frederick argues that these three sets of business values, while all "anchored securely within nature", nonetheless operate on different principles. Economising and power-aggrandising are achieved by "competition and self-centeredness", in contrast, ecologizing can only be achieved through "collaboration and cooperation". Because of this, Frederick identifies the main agenda for business ethicists as being "...*to find ways of reducing the corrosive effect of economising and power-augmentation on ecological integrity*".

Weber's (1993) multi-component model of institutionalising ethics into business

This model is not so much concerned with moral agents' decision process as with organisations' efforts to integrate and institutionalise ethics into their entire decision-making practices. Based on existing theories and empirical evidence, Weber identifies four relevant factors which contribute to an organisation's successful promotion of ethics, as manifested in its organisational practices as well as in its employees' ethical behaviour. These four factors are:

84

(i) *organisational ethical culture*

An organisation's ethical culture refers to its moral values and beliefs. The model contends that the ethical culture of an organisation would affect every sphere of the organisation's practices, including its code of ethics, employee training and the enforcement mechanisms in the promotion of ethical behaviour. Several specific research hypotheses are proposed with reference to the existing classification of organisational culture types by Victor and Cullen (1988). These researchers have identified five types of organisational ethical culture:

(a) *instrumental*

An ethical culture which takes a utilitarian perspective by placing key emphasis on the maximisation of individual employee's self-interest or the interest of the organisation.

(b) *caring*

An ethical culture which emphasises compassion and seeks to maximise all joint interests in the entire organisation.

(c) *independence*

An ethical culture which emphasises employee autonomy. The guiding principles are personal rather than organisational ethical rules.

(d) *rules*

An ethical culture which emphasises the use of organisational ethical principles.

(e) *law and code*

An ethical culture which emphasises the application of more universal ethical principles in the form of law or code of ethics.

The model proposes the use of this framework, upon empirical validation of the typol*ogy, in the assessment of an organisation's ethical culture and its influence on its effort to promote ethics.*

(ii) *organisational code of ethics*

The model proposes that the type of an organisation's code of ethics also affects its efforts to promote ethics. The conceptual framework is that of Berenbeim (1988) who has identified three categories of code of ethics:

(a) *constituency obligation*

This refers to codes of ethics which reflect primarily the organisation's commitment to each individual constituency it serves.

(b) *professional responsibility*

This refers to codes of ethics which prescribe organisation ethical guidelines by emphasising the fulfilment of its various professional obligations.

(c) *corporate mission*

This refers to codes of ethics which clearly identify the mission and objectives of the organisation without providing specific prescriptions of ethical conduct.

(iii) *employee ethics training*
   The model proposes that the institutionalisation of ethics in an organisation is also affected by the type of its employee training programs. Two existing typologies are useful frameworks (Centre for Business Ethics, 1986; Harrington, 1991).

(iv) *organisational enforcement mechanisms*
   The model contends that an organisation's enforcement mechanisms are a necessary motivating force underlying the effective operation of its ethical culture, codes of ethics and its training programmes in the promotion of ethical practices. The model proposes the use of Berenbeim's (1988) classification of ethical enforcement mechanisms into five categories (i.e., termination, suspension, probation, demotion and disciplinary appraisal).

Weber's model serves as a conceptual framework for the understanding of an organisation's attempts of promoting ethical practices. To this end, the model calls for empirical research in three areas: First, in the establishment of consistent classification frameworks with reference to each of the four factors identified; second, in the exploration of the interrelationships among the four factors; third, in the examination of the relationship between organisations' efforts of institutionalising ethics and employees' ethical behaviour. Independent of Weber's model, Carlson and Perrewe (1995) recently made a similar call for institutionalising organisational ethics. They argued for the creation of an ethical climate through transformational leadership in organisations.

Ethical Decision Models in Marketing

Several models have been proposed to account for ethical decision processes in marketing behaviour. These models are:

Ferrell and Gresham's (1985) contingency model of ethical decision-making

This model proposes that the likelihood of ethical marketing behaviour is determined by these factors:

(i) *social environmental factors*
   These factors are treated as exogenous variables in the model. Their main influence pertains to the provision of the societal criteria used to define a marketing issue as involving an ethical dilemma. For instance, deception in advertising or accepting bribes constitute ethical dilemmas. The recognition of these issues as ethically questionable and as requiring an ethical judgement then initiates the entire ethical decision process.

(ii) *individual marketer factors*
The ethical decision process is influenced by several individual factors including each marketer's "knowledge" of the universal moral principles in moral philosophy as well as his/her "personal values, attitudes and intentions". The model posits that individual marketer's knowledge of moral principles affects his/her ethical behaviour through values, attitudes, and intentions about ethical issues. The knowledge is acquired through socialisation and formal education.

(iii) *organisational factors*
Organisational factors that impact on individual marketer's ethical behaviour include:

(a) *significant others*
Through differential association with other organisational members of different power hierarchy, individuals are under peer pressure to behave either ethically or unethically according to peer expectations or norms. The model posits that top management (due to power and authority) has greater influence than peers on an individual's ethical behaviour, and that the likelihood of unethical behaviour is determined by the relative frequencies of an individual's contacts with ethical and unethical patterns of behaviour in the organisation.

(b) *opportunity for ethical/unethical behaviour*
The model proposes that an organisation's code of ethics, policies and the rewarding mechanisms regarding ethical behaviour would influence individual marketer's opportunities to behave ethically or unethically.

Hunt and Vitell's (1986) general theory of marketing ethics

This model proposes that ethical decision-making in marketing involves the following steps:

(i) *issue recognition*
The model begins with a marketer's recognition of a problem as having an ethical content. The perception of an issue as involving an ethical dilemma is a prerequisite for invoking the ethical decision process. The recognition of a moral issue is influenced by four factors: "personal experiences" (e.g., individual's level of moral development, personality traits, or previous socialisation experiences), "industrial factors" (e.g., industrial or societal ethical climate), "organisational factors" (e.g., significant others or peers, professional guidelines, organisational ethical norms), and "cultural environment" (e.g., law, religion, national identity, or customs).

(ii) *identification of alternative actions and consequences of actions*
Having recognised an issue as requiring ethical judgements, a marketer would then need to identify all possible alternative course of actions as well as all

foreseeable or potential consequences for each of the alternative actions identified. These decisions are to be made with reference to each stakeholder group.

(iii) *ethical evaluations of actions and their consequences*

Two kinds of ethical evaluations take place with reference to each alternative action and consequence:

(a) *deontological evaluations*

These judgements are based on the application of deontological moral rules such as rights, duties, justice, honesty. The evaluation results in the judgement of each action or consequence as being "right" or "wrong", "good" or "bad".

(b) *teleological evaluations*

These evaluations are based on the rational-choice notion of subjective expected utility, and involves two sets of judgements with reference to each of the alternative consequences identified. The marketer needs to judge the likelihood of occurrence (how likely that a particular consequence is to occur) and the desirability of consequence (how desirable is each consequence for each stakeholder group). The overall desirability of each stakeholder group is also taken into account in this stage of the evaluation.

(iv) *moral intention*

Moral intention is defined as the likelihood that a particular alternative action will be chosen. The model identifies moral intention as an intervening factor in the link between moral judgement and moral action.

(v) *moral action*

The actual behaviour of marketers is constrained by several situational factors including the opportunities to act out specific alternative actions.

(vi) *effect of actual consequences of moral action*

The model proposes that after the moral act has taken place, the actual consequences of that act will feed back to the first stage of the model (i.e., issue recognition) and henceforth become an integral part of the construct "personal experience". This new set of personal experiences exerts its influence on all subsequent decision processes.

Ferrell, Gresham and Fraedrich's (1989) synthesis model

Ferrell et al. analyse and compare the propositions of three existing ethical models by Kohlberg (1969), Ferrell & Gresham (FG) (1985) and Hunt & Vitell (HV) (1986); as a result, they propose an integrated model by synthesising various constructs from these models. The synthesis model consists of several key stages of ethical decision-making. All these stages are influenced by all the "individual and organisational factors" from the FG model. These stages are:

(i)   *awareness and cognitions of ethical issues*
The awareness of an issue as involving a moral dilemma is primarily determined by all the "socioeconomic, cultural and environmental factors" from both the FG and HV models. The cognitions of the moral issues are constrained by individual marketer's typical stage of cognitive moral development specified by the Kohlberg model.

(ii) *moral evaluations*
The evaluations of a moral issue consist of the deontological and teleological judgements specified in the HV model.

(iii) *moral intention, moral action and actual consequences of action*
These stages follow mainly the propositions of the HV model.

While recognising that the synthesis does not result in a new model, Ferrell et al. contend that this integrative model can "contribute significantly to an improved understanding of ethical decision".

Dubinsky and Loken's (1989) analytic model of marketing ethical decisions

The theoretical framework of this model stems from the Ajzen and Fishbein's (1980) theory of reasoned action, which posits that there are three components in the analysis of ethical decisions:

(i)   *individual's attitudes towards the behaviour*
Attitudes towards a given behaviour refer to an individual's overall evaluation about each behaviour. This attitude variable is typically assessed by the semantic differential rating technique. The semantic differential dimensions frequently used are "good v. bad", "nice v. awful", and "enjoyable v. unenjoyable".

The model further posits that attitudes towards a behaviour are jointly determined by two factors:
(a)   *"behavioural beliefs"*—the perceived likelihood that the behaviour will bring about certain outcomes or consequences
(b)   *"outcome evaluations"*—the evaluation that each of the outcomes is "good" or "bad".

(ii) *individual's subjective norms about the behaviour*
Subjective norms refer to the individual's subjective perception about how his/her "salient referent others" think he/she should engage in the behaviour. Subjective norms therefore are perceived social influences or pressure placed upon the individual to perform a certain behaviour.

The model also posits that subjective norms about a behaviour are jointly determined by two factors:

89

    (a) *"normative beliefs"*—the belief that certain significant others (top management, manager, or a peer) think he/she should perform the behaviour

    (b) *"motivation to comply"*—the willingness to comply to his/her "perceived" wishes of the salient or significant others.

(iii) *intention*

The model proposes that behaviour is primarily determined by the intention to perform that behaviour. Intention is defined as the likelihood that the person will perform a behaviour, which is in turn determined by the person's "subjective norms and attitudes towards the behaviour".

According to this model, an analysis of ethical decision-making in marketing behaviour would begin with the assessment of individual marketer's "behaviour beliefs", "outcome evaluation", "normative beliefs", and his/her "motivation to comply". These four factors then determine the marketer's "attitudes towards the behaviour" and "subjective norms about the behaviour". These two factors in turn determine the marketer's intention to perform that behaviour. Empirical studies of the model have provided convergent support for these propositions (Dubinsky & Loken, 1989).

A POSTMODERN APPROACH TO ETHICAL DECISION-MAKING IN BUSINESS

Rossouw's (1994) Rational Interaction for Moral Sensitivity

As mentioned in the previous chapter, Rossouw argues that moral dissensus is a distinct feature of the present times. Moral dissensus refers to "irreconcilable" moral disputes over, and conflicting moral claims on, contemporary social issues such as euthanasia or affirmative action. Moral dissensus has opposing parties, rather than individual persons, as the frame of reference. Rossouw's approach thus aims at the resolution of disputes between opposing moral viewpoints, rather than the resolution of personal ethical dilemmas. The key features of this approach to moral disputes are:

(1) The stakeholders (disputing parties) engage in a rational dialogue which emphasises (i) reciprocal stating of arguments in terms that can be understood by both parties, (ii) consideration of different values, culture, religion, as well as emotions in the dialogue, (iii) tolerance and respect for one another as equal moral agent, (iv) allowing all parties to freely express their opposing viewpoints.

(2) The rational interaction should avoid an "elitist conception of dialogue", which requires the ability of the parties to state their moral reasoning or to articulate the specific moral tradition to which they subscribe. Such a

requirement would exclude people who are likely to make valuable contributions to the dialogue, due to their inability to meet the requirement.

(3)   The aim of the rational interaction "should not be to reach consensus", but to increase each party's moral sensitivity towards the other and to understand the implications of the consequences of its own stance for the other. It is hoped that, in the light of the opposing views freely expressed in the dialogue, each party will be willing to reformulate its moral viewpoint in a compromising way.

With reference to the participants of the dialogue, Rossouw argued against the need for them to have the knowledge about moral reasoning. However, others argue that it is essential for the participants of such dialogues to have some moral expertise, although the expertise can be aided by moral philosophers. Crosthwaite (1995) has argued that policy decisions that have ethical implications cannot be made *in the absence of understanding the reasoning behind different moral assessments*", and that such moral deliberation about rightness *"is a preliminary to and component of any social policy"* (p.379).

The postmodern approach to irreconcilable moral disputes appears to fit in well with the prevailing climate in most contemporary societies where rights and equality are of paramount concern to their citizens. Cast in that context, an increased sensitivity to others' viewpoints, and an enhanced understanding of the consequences of one's own moral stance for others, become a necessity towards the formulation of a well-informed and well-educated opinion.

Part Two

A Normative-Empirical Dialogue

Chapter 5   Ethics and Justice: The Roles of Philosophy and Empirical Sciences

From the foregoing literature review of moral philosophy, moral psychology and applied ethics, it becomes clear that each has made a significant contribution to current understanding of ethics and justice. Both moral psychology and the practical aspect of applied ethics take primarily an empirical and descriptive approach to the subject; moral philosophy by contrast is inherently normative and prescriptive. The goal of the former is to provide empirical data which describe the factual way people think about and act on morality; the goal of the latter is to prescribe normative and universal rules of morality. Given these differences, the empirical approach serves to describe how ethics and justice are perceived and enacted, whilst the normative approach serves to prescribe what ethics and justice *ought to be*.

Moral philosophy on the one hand, moral psychology and the empirical part of applied ethics on the other, are thus dealing with ethics and justice from different perspectives. Kahn (1990) describes the coverage of the subject by the two approaches as being completely separate, "*...In terms of a Venn diagram, the normative concepts and those who develop them occupy one circle, which remains separate from the circle of contextual (social sciences) concepts and those who develop them*". Because the two content areas tapped by the two approaches do not overlap, Kahn goes on to identify the weakness of existing methods of ethical enquiry, "*...What is missing is the intersection of the two circles, the shaded area in which concepts and methods are created that reflect both normative and contextual understandings*" (p.313).

What Kahn is arguing is a joint effort in a more thorough understanding of ethics and justice, an effort which combines the prescriptive approach of moral philosophy with the descriptive approach of moral psychology and applied ethics. The call for such an integrative effort has been made by scholars researching the subject from diverse perspectives.

For example, in moral philosophy, Buchanan and Mathieu (1986) speak of normative theories of justice, "...*it would be a mistake to assume that..the most reasonable philosophical theory of justice can be achieved simply by refinements in philosophical thinking. On the contrary, it is becoming increasingly clear that philosophical disputes about justice cannot be resolved without significant contributions from the social sciences*"(p.44). Similarly, Etzioni (1989) also advocates a "deontological social science".

In applied ethics, Donaldson (1994) calls for a "symbiotic approach", while maintaining that normative and empirical theories cannot be integrated conceptually. Such an approach gives equal credit to each method of ethical enquiry. Werhane (1994), while rejecting Donaldson's contention that there exists a pure empirical-normative dichotomy in the methodology of applied ethics, argues a similar point on the importance of recognizing that neither method of enquiry is "...singularly The Approach". Further, Werhane believes that only through this recognition that philosophers and social scientists can constructively communicate with, and benefit from, each other.

In moral psychology, Kohlberg (1982) argues for a dialogue across the boundaries of disciplines for the reason that the subject matter can be addressed more fruitfully by both the normative and the empirical approaches. Hann (1982) extends the call for an interdisciplinary cooperation by including "...*psychology and philosophy as well as other social disciplines*" (p.1103). More recently, Waterman (1988) presents a thorough and thoughtful analysis of the nature of philosophical and empirical approaches to ethics. The analysis reveals both the empirical approach's potential contributions to normative ethical enquiry, and its inherent limitations in such an endeavour. As a result, Waterman concludes that "... *the use of psychological evidence in the process of ethical inquiry falls far short of what Kohlberg and Haan urged*". Despite the limitation, Waterman calls for "*generating a dialogue across disciplines with a view to identifying and using those points on which psychologists and philosophers can productively join together in furthering the process of ethical inquiry.*"(p.296).

Therefore, the call for constructive interactions between normative philosophy and empirical social science in ethical enquiry is widespread, although there is also wide disagreement among scholars over the exact mode of such interactions.

NORMATIVE VERSUS EMPIRICAL APPROACHES TO ETHICS AND JUSTICE

Given that moral philosophers and empirical ethicists are increasingly cognizant of the potential contribution each can make towards their common goal of a better understanding of ethics and justice, it becomes necessary to clearly identify the strengths and the weaknesses of each approach to ethical enquiry. To do so, several issues need to be addressed in relation to the nature of each approach; the reasons as to why each will need input from the other; the exact contribution each can make towards the other; and the possible modes of a constructive interaction.

(1) *The Nature of the Normative and the Empirical Approaches*
Kurtines, Azmitia, and Alvarez (1990) in their discussion of science and morality, pin-point the key difference between the two approaches: the normative approach is clearly value driven, while the empirical approach is value-free. In the prescription of normative moral rules, philosophers essentially engage in an evaluation process which is value-laden (i.e., what people "should" or "ought to do" to be moral). However, in describing what people typically think and act, moral empiricists take a natural science or positivism stance towards objectively discovering the facts about moral behaviour. It should be noted that much of the recent literature in the philosophy of science has rejected a strict "value-fact" dichotomy and suggested that science, especially the social and psychological sciences, cannot be free from value (for a review, see Kurtines et al., 1990).

Trevino and Weaver (1994) contrast the two approaches and identify several other key differences between the two.

(a) *difference in academic training required*
The normative approach typically requires formal training in philosophy, theology or liberal arts; empirical approach requires the training of social sciences and scientific methodology grounded in Comte's positivism tradition.

(b) *difference in the vocabulary or language*
The same word (e.g., ethics, good, right, moral) often carries a different definition or connotation in a normative context from an empirical one. According to Waterman (1988), the word "norm" causes much semantic confusion when used in these two different contexts. For moral philosophers, norms are products of reflection thoughts and refer to "standards of conduct or ethical value, principles of right action". For empiricists, norms are obtained from objective observation of behaviour and mean "typical or average patterns of behaviour for specific social groups".

(c) *difference in underlying assumptions about human moral agency*
Normative theories of ethics carry the presumption that moral behaviour is the result of the moral agent's free will and hence the agent acts with autonomy and responsibility. In other words, the "locus of control" of moral behaviour lies in the individual. The empirical approach however rests on the implicit assumption that moral behaviour is determined by characteristics of both the individual moral agent (e.g., ability, personality, free choice) and the external context (e.g., social, situational or environmental influences). Therefore, the "locus of control" of moral behaviour lies both within and without the individual.

(d)   *difference in the purpose, scope and application of theory*
As mentioned earlier, the goal of normative theories is the prescription of universal rules for right and wrong conduct, whereas that of the empirical approach is the description of actual moral conduct without addressing the evaluative question concerning right/wrong or good/bad.

The scope of the normative approach, as compared to that of the empirical, is more abstract, more general and also more independent of the particularities of the context. In terms of application, normative theories are used as a conceptual framework for analysing, critiquing, evaluating and reflecting upon ethical issues. Empirical ethical theories are however used in understanding and explaining moral behaviour as it occurs in a complex social environment, and in predicting its occurrence in other similar contexts.

(2)   *Why Moral Philosophers and Empirical Ethicists Need Each Other and Why Have They Remained Separate?*
The most frequently cited reason as to why moral philosophy needs the input from social sciences is that empirical data can help identify the most "viable" and reasonable moral philosophy which is in line with the reality of daily living (e.g., Waterman, 1988). A similar point has been made by Weaver and Trevino (1994). In addition, Buchanan and Mathieu (1986) identify two other specific reasons:

(a)   *the resolution of many philosophical debates requires the technical expertise of social science*
This reason is primarily relevant to utilitarianism. Moral philosophers have debated over the utilitarian claim that individuals are able to make meaningful and precise interpersonal comparisons in terms of utility gains and losses. Buchanan and Mathieu argue that the problem may be resolved with the help of the technical expertise of some mathematical economists. At a more general level, the concept of utility itself by definition is more of an empirical rather than a theoretical or evaluative notion. Therefore debates pertaining to the utility notion can only be resolved by the empirical rather than the normative approach.

(b)   *the fundamental assumptions on which many philosophical theories rest require the validation of empirical evidence*
Buchanan and Mathieu give several particular examples to illustrate this point.
(i)   Rawlsian justice rests on the assumption that inequality in personal gain is a significant driving force behind productivity. This assumption however is inadequately supported by empirical evidence from psychological and sociological research.
(ii)   Nozick's libertarianism assumes that in a society where wealth is unequally distributed, individuals would behave in a rational manner by voluntarily rendering aid to the needy. Buchanan and Mathieu argue that

this assumption pertaining to "the voluntary practice of the virtue of charity" requires validation from empirical sciences, and that it is not a matter for philosophical reflection.

(iii) Many questions pertaining to the philosophical debate over Capitalistic versus Marxist economic efficiency also require the confirmation or disconfirmation from factual data which can only be provided by empirical sciences.

In the context of business ethics, Velasquez (1996) recently has analysed each empirical study in an issue of *Social Justice Research* and pointed out how each specific piece of research is directly related to the two substantial normative tasks of moral philosophers: *"...first, an attempt to articulate and provide a rational justification for a set of abstract oral principles, and second, an attempt to apply these principles to particular business practices."* (p.102).

Turning the table around, empirical ethicists also need the aid from moral philosophers. Indeed, the field of moral psychology receives most of its theoretical input from philosophical theories of ethics (e.g., Greenberg & Bies, 1992). As mentioned in chapter three the entire empirical literature on organisational justice owes its origin equally to moral philosophy (the distributive justice tradition) and the legal practice (the procedural justice tradition). Victor and Stephens (1994) specifically point out that *"psychological research on moral development would be logically impossible without philosophical theory on morality"*, and that Kohlberg himself has acknowledged Rawls' notion of justice as the basis for his theory of cognitive moral development (p.151).

Given that the two approaches to ethical enquiry obviously derive benefit from each other, the question arises as to why the two have so far remained separate and why so little effort of communication is evident from scholars on either side.

There are several reasons for this:

(a) As mentioned earlier, there are many substantial differences between the two approaches in terms of the nature, the scope of application as well as the underlying assumptions. Due to these differences, each approach may seem either irrelevant or insignificant from the other's perspective (e.g., Weaver & Trevino, 1994).

(b) As previously noted, specialised training is typically required for each approach. Without the demanding extra expertise required for a meaningful dialogue, the attempt to comprehend or to put into use each other's work may result in "fundamental misunderstandings or misapplications" (Trevino & Weaver, 1994). For this reason alone, many scholars are not favourably inclined towards interdisciplinary communications.

(c) Waterman's (1988) analysis of philosophers' objections to empirical inputs has identified several additional reasons for the separation of the two approaches:

(i) Moral philosophers argue that empiricism is subject to the "naturalistic fallacy". Empiricism takes a naturalistic approach to morality and defines moral norms in terms of typical behaviour which can be observed and objectively measured. For empirical ethicists, morality has a factual status. However, most normative ethicists insist that morality has both an objective factual aspect and more importantly, a subjective "value" aspect; the main philosophical task is to evaluate the "rightness" of ethical issues and to prescribe rules of right and wrong. It is this key aspect of evaluation in ethical enquiry that empiricism does not address. Empiricists committing the naturalistic fallacy thus interpret findings of moral facts as meaning both facts and value. In other words, they are making the mistake of "deriving ought from is" (Waterman, 1988, p.292). Because of this, philosophers believe that empirical evidence does not constitute a useful input for the moral philosophers' task of addressing questions of value.

Pertaining also to the general fact v. non-fact dichotomy, the Noncognitivism and the Irrationalism schools of moral philosophy go a step further by arguing that morality does not have a factual status at all; instead, it constitutes expressions of attitudes, feelings and the desires to exert influence over others (Stevenson, 1963). The very denial of morality as having a factual aspect thus renders empiricism totally irrelevant and useless in the philosophical ethical enquiry.

(ii) Normative theories of ethics always carry the implicit assertion that specific standards or norms of behaviour (e.g., specific behavioural consequences or utility) are of value, hence are to be commended. This assertion involves a value judgement, a subject which lies in the core expertise of moral philosophers and is not one for empirical examination.

(iii) Empirical ethicists are biased in their research by their own unique perspective to morality. Empirical work is typically confined within the theoretical framework the researcher adopts in the first place. Questions about morality would be framed and tested in one way by researchers taking the cognitive developmental perspective to morality, but in another way by those taking the taxonomic or the constructionist perspective. Waterman refers to this bias in perspective as the empiricist's "problem of scope".

(iv) There is a great deal of ambiguity in the daily usage of moral language. This presents a thorny problem for empirical research which relies on respondents' own interpretation of the wording of the research questions. This problem seriously undermines the validity of empirical findings and hence their potential contribution towards ethical enquiry.

(v) Empirical findings of ethical issues hold true mainly within the cultural and historical confines wherein the research is conceptualised and conducted in the first place. For instance, Kohlberg's moral developmental theory receives validation from empirical studies carried out mainly in Western countries. This leaves open his assertion about the universality of the sequential stages of moral development (e.g., Simpson, 1974). To the extent that empirically established facts are constrained by sociocultural factors, empirically derived theories of morality simply cannot serve the function of providing absolute moral standards.

(3) *What Contributions Can the Empirical Approach Make in Ethical Enquiry? Its Limitations?*

Empirical research can contribute to ethical enquiry in at least these areas:

(a) *to validate the fundamental assumptions about human nature in moral philosophical theories of ethics*

It has been argued that this is indeed where empirical evidence would be useful in ethical enquiry. Normative theories of ethics have made implicit assumptions about human nature: for instance, the Rawlsian assumption regarding the effect of the "veil of ignorance" (the "original position") on individuals' distributive decisions (cf., Waterman, 1988); and the assumption regarding the sole motivating effect of inequality in personal gain on productivity for the society (e.g., Buchanan, 1983). Other such examples include those mentioned earlier: the Libertarian's assumption regarding the voluntary practice of charity, and the fundamental assumptions in political philosophy regarding the free-market versus socialistic economic efficiency.

(b) *to reveal the factual status of the moral rules prescribed as "shoulds" or "ought-to-bes"*

The key mission of moral philosophers is undoubtedly to prescribe standards of moral conduct. They therefore identify ideals of conduct as those that should or ought-to be carried out. Waterman writes, "...*Any behaviour nominated as instances of moral 'shoulds' can be evaluated against empirical criteria*" (p.295). To clarify this point, consider the moral imperative of ethical egoism, which states that "an act is moral when it produces the greatest amount of net utility for oneself than any other alternative act". Psychologists can effectively do two things:

(1) empirically ascertain the factual aspects of the moral statement, that is, to calculate the net utility for the individual of each possible act hence to identify the one that produces the greatest net utility for that person, and,

(2) empirically ascertain whether such a rule also holds in all contexts of social groups or cultures, other than the one in which the rule was originally proposed.

In other words, psychologists can assess the validity or truthfulness of the factual statement in the imperative and they can also assess the universalisability of that fact. However, the remaining task lies squarely on moral philosophers: the task of evaluating the goodness or rightness of the fact hence justifying its prescription as a moral norm.

(c) *to ascertain the factual relationship between teleological and deontological factors in moral considerations*

While empirical evidence cannot be used to decide or evaluate between alternative philosophical perspectives, it however can shed light on the exact manner in which individuals utilise the key moral standards, presumed in each perspective, in making their ethical decisions. Specifically, empirical evidence can help determine the relative importance individuals accord each moral standard such as right, justice (deontology) or utility (teleology) in their ethical deliberations. Such information serves not only to indicate the applicability of each philosophical perspective to actual ethical considerations, but also to reveal the relative practical utility of each perspective.

While the empirical approach can make a significant contribution in ethical enquiry, the limitations of such a contribution need to be clearly recognised.

(a) Empirical findings from a single experiment always carry a degree of "uncertainty" about the factual status of behaviour, as indexed by the statistical significance level. Furthermore, empirical research is typically guided by the researchers' unique training or preference in the choice of specific theoretical framework and research design. Such differences in the orientation of expertise, together with the known experimenter effect in the actual conduct of the study may contaminate the obtained results. The probabilistic nature of empirical data and the potential for data contamination raise questions about the precision of empirical findings, therefore such evidence "should not be expected to yield definitive conclusions" (Waterman, 1988, p.296).

(b) Empirical evidence inconsistent with normative moral claims cannot be regarded as "refutation" of the claims; rather, it simply reveals the impracticality in terms of the application of the theory. Scholars have illustrated this point by using available empirical evidence on Kant's categorical imperative of "Lying is immoral hence people should not lie". They argue that while empirical findings show that people generally regard some form of lying as perfectly ethical, these findings by no means "undermine" or "alter" the normative status of Kant's theory. This is due primarily to the prescriptive and directive nature of normative moral rules. In Weaver and Trevino's words, "*...the point of ...any...moral theory is to chasten, not to pander to, the status quo... (Normative) principles might be unrealistically demanding, but impracticality alone does not entail the refutation of a normative theory...rather, the moralist can choose between forsaking a general normative principle or delimiting its practical* *value"*(p.135). A similar sentiment has been expressed by Victor and Stephens (1994).

(4) *Modes of Interaction or Dialogue*
Several possible modes of interaction or dialogue between the normative and the empirical approaches to ethics have been suggested in the literature:

(a) *the metaethical mode*
Goodpaster (1983) asserts that applied ethics serve three key functions: the normative function (i.e., to prescribe normative rules), the descriptive function (i.e., to describe typical behaviour), and the analytic or the metaethical function (i.e., to analyse the meaning of ethics and to evaluate its methodologies). Werhane (1994) maintains that interdisciplinary communication can best begin at the analytic or metaethical level whereby different methods of enquiry are analysed, evaluated, and their relative advantages and limitations clearly recognised. Werhane argues that this level of cross disciplinary interaction represents an "analytic integration" which, as a result of the metaethical analysis, helps each side to recognise the importance of the other. Therefore, even though this analytic integration does not involve any real integration of the normative and the empirical, "...*It is on this level of analysis that philosophers and social scientists can communicate with each other and enrich each other's points of view...without metamethodology, the social scientists and philosophers will merely retreat to their more parochial points of view and the unity of analytic integration will be lost*" (Werhane, 1994, p.179).

(b) *the symbiotic mode*
This form of interdisciplinary dialogue involves a pragmatic collaboration whereby each approach derives benefits and guidance from the other, but each remains firmly independent and grounded in its own theoretical, methodological and metatheoretical assumptions (e.g., Weaver & Trevino, 1994). A symbiotic dialogue between moral philosophers and empirical ethicists would entail that the former use empirical evidence to guide the application of their normative theories and that the latter use such theories to formulate their empirical research questions. Successful symbiotic dialogue requires that each learns to understand and keeps an open mind about the other's work. Critical evaluation of one approach from the other does not constitute invalidation or refutation of the fundamental theoretical or methodological stance of that approach.

(c) *the theoretical-integration mode*
While the symbiotic mode of interaction involves a reactive stance of each approach to the other, the mode of theoretical integration entails a proactive stance in developing a new and integrative set of theoretical, methodological and metatheoretical assumptions (Weaver & Trevino, 1994). Such hybridisation can take on differing degrees of conceptual and theoretical

fusion of the normative and the empirical (for detailed discussion on the subject, see Donaldson, 1994; Frederick, 1992; Haan, Bellan, Rabinow, & Sullivan (Eds.), 1983).

Donaldson (1994) however argues that a hybrid "is-ought" theory which attempts to integrate the normative with the empirical at a theoretical level is doomed to failure for the reason *"that the logic of prescription differs from the logic of description"*. Because of this, he calls for a symbiotic mode of dialogue that *"credits the empirical and the normative with equal significance...but which asks each vantage point to know its proper place"* (p.167).

EXISTING RESEARCH ATTEMPTING A NORMATIVE-EMPIRICAL DIALOGUE

Although the exact mode of integrating the normative and the empirical approaches to ethics is still the subject of intense theoretical debate, scholars are in general agreement that a cross-disciplinary dialogue in ethical enquiry is sorely needed. Recently, several empirical ethicists have made constructive attempts at such a dialogue. These research efforts aim at one of two different goals:

(1) to ascertain the factual status of normative assumptions made in philosophical theories of ethics.
(2) to explore the interrelationship among standards of morality prescribed by different schools of moral philosophy.

The following is a review of the existing literature under these two different goals.

The Factual Status of Normative Assumptions

Empirical research has attempted to ascertain the factual status of the following assumptions made in normative theories of moral philosophy: (1) the Rawlsian difference principle, (2) the philosophical claim against rewarding individuals' "native endowments", (3) the Aristotelean claim concerning distribution by merit, (4) the Hobbesian claim about egoism, (5) the utilitarian claim about the utility of merit-based reward systems, (6) the utilitarian claim about the utility of punishment, and (7) the Kantian categorical imperative of truth-telling. The following section reviews the empirical research pertaining to each of these assumptions.

(1) Testing Rawls' Difference (Maximin) Principle
Rawls' difference principle stipulates that people in the hypothetical "original position" (i.e., behind the "veil of ignorance") would endorse a distributive rule which maximises the benefits of the worse-off in the society. Several studies attempted to simulate Rawls' "original" and future society wherein people have no

knowledge of not only their own future place, class position, or social status in that society, but also their future "native endowment" (i.e., genetically-determined natural assets such as intelligence, gender, beauty or race). These studies aim to test the assumption of the difference principle in the allocation of resources. While results of several studies have failed to find support for that principle (see Curtis, 1979; Fisk, 1975; Frohlich, Oppenheimer, & Eavey, 1987a, 1987b; Lissowski, Tyszka, & Okrasa, 1988), results of other studies have found some support for the difference principle. When respondents were uncertain about their abilities in the hypothetical society, they were more inclined to maximise the benefits of the least advantaged (Brickman, 1977). In a cross-cultural study (Bond & Park, 1991), results of Korean, but not Western, subjects have provided supportive evidence to Rawls' theoretical derivation.

Most recently, Mitchell, Tetlock, Mellers, and Ordonez (1993) designed a study to explore the way people make trade-off decisions in income distribution. The maximin principle was contrasted with two other perspectives to the trade-off between equality and efficiency. The three perspectives led to differential predictions of distributive rules.

(1) *the value-guided perspective*
This position would predict that people base their decisions on their personal beliefs and values about political ideology. Political conservatives would prefer efficiency over equality hence an equity-rule in income distribution, whereas liberals or egalitarians would favour equality over efficiency hence an equality-rule.

(2) *the compromise perspective based on Boulding's (1962) position on the efficiency-equality dilemma*
Boulding's proposition involves a two-tier system which sets a "welfare minimum" or "safety net" to satisfy basic needs of the least advantaged group in the society. Beyond that, resource distribution follows the equity rule that is merit-based.

(3) *Rawls' maximin principle*
This principle would predict that people favour a distributive rule that maximizes the income level of the poorest in society.

Respondents were given information about the mean income level and the level of income variability of a hypothetical society. In addition, they were also told the "level of meritocracy" that is operating in the hypothetical society, that is, the degree to which reward is contingent upon individual effort and ability. Three levels of meritocracy were manipulated in terms of "the proportion of income accounted for by individual effort and ability" (i.e., 10%, 50% and 90%).

Results show that people's income distribution decisions are influenced by both individual and situational factors. Rawls' maximin principle was supported when "meritocracy" in the hypothetical society was set either at a low or medium level. When respondents were told that this society places extremely high emphasis on meritocracy (i.e., a 90% correlation between income and effort/ability), they chose the distribution rule consistent with Boulding's compromise solution. Individual differences in political values interacted with level of meritocracy in affecting people's allocation preference: When the hypothetical society is set at medium level of meritocracy (i.e., 50% relationship between income and effort/ability), the liberals favour the equality-based rule and the conservatives the efficiency or equity-based rule. However, when the society is set at the two extreme levels of meritocracy (10% or 90%), comparatively little ideological difference in income allocation was evident.

With specific reference to the maximin principle, the study shows that Rawlsian prediction holds true only if the prevailing political ideology in the hypothetical society is characterised by a low or medium level of meritocracy. If the findings could indeed be extended to real societies, the results would suggest that in a communist or a socialist economy, people would consider the maximin rule as the most fair in the allocation of income. However, in a free-market capitalistic economy, people are more likely to consider the Boulding solution (equity-rule above minimum welfare) as the most fair. Therefore, the study has two significant implications. At a pragmatic level, an income distribution which is consistent with the prevailing political climate tends to be seen as more fair than other alternatives. At a more theoretical level, justice or fairness then is not "a stable, well-defined ideal end-state", rather, it has "a cybernetic component" that makes it "responsive to shifting features of the social order and that ensures that no one position will be dominant for long" (p.637).

In a recent effort to establish the contribution of the empirical research on organisational justice towards normative ethical inquiries, Greenberg and Bies (1992) first identified several assumptions (other than the maximin principle) implicit in the normative theories of ethics. After reviewing the existing empirical evidence pertaining to each assumption, they then drew a conclusion concerning the factual status of each normative claim. The following normative claims were identified and relevant empirical research was included in that review:

(2) *The philosophical claim against rewarding individuals' "native endowments"*
Some philosophers (e.g., Rachels, 1986) have claimed that it would be unfair or unjust to reward people for their native endowments (e.g., beauty, gender, race). Such inalienable aspects of individual characteristics are referred to by Rawls as "the natural lottery" over which people have no control. Greenberg and Bies (1992) reviewed empirical studies pertaining to fairness perceptions of using such non-merit criteria in income or reward allocation. Based on existing empirical evidence, they concluded that "...*although people are reluctant to take rewards based on completely random criteria, they do believe that it is fair for them to reap the benefits of any victories received in the natural lottery*" (p.436).

(3) *Aristotle's claim that distribution by merit is universally considered as the fairest means of allocating resources*

Greenberg and Bies's (1992) review included empirical evidence based on equity theory and other distributive principles. The review found support for Aristotle's claim, but evidence also suggested that people define "merit" in a variety of conflicting ways. For instance, research pertaining to gender-based pay inequity suggested that being a male was seen as "meritorious" (p.430). When merit was so defined, it then followed naturally that females would receive less pay than males in jobs of equal worth.

(4) *Hobbes' egoism claim that people seek to maximise self-interest*
Greenberg and Bies' review suggested that self-interest significantly affects people's fairness perception of various allocation rules: people typically consider as the most fair the allocation rule that maximises their own self-interest. However, results of studies on reward allocation also showed that people often had concerns for others' interest and did not always seek to maximise their own gain. In other words, there was a limit to the egoistic pursuit of self interest. This pattern of results were observed under experimental conditions when respondents expected to maintain a long-term interpersonal relationship with others and when others were in a less powerful or disadvantaged position.

(5) *The utilitarian claim about the utility of merit-based reward systems*
The claim is that reward by merit would result in the "greatest good for the greatest number of people". Empirical research has focused on pay systems based on merit. Two specific criteria of "good" were considered: organisational productivity and employee job satisfaction. Results of these studies suggested that merit-pay system did not "consistently lead to increases in productivity", but it tended to enhance employee work satisfaction. This evidence, however, does not constitute sufficient data for a test of the utilitarian claim, as the validation of the claim would have to involve not only systematic comparisons of the utility of all alternative reward systems, but also a valid and complete set of the criteria of "good". Until results of such a comprehensive study are available, the factual status of this claim will remain uncertain.

(6) *The utilitarian claim about the utility of punishment*
The claim is that punishing harmdoers would result in more good than harm to the society. Two criteria of "good" were included in the review: the prevention and deterrence of future harmdoing, and the rehabilitation of harmdoers. Results suggested that punishment did have a significant deterring effect, but rehabilitation programmes failed to consistently benefit the harmdoer. It is obvious that these results are not sufficient in providing a clear indication as to whether punishment does indeed produce "more good than harm to society". As the validation of such utilitarian claims require similar systematic research as outlined above, existing empirical evidence again is not sufficient to serve such a purpose.

(7) *Kant's categorical imperative of truth-telling*
Two claims that are empirically verifiable were identified in the review: that lying is morally unacceptable, and that being lied to constitutes an attack on the person's basic human dignity. Regarding the acceptability of lying, empirical evidence suggested that people considered certain type of lying as morally justifiable hence acceptable. However, direct empirical evidence was not available in validating the latter claim, although relevant evidence suggested that people typically considered honesty as the most important fairness determinant in interpersonal interactions. More recently, in the literature of organisational justice, scholars are in agreement that interactional justice serves to affirm basic human dignity (e.g., Folger, 1988; Lane, 1988; Lind & Tyler, 1988). Accordingly, a theoretical link between lying (honesty) and dignity does exist beyond the domain of normative theories of ethics. However, empirical research which allows a direct test of this claim is needed.

The Interrelationship Among Standards of Morality

Given the multiplicity of normative moral viewpoints, an obvious question concerns the relative position of the moral standards espoused by different viewpoints. Several moral philosophers have identified the teleology-deontology division as representing the most dominant polarisation in the philosophy of morality. Given the teleological emphasis on the consequences and utilities of moral actions and the deontological emphasis on justice, rights and duties, the former takes an "impersonal, spectatorial" stance, whereas the latter, a more "personal, participative vision" (e.g., Goodpaster, 1985). While moral philosophy collectively considers utility, justice, and right as key aspects of morality, it has not specifically prescribed the relative importance of each constituent in overall considerations of morality. A likely reason for this is that philosophers adopting a different moral perspective tend to claim priority relative to the other positions (Goodpaster, 1985).

However, Velasquez (1982) has provided a general guide-line on the relative importance of the three key moral standards. He argues that standards concerned with moral rights, by virtue of their being foundational to human existence, are typically given the greatest weight in moral considerations. A greater weight is also typically accorded justice than utilitarian concerns. However, Velasquez argues that the relative importance may differ in different contexts. Velasquez writes, "...*We have at this time no comprehensive moral theory capable of determining precisely when utilitarian considerations become 'sufficient large' to outweigh narrow infringements on a conflicting right or standard of justice....Moral philosophers have been unable to agree on any absolute rules for making such judgements*" (p.92). What Velasquez is emphasising here is the importance and the uniqueness of contextual influences on moral considerations. The answer to the question of relative importance appears to be context-dependent. To the extent that the answer may be contingent upon the particularities of the ethical dilemma, the empirical approach may then be appropriate in addressing the issue.

The empirical literature pertaining to morality exists in three distinctive domains: moral psychology, applied ethics (business ethics), and organisational justice. Both moral psychology and business ethics are primarily concerned with empirical testing of the overall rightness or goodness of a moral act. The key research question typically involves judgements of "ethicality" (or perceived overall goodness or rightness). On the other hand, the organisational justice literature has a unique focus on the notion of justice. The key research question typically involves judgements of fairness and associated mental processes. Despite the moral philosophical premise that justice is an integral part of morality, organisational justice research has remained separate and independent of research on judgements of overall ethicality. Research designed to bridge this gap by assessing judgements of fairness and overall ethicality within the same experimental context can help to ascertain the factual status of the philosophical assumption that justice is indeed an integral part of morality.

While the research on justice is extensive and exists as an independent literature, empirical research into the notions of utility, rights and duties is relatively scarce. Although the question of utility is often addressed in the economics literature, there is little research addressing its relationship either with judgements of overall ethicality, or with other constituents of morality. Because of this, the factual status of the "perceived" relative importance of utility, rights and justice in ethical considerations is also unclear in the empirical literature.

Given the centrality of these teleological and deontological notions in normative moral philosophy, the author has recently designed studies which aim to contribute to the normative-empirical dialogue by addressing these specific questions:

(a) Is justice an integral part of considerations of morality as implicated in moral philosophical theories of ethics. Translated into empiricist or hypothesis-testing language, the question becomes, "Is judgement of fairness an integral aspect of judgements of overall ethicality?" or "Is fairness consideration a significant predictor of overall ethicality judgement?"

(b) What are the interrelationships among various constituents of morality? Specifically, there are two aspects to this question: ·

    (i) Does morality entail considerations of rights, justice and utility as implicated in philosophical theories of ethics? In empiricist language, the question becomes, "Are considerations of rights, fairness and utility significant predictors of the overall ethicality judgement?"

    (ii) What are the relative importance of the three key constituents of morality (rights, justice and utility) in overall moral considerations? Framed in empiricist language, the question becomes, "What are the relative weights placed upon rights, fairness and utility in the overall ethicality judgement?".

Studies Addressing the Empirical Link between Justice and Ethics

These studies employ a scenario approach whereby hypothetical ethical dilemmas were presented to respondents. Each scenario depicts a moral agent (i.e., the decision maker) making a decision which has clear ethical implications. After reading the scenarios, respondents made judgements of the fairness and ethicality of that decision.

The theoretical framework of these studies is grounded in Jones' (1991) moral intensity model of ethical decision making. Unlike other existing models which emphasise the roles of the moral agent or the moral climate, Jones' model focuses on the effect of the characteristics of the moral issue itself on ethicality judgements. As perceived fairness is an essential feature of the moral issue, the Jones model appears to be more appropriate than other models in serving as a framework for the present studies. Although the Jones model has been briefly reviewed in Chapter 4, its relevance to constituents of morality needs to be elaborated for the purpose of the studies.

The Jones Model and Issue Fairness

The model contends that ethical decisions are primarily contingent upon the characteristics of the ethical issue. In making ethical judgements, individuals evaluate the intensity of the characteristics of the issue. The overall intensity of a moral issue is determined collectively by the *magnitude of consequence* of moral acts; the degree of *social consensus* that the moral act is unethical; the *likelihood* that the act would take effect; the *temporal immediacy* of the effect of the act for the target person; the *proximity* or feelings of closeness to the target person; as well as the *concentration* of the effect. The model further posits that the perceived overall intensity of the moral issue would influence issue recognition and judgements, moral intent, as well as the engagement of a moral act.

Several issue dimensions in the moral intensity model appear to closely correspond to various constituents of morality. The notion of consequence in the teleological models features prominently in the Jones model where the consequence of a moral issue is said to be evaluated from several angles: its size (i.e., *magnitude of consequence*), its probability (i.e., *likelihood of consequence*), and its nearness in time (i.e., *temporal immediacy*). This emphasis on the consequence of a moral issue in ethical judgements also corresponds to the Piagetian concept of *severity of consequence* in moral development (e.g., Piaget, 1965).

The inclusion of the *social consensus* dimension gives credence to the importance of social influence on individuals' ethicality judgements. In theories of ethics, the status accorded to social influences on morality varies greatly. While ethical absolutists imply that universal moral rules are immune to social influences, ethical relativists claim that what constitutes morality is society- or culture-specific. The significance of social influence on morality is also explicit in most models of moral psychology: In Hogan's (1973) ethics of social responsibility, morality consists of "socially responsible rule following" (Waterman, 1988). In Kohlberg's (1976) notion of conventional morality, the primary motivation for morality is a desire to conform, and the main moral consideration is socially-agreed-upon rules. Further, in the interactional models of ethics (Haan, 1983; Rossouw, 1994), the *social consensus* notion most explicitly features in the dialogue process by which moral solutions are to be reached.

The inclusion of the *proximity* (i.e., feelings of nearness) issue dimension in the Jones model deserves special attention. The model's contention here is that the degree of feelings of closeness to the target person of a moral act would affect perceived intensity of that act, and hence the judgement of its ethicality. Although *proximity* is defined in terms of either social, cultural, physical or psychological nearness in Jones model, it is the social psychological aspect (i.e., friendship, liking or personal concerns) that was addressed in this study. This is because the role of subjective feelings or concerns for others in morality has been at the core of the debate over whether morality has a *care* or *justice-* focus. Traditional theories of ethics place morality strictly within the domain of pure reason and intellect to the exclusion of any influence of subjective feelings. Noting the inadequacies of that perspective, some more recent theorists (e.g., Flanagan, 1982; Kagan, 1984) have argued for a significant role of subjective personal feelings in morality. The idea of concern for others is central to Gilligan's (1982, 1986) "care-based morality", Kitwood's (1990) "psychology of moral life" and Forsyth's (1980, 1992) personal moral philosophy of "idealism". In all these contexts, "concerns for others" refers to an intrinsic aspects of human behaviour in that people are fundamentally concerned about the welfare of other fellow beings; the idea here is akin to Lerner's (1977, 1982) notion of a justice motive. However, the degree to which a person possesses such concerns and its consequences for morality vary in each theory. In Gilligan's theory, concerns for others is related to gender group status (i.e., the ethics of care features predominantly in female rather than male morality). In Forsyth's theory, the degree of concern for others defines the individual differences dimension of idealism. The morality of people who are highly "idealistic" is more likely to have a care-focus. In the Jones (1991) model, the degree of concerns is contingent upon the feelings of proximity or closeness to the target (or victim) of the moral issue.

While the model has identified several key characteristics of a moral issue upon which ethical decisions are said to be contingent, it has however ignored one other essential feature, that is, the issue's perceived fairness. Given the philosophical link between justice and ethics explicit in the deontological models, and Rawls' (1971) definition of justice in terms of fairness, it is then logical to add *fairness* as an additional issue dimension to those identified in the Jones model. This leads to an extension of the model's prediction: ethicality judgments would involve an evaluation of the intensity of the fairness dimension of the moral issue, in addition to the issue dimensions as defined in the Jones (1991) model. This extended framework thus allows a direct test of the empirical relationship between judgements of ethicality and fairness.

Description of the Studies

Details of the studies were originally reported in Singer (1996). In the studies, two samples of respondents were recruited:

(a) *managerial professionals:*
Altogether 160 (93 male and 67 female) managers were recruited from commercial firms and private sectors. These professionals were working as bank managers, owner-managers in commercial firms, accounting managers or lawyers in law firms. They were located in cities of Auckland (n=70), Christchurch (n=75) and Ashburton (n=15). The age of male managers ranged between 21 and 65 years with a mean of 39.2 years. The age of female managers ranged between 21 to 53 years with a mean of 35.4 years.

(b) *general public:*
This sample consisted of 164 people (77 males and 87 females) outside the business and the university communities. The age range was between 19 and 78 years (mean=44.4). These respondents were randomly recruited from 30 suburbs in the Christchurch area. All respondents were visited by the same research assistant in their homes.

Respondents were given a questionnaire which consisted of hypothetical scenarios of ethical decision making. Some scenarios depicted cases whereby the target person unduly benefited from the decision made by the moral agent, others depicted a decision which unfairly harmed the target person. The scenarios were chosen as pilot research showed that respondents perceived them as having high relevance and realism for ethical decision making. The following is an example of the scenarios depicting decisions resulting in harmful consequences for the target person:

"Several months ago, Jackie asked Lucy to help her with a special design assignment which she has contracted for a lucrative commission. Jackie said if Lucy took on and completed half of the assignment, Lucy should have half of the commission. Lucy agreed to take the offer. Since then she diligently worked on the design. Three weeks ago, Lucy completed her part of the design and showed it to Jackie. Jackie said she loved it and suggested some minor alterations. Lucy made these changes in the design and gave the final product to Jackie. However, Lucy received a letter from Jackie yesterday saying that she just decided that Lucy's design would not fit in with her part of the fashion assignment, so she was not going to use Lucy's work. As a result, there will be no pay for Lucy."

The following is an example of the scenarios depicting hypothetical cases whereby the target person unduly benefitted from the decision made by the moral agent:

> "...Ben and John are both studying science in the university. During the last few months, Ben has been dating a young woman in his class. Because of this, he has been very much behind in his study. Ben asked John if he could copy one of John's assignments for Applied Maths, as he had not been able to find the time to do it himself. John agreed to offer the help..."

Following each scenario, respondents made judgements about the decision. Seven judgements were assessed: (1) *overall ethicality* of the decision (e.g., "To what degree do you think that the decision was morally unsound?", (2) *magnitude of consequence-* of the decision (e.g., "How would you estimate the seriousness of the consequences of the decision?"), (3) *social consensus-* over the decision (e.g., "How likely is it that there is a general consensus among people that the decision is unethical?"), (4) *likelihood of action* (e.g., "In your opinion, how likely is it that the decision maker might change his mind ?", (5) *likelihood of consequence* (e.g., "What are the chances that the decision will result in the expected consequences?"), (6) *temporary immediacy* (e.g., "How likely is it that the decision will have long-term consequences?", and (7) *perceived fairness* of the decision (e.g., "In your opinion, how would most people rate the fairness of the decision?").

Results of Studies

Results from all scenarios were pooled together and analysed. Seven scores were computed for each respondent: scores on overall ethicality, magnitude of consequence, social consensus, likelihood of action, likelihood of consequence, temporal immediacy and perceived issue fairness. Each score was calculated by summing up respondent ratings on all items assessing that variable. A regression analysis was used to ascertain whether judgements of ethicality are influenced by the perceived fairness of the moral issue as well as by the intensity of other issue characteristics identified by Jones. The predictors were fairness ratings and ratings on the moral intensity variables. The overall ethicality score was the dependent variable.

Results of the regression analysis for the managerial sample show that managers' overall ethicality score could be significantly predicted by three issue intensity scores: social consensus (β=.38, p<.01), magnitude of consequence (β=.27, p<.01), and issue fairness (β=-.22, p<.01). Results for the general public sample show that these respondents' overall ethicality scores were predictive by two issue intensity scores: magnitude of consequence (β=.51, p<.01), and issue fairness (β=-.18, p<.01).

Consistent for both respondent groups, the perceived fairness of a moral issue was a significant determinant in the judgements of its overall ethicality. These results thus show a significant empirical relationship between judgements of fairness and judgements of ethicality.

A Further Study

A recent comprehensive review of the research using scenarios reveals that this approach has been an integral part of applied ethics (Weber, 1992). Compared with other approaches to ethics research, scenarios are less susceptible to the social-desirability response set bias (e.g., Armacost et al., 1990, cited in Weber, 1992). Several researchers have argued for the importance of "relevance" and "realism" in the design of scenarios (e.g., Fredrickson, 1986; Elm & Weber, 1994) on the grounds that scenarios so perceived by respondents are more likely to elicit a greater extent of involvement and hence more realistic responses. The two studies reported above involve the "non-personal" scenario design typically deployed in applied ethics research. This further study, which is part of a larger research project by the author, aims to improve upon the degree of personal involvement and relevance of the design by requiring respondents themselves to name people known to them as characters in the ethical dilemmas. This serves to engage respondents more fully than the standard "non-personal" scenario approach.

Specifically, the experimenter briefly described the scenarios used and asked the respondent whether the scenarios were likely to happen to any people they know. When the respondent decided upon the two names (the moral agent and the target person), the experimenter filled the two names into the appropriate blank spaces throughout the scenarios before giving them to the respondent to read. The scenarios and questionnaire used in this study were near identical to those used in the previous studies. A total of 120 respondents were recruited from the general public. Results of this study concurred with those of the previous two studies in showing a significant relationship between judgements of fairness and judgements of ethicality.

Implication of Findings

Results of these studies addressing the empirical link between justice and ethics consistently confirm that fairness consideration is a key determinant of people's overall ethicality judgement. The observed empirical link thus parallels the moral philosophical claim that justice is an integral part of morality. Therefore, the studies have provided empirical validation of a major philosophical assumption.

Studies Addressing the Interrelationship among Utility, Rights, Justice and Ethics

While the scenario approach is widely used in empirical studies of morality, it is highly context-dependent. Respondents' ethicality judgements are constrained by particularities of different ethical dilemmas. By contrast, interviews can explore individual's "ethics schema" more directly and thoroughly. In the following study, an interview was conducted first to explore what people typically believe to be the main determinants of ethical and fair behaviour. As managerial professionals were interviewed, the questions were framed in the context of work behaviour. The factors managers identified as main determinants of ethical behaviour at work were analysed and sorted into non-repetitive statements by independent judges. These statements were then used to construct a twenty-one item Likert-type questionnaire of ethical behaviour. To complete the questionnaire, respondents were required to rate the importance of each item as a determinant of ethical or unethical work behaviour. An example of the items reads, "*acting to intentionally promote community welfare or collective interest*".

The same procedures were repeated for the construction of a Likert-type questionnaire to identify determinants of fair or just behaviour at work. The questionnaire consisted of fifteen items: an example reads, "*keeping employees well informed of work-relevant information*".

The questionnaire assessing ethical work behaviour was given to a sample of 210 managerial professionals. The other questionnaire assessing fair work behaviour was given to an independent sample of 161 managers. These professionals were recruited from a total of 114 commercial companies, private and public offices including airlines, clothing firms, accountant offices, real estate agencies, bookshops, law firms, supermarkets, investment office, retail companies, government Departments, teaching institutions, consultancy firms and hotels. The offices are located in the cities of Auckland, Christchurch and neighbouring areas.

For each questionnaire, respondents' importance ratings were analysed by the statistical technique of the Principle Components Factor Analysis with varimax rotation. Results of the analysis on ethical work behaviour reveal five key factors. These factors together accounted for 61.4% of the total variance of ethical behaviour at work. The factors are listed below, together with the individual items having significant loadings on each factor.

Factor 1: "*acting to promote utility for collective interest or public good*" (36.2% of total variance)
    (1) "acting to intentionally promote community welfare or collective interest" (item loading=.81)
    (2) "acting to intentionally benefit the community despite personal sacrifices" (item loading=.74)
    (3) "acting out of a concern for people or environment, rather than for money" (item loading=.63)

Factor 2: "*being just, respecting others' rights and equal treatment of others*" (7.9% of total variance)
    (1) "being fair and just" (item loading=.76)
    (2) "respecting others' rights" (item loading=.71)

Factor 3: "*going beyond normal acceptable behaviour and being caring*" (6.2% of total variance)

(1) "going beyond what is normally considered acceptable behaviour" (item loading=.71)
(2) "acting in a caring manner" (item loading=.65)

Factor 4: *"not acting solely out of self-interest or abusing power" (5.9% of total variance)*
(1) "acting solely out of self-interest" (item loading=-.77)
(2) "not abusing power" (item loading=.65)

Factor 5: *"acting according to moral principles and conscience" (5.2% of total variance)*
(1) "putting principle before profit" (item loading=.73)
(2) "acting on moral grounds despite personal financial loss" (item loading=.69)
(3) "acting according to one's conscience" (item loading=.69)

For fair work behaviour, three main factors emerged as significant determinants. The three factors together accounted for 57.9% of the total variance. The factors and associated individual items are:

Factor 1: *"respecting, valuing, informing and including each individual" (40.0% of total variance)*
(1) "giving individuals the power to decide for him/herself" (item loading=.74)
(2) "putting staff welfare before profit" (item loading=.76)
(3) including others rather than excluding or ignoring others" (item loading=.68)
(4) "keeping employees well informed of work-relevant information" (item loading=.58)
(6) "being responsible to others" (item loading=.56)
(7) "being thoughtful and considerate to others" (item loading=.55)

Factor 2: *"getting due rewards and being unbiased"* (9.4% of total variance)
(1) "getting what one deserves" (item loading=.75)
(2) "getting what one is entitled to" (item loading=.68)
(3) "being unbiased" (item loading=.61)

Factor 3: *"equal treatment of others and being honest, trustworthy and moral"* (8.5% of total variance)
(1) "treating everyone the same and not discriminating or showing favouritism" (item loading=.72)
(2) "applying the same standards to all" (item loading=.68)
(3) "being moral" (item loading=.57)

(4) "being honest and trustworthy" (item loading=.56)

Implications of Findings

These results have shed light on the empirical relationships among the three key standards of morality. When asked directly to think of the key standards of ethical behaviour in a work context, people identify five such standards. The first two most important ones so identified clearly concern the "utility for collective good" (i.e., Factor 1) and "justice and rights" (i.e., Factor 2). Further, Factor 1 accounted for a significantly greater proportion (i.e., 36.2%) of the total variance of overall ethicality than did Factor 2 (7.9%). These findings suggest that, in judging the goodness of work-related behaviour, people tend to place a much greater weight on community utility concerns than on standards of justice and rights.

Three other minor factors have also been identified as determinants of ethical work behaviour: Factor 3 concerns the practice of caring behaviour; Factor 4, the prohibition of self-interest; and Factor 5, the abiding-by of moral principles and conscience. While Factors 4 and 5 are consistent with a fundamental and well-accepted view of morality, the identification of the practice of caring behaviour as a key aspect of ethical work behaviour deserves further discussion. The finding points to the importance of "care" and "compassion" in moral considerations. Although moral philosophers agree that justice is the basis of morality, they disagree over the status of compassion and care in morality. Only a handful of theorists such as Gilligan and Forsyth have placed care, alongside justice, at the core of morality. Results of these empirical studies have shown that people indeed consider care and compassion as important aspects of ethical work behaviour. The individual items which had the highest loadings on this factor and hence can best define the factor include, "going beyond what is normally considered acceptable behaviour" and "acting in a caring manner". Given that acceptable behaviour is typically considered obligatory, behaviour going beyond that seems to fall in the domain of supererogatory and other non-obligatory categories of moral acts (Baron, 1987; Kolnai, 1973; Mellema, 1994). Viewed this way, the present results taken together suggest that the five criteria private citizens use in judging ethical work behaviour not only encompass the entire range of moral standards prescribed by normative theories of ethics, but also include those additional moral acts which are "beyond the call of duty".

Turning to the results on fair work behaviour, while Factor 2 confirms the importance of "due rewards" in the concept of justice, Factors 1 and 3 pertain to the quality of interpersonal treatment. The identification of these two factors (1 and 3) suggests that what people see as fair work behaviours appears to be acts that follow the standards of "rights" identified by Velasquez (1982, p.91): to respect and value others, to allow others the freedom to choose, to ensure the availability of relevant information, or to ensure no deception or manipulation is used against others.

In moral philosophy, the core focus of justice tends to be the fairness of distribution as implicit in the Rawlsian notion. However, the focus of rights appears to be on interpersonal interactions or treatments. While these two key deontological concepts are closely related, the Rawsian notion of justice takes a somewhat impersonal perspective to distribution and requires people to behave in the hypothetical "original position". The ultimate goal of justice thus zeroes in on the fairness of the final distribution. The notion of rights, on the other hand, has a totally personal focus with the ultimate goal being the affirmation of fundamental human dignity.

In the applied ethics literature, the distinction between "due-reward" (justice) and "affirmation-of-dignity" (rights) is blurred by the fact that both notions are examined under the rubric of "organisational justice". In the organisational justice literature, no attempt has been made to clearly distinguish justice from rights. For instance, researchers have equated justice to "dignity" (e.g., Folger, 1988). In addition, although due-reward is analysed within the theoretical frameworks of both outcome justice and procedural justice, affirmation-of-dignity is analysed within the procedural framework under the special case of "interactional justice" (e.g., Bies & Moag, 1986; Lind & Tyler, 1988). Here, interactional justice is defined in terms of the quality of interpersonal treatment an individual receives in the process of resource distribution. Several studies have identified the key criteria of interactional justice in different interpersonal contexts. The criteria include "open and honest communications", "providing vital information and discussing expectations", "seriousness of treatment", "sincerity" and "not harming people" (for a review, see Singer, 1993). These criteria are in close agreement with those identified by Velasquez as moral standards of rights. Given that the importance of interactional justice lies in its potential in sustaining human dignity and enhancing self-esteem (Lane, 1988, p.316), what organisational justice researchers refer to as "dignity" (Folger, 1988) or "interactional justice" is thus in fact the deontological standard of "rights" in philosophical terms.

Turning back to the present study, results show that private citizens identify standards of action that "affirm human dignity" (i.e., Factors 1 and 3; 48.5% of total variance) as a more important criterion than those ensuring "due reward" (Factor 2; 9.4%) in determining "fair" work behaviour. What the results suggest is that in the context of work behaviour, people believe that the affirmation of others' rights, more so than due rewards, is what justice is all about.

To sum up, the findings of these studies have shed light on the relative weights private citizens or ordinary people place on the criteria of utility, justice and rights in their judgements of ethical behaviour. In the specific context of work behaviour, considerations of utility in terms of consequences for public good appear to be of foremost importance. Given that affirmation of rights, rather than fairness in allocation, is seen as the core of fair work behaviour, it is plausible to conclude that considerations of rights are accorded a greater weight than those of justice in people's moral judgements. Although moral philosophers argue that considerations of rights typically override those of justice and utility (Velasquez, 1982), the findings obviously suggest that at least in the context of work behaviour, utility considerations are perceived by people as being "sufficiently large" to outweigh the standards of rights and justice. However, it is important to note that in people's perception, it is the community welfare or public good, rather than self-interest, that defines such utility considerations.

Chapter 6 Ethics and Justice in Organisational Recruitment and Selection

Organisations interface with society through many of their functions. Personnel recruitment and selection is one such example. From the organisation's perspective, the goal of recruitment is to optimise its human resources and hence its productivity and efficiency. Utility research into economic efficiency consistently shows that organisational productivity can be significantly enhanced by selection procedures that are based on the principle of meritocracy (e.g., Cascio, 1982; 1991; Schmidt, Hunter, McKenzie, & Muldrow, 1979; Schmidt, Ones, & Hunter, 1992; Schmitt & Noe, 1986). Recruitment by merit therefore would best serve the interest of the organisation. However, historically, merit-based selection has persistently resulted in the hiring of predominantly "majority" (as defined by gender, ethnic origin, etc.) job candidates to the exclusion of "minority" applicants. The reason for the differential hiring rate has only become clear towards the beginning of the 1990s after two and half decades intensive psychometric research. In the case of ethnic groups, it is due primarily to the existence of significant subgroup differences in job-related abilities (for a review, see Singer, 1993a). In the case of gender groups, psychological processes other than objective ability differences appear to be the likely reason for the lower hiring rate of female candidates. Regardless of the nature of the mechanisms underlying the differential hiring rates, the observable fact is that minorities are underrepresented in the workforce, and in particular, the higher echelons in the workplace hierarchy.

From the perspective of a society in which people have fundamental egalitarian concerns, such recruitment programmes are seen as having failed to "fairly and justly" distribute among its members one of the most sought-after resources, i.e., employment opportunities. Given that the society ultimately aims to ensure that all its members are "fairly" treated and their basic needs are well catered for, the societal goal therefore appears to be persistently contradicted by the merit-based recruitment programmes adopted by business organisations. Because of this, employment recruitment becomes a thorny issue of distributive justice in society. Some moral philosophers have long argued for the implementation of affirmative action and preferential selection programmes to redress the injustice in employment distributions. However, others have grave doubts about the very "justice" of such programmes themselves. The philosophical debate over affirmative action and preferential selection has been well documented in the business ethics and social justice literatures.

Philosophical debates aside, the public disquiet over the inequality in subgroup hiring rates eventually led to the legislation and court rulings which stipulate that organisations adopt various affirmative action programmes to achieve a fairer and more equitable representation of minorities in the workforce. However, such recruitment programmes, rather than solving the distributive justice problem, have created a new set of ethical dilemmas. Empirical research has provided insight into the nature of such dilemmas. Elsewhere the author has provided a review of the legislative and legal history of affirmative action in the United States (Singer, 1993a). Interested readers are referred to the book for discussions of the psychometric and social background to the legal development of employment nondiscrimination during the past three decades.

Given that the focus of the present book is on ethics and justice and that preferential treatment of minority candidates is a key controversial issue in applied ethics, this chapter aims to contribute to the normative and the empirical dialogue on the ethics and justice of preferential selection. The dialogue pertains to two different aspects of the selection practice:

(1) the justifications for the selection practice

The chapter reviews the philosophical and the empirical literatures on the justifications for diversity versus merit selection. The moral philosophical literature documents the debate over the ethics of diversity selection, the empirical literature focuses on the description of people's typical reactions to and judgements about these philosophical justifications.

(2) the overall "rightness or goodness" (in philosophical terms) and "perceived ethicality" (in empirical terms) of selection practices

Moral philosophy presumes that utility, justice and rights are key constituents of ethics, the rightness or goodness of an act is to be determined by considerations of these three aspects of the act (Goodpaster, 1985; Velasquez, 1982). In this chapter, such a normative prescription is applied to the evaluation of diversity-based and merit-based selection. To this end, the evaluation of the overall goodness of the programmes would need to embrace deliberations over issues of consequence, fairness and individual rights. Therefore, the chapter first reviews the empirical evidence on (a) the relative utility or consequences of the selection practices, (b) the perceived justice or fairness of the programs, and (c) issues of individual rights and selection. It is hoped that such a systematic evaluation can shed light on people's typical judgements of the overall goodness of selection practices.

DIALOGUE CONCERNING JUSTIFICATIONS FOR AND EMPIRICAL EVIDENCE ON SELECTION PRACTICES

In this section, a normative-empirical dialogue is generated by applying empirical tests to the philosophical justifications for each of the two selection practices. The empirical tests are in the form of attitudinal questionnaires. To this end, moral philosophers' justifications for diversity-based and merit-based selection are first reviewed. After the review, the section reports an empirical study which was designed to systematically examine and compare people's typical reactions to the philosophical justifications for the two selection practices.

Justifications for Selection Based on Diversity versus Merit

Justifications for Diversity Selection

Proponents of diversity selection have provided five key compelling reasons for granting differential treatment to minority job candidates.

(1) Diversity selection obeys the compensatory justice principle in providing compensations to minorities for past discriminations they suffered
This is one of the most compelling justifications for granting differential treatments to minorities in employment selection (e.g., America, 1986; Broxhill, 1972; Minas, 1977; Taylor, 1973; Thomson, 1973). There are three essential but somewhat independent components to this argument:
(i)   a recognition of the fact that minorities were treated unfairly in the past;
(ii) a recognition of the need for paying some form of reparations to those suffered; and
(iii) a suggestion that differential treatment in hiring is a just form of reparation.
Nowadays few, if any, would deny the truth of the first component of the argument. In a survey of American Whites (Sniderman & Hagen, 1985), the majority believed that the current less than desirable social and economic circumstances of the Blacks are the direct effect of generations of discrimination and slavery.
People's views regarding the need of paying reparations seem to be somewhat diverse. For gender-based hiring, studies by Tougas and Veilleux (1988, 1989) showed that females would prefer hiring programs emphasising current equality to those designed to compensate for past inequality. However, whites in general support the idea that special efforts should be made to help Blacks and other minorities to improve their circumstances (Kluegel & Smith, 1986). Seltzer and Thompson (1985) reported that a majority of their respondents (both whites and

blacks) supported the idea that those who were discriminated against in the past should be compensated for and should get a "better break" in the future. A survey of university administrators also showed that a majority considered additional efforts as "necessary to overcome past discrimination" (Tickamyer, Scollay, Bokemeier, & Wood, 1989, p.132).

Regarding the third component of the argument, people in general disagree with the suggestion that diversity selection is a just form of reparation. The Gallup Polls (1984) conducted between 1977 and 1984 on this very argument consistently showed that only a small minority (10% to 11%) agreed with this idea. Tougas and Veilleux (1989) also found that both women and men opposed differential treatment in hiring as a just form of improving females' social and economic conditions. In a national survey of white Americans, Kinder and Sanders (1990) found that the majority (over 85%) opposed giving differential treatments to minorities in hiring or promotion decisions in order to compensate for past discrimination. Although the majority of studies addressing this issue report negative attitudes towards diversity hiring, there are a few exceptions. For instance, in the Tickamyer et al. (1989) survey of university administrators, those administrators responsible for implementing affirmative action programs showed strong support for diversity hiring goals (p.131).

These results suggest that people are supportive of the general idea of paying compensation to minorities. However, with a few exceptions (e.g., Goldsmith, Cordova, Dwyer, Langlois, & Crosby, 1989; Tickamyer et al., 1989), most people do not favour the idea of giving minority candidates differential treatment in employment decisions. Lipset and Schneider (1978) attributed the observed attitudinal discrepancy to a conflict in values between individualism and egalitarianism. Paying reparations for past wrongs are seen as an egalitarian act, but giving differential treatment to a specific class of people is viewed as contradicting the principle of individualism and fair competition.

(2) Diversity selection helps to equalise life chances so that minorities can compete with nonminorities on equal terms

This argument focuses on individual competitiveness. The ideology of a free market economy carries the presumption that individuals compete for the limited economic or societal resources on an equal basis (e.g., Fishkin, 1983). An equal basis would mean both the absence of external barriers and the equality of life chances (Hartigan & Wigdor, 1989; p.33). This argument also involves two components:

(i)   a recognition that minorities should have an equally good chance of getting any societal or economic resources as the nonminorities;

(ii) a suggestion that differential treatment of minorities in job allocations can ensure a fair competition for employment opportunities.

Again, few would dispute the first argument. A survey of white Americans in 1972 showed that an overwhelming majority (97%) supported the view that

Blacks should have "as good a chance as White people to get a job" (Schuman, Steeh, & Bobbo, 1985). Although there has been no direct empirical testing of people's views on the the second component of the argument, some argue that differential treatment itself would render any competition unfair (e.g., Lipset & Schneider, 1978). Indeed, there has been convergent evidence showing that people perceive diversity hiring as unfair (to be reviewed later in the chapter).

(3) Diversity selection helps to broaden the talent pool of organisations
This justification (e.g., Shaw, 1988) focuses on the possible gains for the recruiting organisation. Through actively recruiting minority employees, organisations widen their search for suitable candidates by incorporating the so-far underutilised population into their potential talent pool. Scott and Little (1991) also argue that firms having minority employees would "gain a competitive advantage in market share" (p.180). Further, because minorities make up almost one quarter of the US population, in order to provide services that best fulfil the needs of these customers from a diversified background, employers need to have minority service providers or decision makers who can best understand such needs. This argument carries two presumptions:
(i)   the current workforce underutilises minority talents
(ii)   diversity hiring may enhance the competitiveness of the employer.
      Whether the workforce underutilises minority talents is an empirical question. The answer requires a "workforce analysis" and a "utilisation analysis" (e.g., Cascio, 1989). Available utilisation analyses carried out as Court orders or research interests (e.g., Bronstein & Pfennig, 1989) often reveal such an underutilisation.
      Regarding the second component of the justification that diversity hiring may enhance the employer's competitiveness (e.g., Scott & Little, 1991), there is no direct empirical data for this claim. Existing utility analysis seems to suggest that diversity hiring may cause a loss in economic efficiency or productivity (to be reviewed later in the chapter). However, it needs to be pointed out that the competitive edge stressed by Scott and Little takes a distinctive moral-philosophical and social psychological perspective which is largely ignored by the traditional economic cost-benefit approach underlying the utility analysis. This difference highlights the dilemma between the two goals of diversity-based hiring programs: the goal for social justice and the goal for economic efficiency. Schmidt et al. (1992) argued that this conflict cannot be resolved by empirical research. Therefore the answer to this question would require a thoughtful and balanced consideration of both social justice and economic issues.

(4) Diversity selection ensures having minority role models in the workforce
This justification focuses on the long-term advantageous effect of diversity hiring on minorities' socialisation and development. Scholars have argued that there exists systemic barriers that act as a "glass ceiling" in preventing minorities from

advancing through the professional hierarchy (e.g., Morrison & Von Glinow, 1990). One of these barriers is the lack of role models (e.g., Irons & Moore, 1985). Proponents argue that diversity-based hiring can ensure having role models in the workforce for minorities. This may not only help their career development but also their socialization process (e.g., Jackson, Stone, & Alvarez, 1992).

(5) Diversity selection helps to promote societal welfare by attending to the needy
Proponents argue that diversity hiring cares for the needy in society (e.g., Nagel, 1973; Nickel, 1974). Attending to the needy will ultimately improve the welfare of the society. Since members of the minority groups typically constitute the needy in society, diversity selection can help to improve their disadvantaged situation by a redistribution of employment opportunities (e.g., Fiss, 1976; Nagel, 1973; Sher, 1975). Compared to the justification based on the principle of compensatory justice, this need-based justification has a different temporal focus: satisfying present needs, rather than rectifying past ills.

Justifications for Selection by Merit

In a free market economy, the allocation of employment opportunities traditionally follows the principle of meritocracy. There are several philosophical justifications for this.

(1) Merit selection maximises workforce productivity and efficiency
When jobs are performed by people having the best job-relevant qualifications and competence, a highest possible workforce efficiency is most likely to be achieved (e.g., Daniels, 1978). It has also been argued that the fundamental tenets of meritocracy in a free market economy are the principles of efficiency and fairness (e.g., Fishkin, 1983; Hartigan & Wigdor, 1989). Utility analysis has shown that selection by merit optimises workforce efficiency (to be reviewed later in the chapter).

(2) Merit selection obeys the principle of justice
The formal principle of equality requires that people who are equal in job-related merits are to be treated equally in job allocations. Selection by merit honours this formal principle. Rawls' principle of equality also stipulates that social and economic opportunities should be open to everyone "under conditions of fair equality of opportunity". However, diversity selection by granting preferential treatment to minorities, violates such principles (e.g., Cohen, 1975; Newton, 1973; Sowell, 1990; Steele, 1990).

(3) Merit selection inspires excellence in society by rewarding the most merited candidate

The ideology of a free market economy by tradition defines an individual's merit in terms of the contributions he/she makes to society. Overlaet (1991) argues that the concept of merit consists of three basic components: *effort, competence* and *result*. Effort (defined as commitment and sacrifice) and competence (defined as talents or gifts) are the characteristics or traits of an individual; "result" however refers to the manifestation of these two personal characteristics in terms of measurable or observable output or productivity. Applying Overlaet's notion to an employment hiring context, a job candidate is considered "meritorious" if his/her effort, competence and results are valued by the organisation or the society in general.

However, there is intense debate over which of these three factors should be used to define "merit" in allocating societal rewards. While some scholars assert that individual *effort* should be the basis for resource allocation (e.g., Griswold, 1934; Rodgers, 1978), others argue that *results* or productivity should be the key criterion of merit and allocation (e.g., Rescher, 1966; Ryan, 1941), still others (mostly liberal theorists) argue that talents or *competence* should be the major consideration in allocation (e.g., Nozick, 1974). However, according to Overlaet, an ethical view on merit would use *effort* as the primary criterion in resources allocation, whereas an economic transactional view on merit would use *result* as the main allocation criterion. He further argues that individual employees are likely to take the former view while the organisation is more inclined to take the latter perspective in making allocating decisions.

Overlaet tested the relative importance people place on *effort* and *result* in making allocation decisions involving assigning income differentials. His results showed that respondents awarded a higher income to higher efforts associated with a higher level of productivity. However, when extra efforts failed to result in an increase in productivity, respondents awarded income proportional to the output level. The findings indicate that both effort and result are important criteria in allocation decisions, although the most important of all was when effort does lead to results. In employment selection, similar findings have been reported (Singer, 1994, 1996). These studies are reviewed in the next section of the chapter.

The debate over the rights and wrongs of diversity and merit hiring is still very much alive in the applied ethics and philosophical literatures. However, apart from the very limited and scattered data from public opinion surveys reviewed so far, studies by the author have explored in a systematic way people's reactions to these philosophical arguments within the same research design.

Empirical Studies of People's Reactions to Justifications for Merit Versus Diversity Selection

The main aim of the study is to assess the extent to which people agree or disagree with the philosophical arguments in the debate. To this end, the study conceptualises people's choice between the two selection practices as a result of a decision process involving thinking through possible consequences of the two alternative hiring practices. The theoretical framework stems from the valence model (Vroom, 1964; Feather, 1982). The research findings reported here are parts of three larger studies (Singer, 1993b, 1994; Singer & Lange, 1994).

Description of the Studies on Gender-Based Selection

The valence model proposes that in making choices, an individual systematically evaluates possible consequences of alternative choices. In the present research, the five justifications for diversity-based selection were provided to respondents as possible consequences of that selection practice; similarly, the justifications for merit selection were provided as possible consequences of merit hiring. All justifications were phrased in terms of gender-based selection. Separately for each of the two selection practices, respondents were asked to think through each given consequence by making two evaluations: (a) the "likelihood" of the hiring practice bringing about that consequence, and (b) the "value" they attach to that consequence. According to the valence model, the "valence" (i.e., the product of the likelihood and value ratings) of each consequence is indicative of the level of significance that consequence is perceived by the individual. The valence model is the psychological version of the economic man model of rational choice; its computational procedures are similar to those of the subjective expected utility.

Three respondent samples were tested:
(a) *general public*
  This sample consisted of 204 residents in the Christchurch area, of whom 105 (55 males and 50 females) were unemployed and 99 (48 males and 51 females) were employed. All respondents were recruited by a male research assistant.
(b) *university students*
  Altogether there were 291 students (129 females and 162 males) recruited from the University of Canterbury and Lincoln University in Christchurch. They were completing a degree in either Commerce, Political Science or Engineering.
(c) *managerial professionals*
  A postal survey method was used for this group of respondents. The research questionnaire (see below) was posted to 400 managers chosen randomly from the WISES 1991 New Zealand Business Directories. Seventy-eight questionnaires were returned (response rate=19.5%), 62 of those were complete hence were used for analysis. There were 48 male and 14 female managerial professionals in the final sample.

Results

The findings concerning people's overall views on merit versus gender hiring are consistent with existing literature showing that people in general endorse merit-based hiring and oppose diversity-based hiring (e.g., Kinder & Sanders, 1990; Warner & Steele, 1989). Based on the ratings of overall support for merit versus gender-based selection, results show that among respondents from the general public, 54.4% could be classified as supporters of merit hiring and 3.9% were supporters of gender-based hiring. Altogether 59% and 6.8% of the students could be classified as supporters of merit selection and gender-based selection respectively. Therefore these results suggest that respondents espouse a traditional conception of meritocracy. In addition, the main findings of the present study concern people's views on individual philosophical arguments for merit and diversity hiring. The mean valence ratings are given below. These ratings are out of 100 with 50 as the neutral point. Consequences with a mean valence rating above 50 are considered both important and obtainable, with higher ratings being indicative of greater importance and increasing likelihood to obtain. Consequences with a mean valence rating below 50 are considered either unimportant and/or unlikely to obtain through the given selection practice. The mean valence ratings for outcomes of merit selection for the three respondent groups are:

(1) *"getting the most effective person for the job"*
(mean valence score=74.62)
(2) *"rewarding the most merited candidate based on job-relevant qualifications"*
(mean valence score=70.96)
(3) *"ensuring a highest possible productivity"*
(mean valence score=67.86)
(4) *"inspiring excellence in performance in society"*
(mean valence score=66.05)
(5) *"achieving fairness in employment competitions in society"*
(mean valence score=45.55)

The following are respondents' overall valence ratings for each of the six outcomes of ethnicity-based selection:

(1) *"achieving equality in employment opportunities in society"*
(mean valence score=37.17)
(2) *"maximising the utilisation of Maori's talents"*
(mean valence score=37.13)
(3) *"having a fair representation of Maori employees in the workforce"*
(mean valence score=34.74)
(4) *"having role models in the workforce for Maoris"*
(mean valence score=29.66)
(5) *"rewarding the most needy candidate"*

(mean valence score=26.37)

(6) *"compensating for the disadvantages suffered by Maoris in the past"*
(mean valence score=24.07)

A Study on Ethnicity-based Hiring

A study with the same design was carried out to ascertain people's views on diversity hiring based on candidates' ethnic origin. In the instructions given to respondents and in the questionnaire used, all statements concerning candidate gender were replaced with candidate ethnic origin (i.e., Maoris versus European New Zealanders). The respondent sample consisted of 215 (54 male and 161 female) psychology students at the University of Canterbury (for the entire study, see Singer, 1996).

Results concerning respondent reactions to philosophical justifications for merit versus ethnicity-based selection are consistent with those obtained in the previous study. People in general support merit selection and oppose selection by candidate ethnicity. Respondents' valence scores for each of the five consequences of merit selection are arranged in descending order:

(1) *"getting the most effective person for the job"*
(mean valence score=72.31)
(2) *"rewarding the most merited candidate based on job-relevant qualifications"*
(mean valence score=69.42)
(3) *"inspiring excellence in performance in society"*
(mean valence score=60.77)
(4) *"ensuring a highest possible productivity"*
(mean valence score=60.00)
(5) *"achieving fairness in employment competitions in society"*
(mean valence score=47.57)

The following are respondents' overall valence ratings for each of the six outcomes of ethnicity-based selection:

(1) *"achieving equality in employment opportunities in society"*
(mean valence score=46.75)
(2) *"maximising the utilisation of Maori's talents"*
(mean valence score=45.10)
(3) *"having role models in the workforce for Maoris"*
(mean valence score=42.66)
(4) *"having a fair representation of Maori employees in the workforce"*
(mean valence score=40.37)
(5) *"rewarding the most needy candidate"*
(mean valence score=32.84)

(6)   *"compensating for the disadvantages suffered by Maoris in the past"* (mean valence score=27.58)

Implications of Findings

Consistently for all four studies, results show that all valence scores associated with four of the five consequences of merit selection are higher than the neutral point 50. This suggests that people believe that these four outcomes of merit selection are important and achievable goals of organisational recruitment. In other words, people see it as important for an organisation to aim at achieving these outcomes through its recruitment practice. Furthermore, the findings also shed light on what people typically believe to be the key criterion in determining a candidate's "merit". Respondents in all studies give the highest valence ratings to the outcome "getting the most effective person for the job", and the second highest ratings to the outcome "rewarding the most merited candidate based on job-relevant qualifications". These two criteria differ in their focus on effort and result as defined by Overlaet. The latter takes an individual's perspective and focuses on effort or qualifications alone. However, the former criterion appears to have a focus on both individual's effort and the result of that effort for the organisation: the person has to be "effective" (due to either effort or talents) and has to be effective "for the job" (result). These results indicate that the criterion, "effort-leading-to-result" is also the most crucial in people's decisions involving the allocation of employment opportunities. Therefore the present findings concur nicely with Overlaet's (1991) conclusions about what constitutes merit in making income awards.

With reference to diversity selection, results of all studies show that without exception, all valence scores associated with consequences of diversity selection are lower than 50. This indicates that respondents do not think that these consequences should be seen as being the aim or the goal of an organisation's recruitment practice. In other words, they do not believe that an organisation should be made responsible for achieving these outcomes through its recruitment practice. Among the six philosophical justifications of diversity hiring, the least convincing for all respondents appears to be the one based on compensatory justice (i.e., "to compensate for disadvantages suffered by women, or Maoris, in the past"). The comparatively more convincing justifications appear to be "to maximise utilisation of minority talents" and "to achieve equality in employment opportunities in society". From a practical point of view, these findings are useful for the implementation of a diversity selection programme. It is likely that when used to justify this selection practice, each of these philosophical justifications may invoke a different reaction or a different extent of psychological reactance.

DIALOGUE CONCERNING THE "RIGHTNESS OR GOODNESS" AND THE "PERCEIVED ETHICALITY" OF SELECTION PRACTICES

In this section, a normative-empirical dialogue is generated by applying philosophical prescriptions for determining goodness to the evaluation of selection practices. The moral philosophical norm for determining the goodness of an act requires that consideration be given to the utility, rights and justice of that act. Specifically, the evaluation of the relative goodness of merit versus diversity selection would involve a comparison of the relative effects of the two selection practices on utility, rights and justice issues. Accordingly, the empirical findings of the consequences (both economic and social-psychological) of the selection practices are reviewed first. The review then covers empirical studies examining the effects of the selection practices on individuals' moral rights (e.g., equality of treatment, sense of self-esteem and basic human dignity), as well as research findings concerning the perceived fairness or justice of the two selection practices. The empirical evidence collectively is used to index the "overall ethicality" of the selection practices, as people typically perceive it.

Therefore, the use of the normative criteria of goodness to evaluate the selection practices has created a dialogue between the normative and the empirical approaches to ethical enquiry. Such a dialogue, hopefully, can contribute to a pragmatic resolution in the choice between two competing selection practices.

Empirical Studies Pertaining to the Utility or Consequences of Diversity Selection

In reviewing the existing literature on the utility or consequences of diversity-based hiring, the economic consequences are examined first with an emphasis on the application of utility analyses. The social and psychological consequences are then examined. The focus is on the effects of diversity hiring on intergroup relations and on society as a whole.

Economic Consequences of Diversity Hiring

Research shows that people typically hold the view that a hiring practice should aim primarily at getting the most effective person for the job. They also believe that this goal can best be achieved if meritocracy is the main hiring criterion. So when a non-merit criterion is used, one logical question would be, *"How is the overall efficiency or productivity affected?"* To answer this question, some psychologists working in this area have applied the utility analysis technique traditionally employed by economists in estimating, in dollar terms, the cost and benefit of economic programs. Others have examined the question by employing typical psychological research methods or using existing Census data.

Studies Using Utility Analysis

In the economics literature, several studies have carried out the cost and benefit analysis of preferential treatments among job candidates. The general conclusion appears to be that job discrimination adversely affects productivity and efficiency (for reviews, see Becker, 1971; LaMond, 1977). In the psychological literature, utility analysis was first applied to the issue of minority hiring by Hunter, Schmidt, and Rauschenberger (1977). Utility analysis carries the assumption that the hiring ratio, the base rate, the SD of job performance in candidate pool, and the validity of the test used in selection are the key determinants of the final utility. In a study comparing the utility of merit and diversity hiring, Hunter et al. (1977) estimated the average productivity gains over random hiring separately for merit-hiring and quota hiring under the various value combinations of hiring ratio, base rate and validity coefficient. The general finding is that the productivity gains associated with quota hiring are consistently lower than those associated with merit-hiring using the Cleary method.

Schmidt, Mack, and Hunger (1984) directly compared the productivity gains (over random hiring) of three hiring practices for hiring forest and park rangers: (1) strict top-down merit hiring, (2) lowering test score cut-off to the mean test score of the candidate pool, and (3) lowering test score cut-off at one SD below the mean. They found that by lowering the hiring standard, a significant amount of possible productivity gain is lost. The loss amounted to between 55% to 84% of the gain associated with strict merit-hiring.

The relative loss in productivity associated with quota hiring is difficult to measure because it depends on other market factors such as the relative job acceptance rate and performance differences between minority and nonminority candidates (e.g., Murphy, 1984; Schmitt & Noe, 1986). Most other utility studies reached a similar conclusion to that of Schmidt et al. (1984): diversity hiring is associated with some loss in overall productivity (e.g., Gross & Su, 1975; Kroeck, Barrett, & Alexander, 1983; Steffy & Ledvinka, 1989; Widgor & Hartigan, 1988). This means that the organisational goal of maximising productivity and the goal of diversity hiring (i.e., increasing minority hiring rate) are certainly to be in conflict (e.g., Schmitt, 1989; Schmitt & Robertson, 1990). According to Schmidt et al. (1992), this conflict simply "cannot" be resolved by research (p.662).

Given that quota hiring would always result in some productivity loss, an important question is then *which quota method would result in the least amount of productivity loss.* Utility analysis has been applied to the identification of the best trade-offs between maximising productivity and increasing minority hiring rate (e.g., Cascio, 1981; Cronbach & Schaeffer, 1981; Cronbach, Yalow, & Schaeffer, 1980; Gross & Su, 1975; Hunter et al., 1977). Results show that a *top-down within-group method* results in about 5% loss as compared to a strict merit-hiring practice (e.g., Cronbach & Shaeffer, 1981; Hartigan & Wigdor, 1989; Hunter & Hunter, 1984). The top-down within-group method involves the hiring of the best qualified candidates within each minority and nonminority group. Because of its small utility loss, this method is recommended as the best of the diversity-based hiring practices.

To sum, utility analysis assessing the economic consequences of diversity-based hiring has shown that:

(1) Merit-hiring results in significant and substantial amount of productivity gains over random selection without using tests. Relative to the gains of merit-hiring, any diversity-based hiring program would result in less gains, or even a loss in overall workforce efficiency.

(2) The top-down within-group method significantly increases minority hiring rates and at the same time, results in the least amount of loss in workforce productivity.

Results of utility estimates therefore indicate that diversity-based hiring (these utility studies deal primarily with ethnicity-based hiring) has negative economic consequences in terms of workforce efficiency and productivity. However, some scholars have warned against the use of utility analysis to estimate the consequence of a hiring programme for the economy as a whole. For instance, Hartigan and Widgor (1989, p.248) argue that because "the current state of economic knowledge does not permit estimation" of the aggregate effect of merit-hiring on the productivity of the economy-wide workforce, policy makers should therefore "refrain from" making such a global estimation. Furthermore, recent research shows that utility estimation associated with using valid tests in selection results in a range of possible utility values, rather than a single utility value as previous research has suggested (e.g., Hunter, Schmidt, & Coggin, 1988; Anderson & Muchinsky, 1991). The range of utility values varies according to several criteria including the definition of the level of satisfactory or desired job performance.

Studies on Workforce Efficiency Using Other Research Methods

There have been studies on the economic consequences of ethnicity hiring programmes without the use of utility analysis (e.g., Heckman, 1989). Other studies have assessed the economic impact of gender-based hiring in policing (e.g., Lovrich, Steel, & Hood, 1986; Lovrich & Steel, 1983; Steel & Lovrich, 1987). These studies compared the efficiency of police functioning between two groupings of cities: cities in which police departments placed high emphasis on gender hiring goals, and cities in which police departments gave low priority to gender-based hiring. The comparisons on a number of measures of police productivity and efficiency revealed no difference between the two kinds of cities.

This was interpreted as indicating that gender-based hiring in policing had little negative consequence on workforce efficiency. However, field studies such as these typically suffer from inadequate controls, so caution should be exercised over the interpretations of these findings.

The effect of diversity in top level management teams on organisational performance has also been explored in several studies. These studies found that the degree of diversity in the leading teams of an organisation typically is associated with greater innovativeness and enhanced financial performance (e.g., Bantel & Jackson, 1989; Finkelstein & Hambrick, 1990; Murray, 1989). Other studies also reported beneficial consequences of a diversified workforce on the organisation (e.g., Bok, 1985; Thomas, 1990).

To sum, results of these studies tend to be in conflict with those using utility analysis. Diversity in an organisation may indeed have beneficial consequences for certain specific aspects of the organisation's performance and efficiency.

Studies Using Census Data

At the societal level, an obvious question concerning the economic consequences of diversity hiring is whether there has been an economic gain for minorities. The question consists of two aspects: "Has there been an economic gain for minorities as a group?", and "Is economic gain distributed evenly among all minorities?". Crosby, Allen, and Opotow (1992) have the answer for both questions. Using data on income concentration compiled by the Bureau of the Census, they conclude that there has been little income concentration change among Blacks since 1965 when these programs were first implemented. In other words, "...*After 20 years of affirmative action, there has been no clear redistribution of wealth among black and white Americans*" (p.340).

Turning to the question of whether affirmative action policies have benefited American Blacks equally as a group: While several authors have speculated upon a widening economic gap between the educated and professional Blacks and the uneducated and unskilled Blacks (e.g., Carter, 1991; Garcia, 1989; Gelman, Springer, Brailsford, & Miller, 1988; Steele, 1990; Wilson, 1987), Crosby et al. (1992) conclude that there has been no bifurcation among either White or Black families since 1967. The Census data therefore have rejected the claim that affirmative action policies have widened the economic gap between the "haves" and "have nots" among Blacks.

Social Psychological Consequences of Diversity-Based Hiring at Macro level

Research has been carried out to examine the social psychological consequences of diversity hiring at both a micro and a macro level. At the micro level, research concerns the effects on *individual beneficiaries* (women and minorities) and on *individual nonbeneficiaries* (white males). At the macro level, research focuses on the impact of diversity hiring on *intergroup relations* (gender or racial subgroup) and on *society* in general. However, given that utilitarianism evaluates morality from the perspective of society as a whole rather than from that of individuals (Velasquez, 1982, p.61), this section on the utility of diversity hiring will only review its social psychological consequences at the macro level.

Consequences of Diversity Hiring for Intergroup Relations

Diversity hiring can create intergroup conflict. The special treatment one group receives may be at the expense of the other group. When group interests are in conflict, intergroup relations are often adversely affected. Barnes Nacoste (1992) has suggested that diversity hiring may have negative consequences for intergroup relations if the beneficiary and nonbeneficiary groups react in a certain specified manner to the hiring practice. These consequences include "strained social interactions", "over-surveillance of and avoiding working with the beneficiaries", "defensiveness, oversensitivity to negative feedback", "ill at ease in mixed interactions" and "hostility and tension in work teams".

Studies have shown that diversity in work teams can have negative impact on group cohesiveness (e.g., Block, Robertson, & Neuger, 1995; Jackson et al., 1992; Tsui, Egan, & O'Reilly, 1992). Several authors have also identified the negative effects of diversity hiring programs on intergroup relations among African Americans. Bell (1989) suggests that these programs may have caused a greater disparity between Black males and females in social and economic advancement. Garcia (1989) writes about the negative effect of diversity programs on relationships between the middle-upper class and the underclass among Black women. It was argued that there emerged a widening gap between Black women who have achieved through affirmative action programs and those women who failed to benefit and remained on welfare; the former carried an increasing burden of moral responsibility for the latter.

However, diversity hiring can also have positive consequences for intergroup relations. Studies (Tougas, Dube, & Veilleux, 1987; Veilleux & Tougas, 1989) have shown that men who experienced "relative deprivation on behalf of women" (Runciman, 1966, 1968) were more supportive of affirmative action programs and more committed to the improvement of women's welfare and circumstances. This kind of empathy certainly enhances intergroup relations. Barnes Nacoste (1992) also identifies one condition which may foster positive intergroup relations: when nonbeneficiaries believe that beneficiaries are qualified and when beneficiaries have low evaluation apprehension. He argues that under this condition, the intergroup relation is harmonious, the development of informal social groups consisting of mixed members is relatively easy, and a positive work group climate prevails.

Consequences of Diversity Hiring on Society as a Whole

The macro-level consequences of diversity-based hiring on society as a whole are much more complicated and difficult to assess than the program's micro and individual level impact. The societal level impact can most directly be evaluated with reference to the major goal of diversity hiring: increasing the minority hiring rate in the workforce. Studies have been carried out to ascertain whether there has been an increase in minority hiring rate in various workforces. The workforces include federal government (Benokraitis & Gilbert, 1989), federal contractors (US Department of Labour, 1984), serving industry (Woody, 1989), law enforcement (Horne, 1979; Sichel, Friedman, Quint, & Smith, 1978; Walker, 1983; Warner & Steel, 1989) and higher education (e.g., Bronstein & Pfennig, 1989; Finkelstein, 1984; McCombs, 1989; Tickamyer et al., 1989). Results of these studies show that there appears to be a slight increase of female and minority hiring rates during the last two and half decades in the workforce in the United States. The trend however is that these new jobs are concentrated more in the lower level of positions, and their average salaries appear to be lower than their male counterparts in similar job categories. Similar trends are also evident in the workforce in Canada where affirmative action and diversity-based hiring policies have been in place for the last two decades (Tougas & Beaton, 1992).

Empirical Studies Pertaining to the Fairness or Justice of Diversity Selection

Taken in its entirety, research on selection fairness consistently shows that selection by merit is perceived as fair whereas selection involving differential treatment of minority candidates is seen as unfair. It has also been repeatedly shown that the main reason for most people to oppose diversity hiring is that the program is believed to violate the principle of meritocracy and hence is considered unfair (e.g., Clayton & Tangri, 1989; Lipset & Schneider, 1978; Norvell & Worchel, 1981; Tougas & Beaton, 1992; Veilleux & Tougas, 1989). It seems ironic that the program is seen as unfair, given that achieving justice is its very fundamental goal in the first place. Because of this, many researchers view the judgements of the program's fairness to be the primary factor in determining its success or failure (e.g., Clayton & Tangri, 1989; Optow, 1992). Crosby and Clayton (1990) assert that affirmative action programs can only achieve their ends under the condition that the programs "*must be, and also must appear to be, fair*" (p.73). Accordingly, there has been ample research focusing on the identification of key variables which can significantly affect and enhance the perceived fairness of the program. Most of these studies have taken a theoretical approach, stemming from current organisational justice theories (e.g., Greenberg, 1987; 1990a). A smaller number of other studies fall outside that theoretical framework.

Fairness Research Stemming from Organisational Justice Theories

Research taking this approach attends to two different aspects of justice or fairness: fairness of the outcomes of diversity-based hiring and fairness of the program's procedures. Other studies have applied the "provision of justification" notion in examining the fairness of the program.

(1) *Outcome fairness*
The outcome fairness of diversity hiring has been examined within the conceptual framework of the theory of relative deprivation (e.g., Davies, 1959; Gurr, 1970; Pettigrew, 1967). These studies have identified several factors that can significantly affect the *perceived fairness of the outcome* of diversity-based hiring programs (e.g., Singer, 1992, 1993c; Tougas & Beaton, 1992; Veilleux & Tougas, 1989).

(a) *The beneficiary vs. nonbeneficiary status of the perceiver*
Beneficiaries tend to perceive diversity-based hiring as less unfair than do nonbeneficiaries. This factor also interacts with the next two factors.

(b) *The strength of identification with one's group*
The stronger a beneficiary identifies with his/her group, the less unfair diversity-based hiring is perceived to be. Similarly, the stronger a nonbeneficiary identifies with his/her group, the more unfair the program is judged.

(c) *Felt deprivation for one's own group or on behalf of others*
For beneficiaries, collective deprivation for their own group tends to enhance their fairness perception about the program, whereas collective deprivation on behalf of the nonbeneficiaries tends to have a fairness-reducing effect. For nonbeneficiaries, the opposite effects are likely to prevail.

(2) *Procedural fairness of diversity-based hiring*
Studies have identified several factors that can significantly affect the perceived fairness of the procedures of diversity-based hiring programs:

(a) *The procedural criterion used in making the judgement of procedural fairness*
The theoretical framework for the analysis was based on the procedural fairness models of Leventhal, Karuza, and Fry (1980) and Lind and Tyler (1988). These theorists proposed that fair procedures of an allocation would adhere to six fairness criteria (i.e., representation, consistency, impartiality, accuracy, correctability, and ethicality). Fairness judgements of diversity hiring vary according to the exact procedural criterion used in the judgements. The program is most likely to be judged as fair so far as the consistency of its procedures are concerned; it

is judged as less fair from the point of view of ethicality or impartiality (e.g., Ayers, 1992).

(b) *The relative weights placed on merits and group membership in making the diversity-based hiring decision*
In a series of studies, Barnes Nacoste (1990, 1992) manipulated the procedures of diversity-based hiring by varying the relative weights given to candidate merit and group membership. Results showed that people's fairness judgements of diversity-based decisions are influenced by these procedures and in general, the more weight the procedure gives to membership (hence less weight to merit), the less fair the program is judged.

(c) *The judged outcomes of the programme*
In Barnes Nacoste and Powell's (1991) procedural model of perceived fairness, procedural evaluations determine an individual's judgements of the program's likely outcomes, which in turn influence overall fairness perceptions.

(3) *Perceived fairness of diversity hiring as a result of the provision of justification*
Fairness perceptions, according to Bies (1987a), are a product of "a process of argumentation or persuasion" (p.304). People's perceptions of fairness or unfairness about the outcome of an allocation are therefore determined to a greater extent by the provision of a social account (or an explanatory justification) for the outcome than by the sheer favourability of the final outcome. Bies argued that perceptions of unfairness associated with unfavourable outcomes are primarily due to the inadequacy or absence of justifications; when adequate justifications are provided, perceived unfairness would be significantly reduced. Several studies have found that the provision of justifications typically had a fairness-enhancing effect (e.g., Bies, 1987a, 1987b; Bies & Shapiro, 1988; Brockner, 1990; Folger & Bies, 1989; Greenberg, 1990b; Tyler & Bies, 1990).

In the context of diversity-based hiring, several studies examined the effect of the provision of justification on fairness perceptions of a hypothetical case of diversity-based hiring (Singer,1990; 1993c). These studies explored the effect of either an "ethical justification" (i.e., emphasising the moral and ethical reasons for diversity-based hiring) or a "legislative justification" (i.e., emphasizing the legislative or legal requirement for minority hiring). Results showed that either form of justification further exacerbated perceptions of unfairness. Respondents perceived the hypothetical diversity-based decision without any justification as unfair: they perceived the same decision as even more unfair when either the ethical or the legislative justification was provided.

Research which Identifies Variables Affecting Perceived Fairness of Diversity Hiring

Other research outside the organisational justice framework has identified other factors that can significantly affect the support for or perceived fairness of the program. These factors are:

(1) *Merit discrepancy*

This refers to the size of the discrepancy in job-related merit or qualifications between the minority appointee and the most qualified nonminority candidate. Singer (1990; 1992; 1993c) showed that when the overall-merit score of the minority appointee became increasingly lower than that of the highest scoring nonminority candidate, the decision was judged as increasingly unfair. These results concur with those of Nacoste (1985, 1987) and Nacoste and Lehman (1987) in showing that as the hiring procedure places increasing weight on membership (i.e., greater merit discrepancy), the selection is likely to be judged as increasingly unfair.

(2) *Beneficiaries' minority membership status*

An early study (Smith & Kluegel, 1984) compared people's reactions to diversity selection with reference to different minority categories of beneficiaries (i.e., gender or race). Results show that while only a small percentage of male respondents believed that women receive unfair advantages from these programs, a significantly larger proportion of white respondents believed that the programs unfairly benefit Blacks. A more recent study concurs with that study (Clayton, 1992) in showing that white males were more supportive of gender-based programs than ethnicity-based programs. Reid and Clayton (1992) analyzed in detail the effect of beneficiary minority membership status on people's attitudes towards and fairness perceptions of diversity-based programs. The analysis reveals a greater resistance to ethnicity-based than gender-based program and the resistance appears to be greatest for people of double minority status (e.g., black women). Murrell et al. (1994) reported a higher level of resistance to affirmative action policies when the target group was Blacks, as compared with other target groups including physically handicapped people and elderly persons.

(3) *Differences in minorities' personal experiences with discrimination*

Tougas , Beaton and Veilleux (1991) found that while most women opposed gender-based hiring, women who had personally experienced gender-related discriminations at work, were supportive of the hiring practice. A review of French-Canadian women's attitudes towards diversity-based hiring reveals that over the years between 1983 and 1991, they have become increasingly more supportive of preferential treatment for women (Tougas & Beaton, 1992). These studies together have shown that beneficiaries' personal experience with and/or awareness of work discrimination can influence their reactions towards the program.

(4) *"Informant's" group membership status*
Singer (1993b) applied findings in the persuasion literature to gender-based hiring and reasoned that a female informant arguing for a gender-based hiring practice would be more likely to be seen as self-serving; whereas a male informant putting forward the same case would be seen as arguing against his own interest. Fairness judgements would be affected accordingly. Results show that while all respondents judged gender-based hire decisions as unfair, they judged the decision as significantly less unfair when the informants were of the same gender as the respondents. Similar findings exist for ethnicity-based selection (Singer, 1996).

(5) *Frame of the information about diversity selection*
The concept of frame has its origin in the cognitive and decision making literature (e.g., Bruner, 1986; Minsky, 1975; Tversky & Kahneman, 1981). Kinder and Sanders (1990) found that while the frames did not affect respondents' (Whites') general opposition to the practice, their emotional reactions towards the hiring practice were more negative when the practice was framed as "unfair advantage for Blacks" rather than "reverse discrimination against Whites".

In another study (Singer, 1996), identical preferential treatment in selection was framed as either "diversity-based selection" or "preferential selection". Results show that under certain experimental conditions, respondents perceived the same selection outcome as less unfair when the frame "diversity-based selection" was used.

Empirical Studies Pertaining to Individual Rights of Diversity Selection

Moral philosophy asserts that individuals have fundamental moral rights including the rights to life and to freedom. The United Nations Universal Declaration of Human Rights stipulates that all human beings are entitled to basic human rights which ensure "an existence worthy of human dignity". While diversity hiring aspires to the affirmation of minorities' basic sense of human dignity, it may nonetheless deprive members of majority groups of their rights to equality of treatment. Several researchers have applied the relative deprivation notion to males' reactions to gender-based selection (e.g., Veilleux & Tougas, 1989; Singer, 1993c). Results of the studies show that differential treatment in hiring decisions induced strong feelings of deprivation among males. They felt that they are deprived of equality of treatment which they deserve and are rightly entitled to.

From the perspective of the intended beneficiaries of the diversity hiring practice, several philosophers have argued that the practice may have unintended adverse consequences for minorities' self-esteem and basic sense of dignity. These arguments are:

(1) The practice carries the presumption that minorities are inferior hence are in need of special considerations (e.g., Goldman, 1976; Howard & Hammond, 1985; Loury, 1986)

(2) The practice may also cause people to denigrate minorities' real achievements (e.g., Decter, 1980; Roberts, 1981; Shaw, 1988)

(3) More importantly, the practice may negatively affect minorities' self-perceptions about their own abilities (e.g., Boxill, 1984; Eastland & Bennett, 1979; Sowell, 1978).

Witt (1990) reported survey data bearing on the first two consequences. Witt asked university faculty members whether they agreed with the statement: *"affirmative action perpetuates a myth of minority and female inferiority"*. Results showed that 21% of White males , 15% of White females, 11% of Black males and 8% of Black females in the whole sample agreed with that statement.

When asked if they agreed with the statement, *"affirmative action robs women and minorities of a deserved sense of accomplishment"*, 17% of White male, 17% of White female 10% of Black male and 8% of Black female faculties agreed with that statement.

These survey results have not provided convincing support for the philosophical arguments about the negative consequences of diversity hiring for human rights and sense of dignity. However, laboratory research has provided ample empirical support for the claim that diversity hiring has unintentional adverse consequences for minority appointees in terms of their own sense of worth as well as others' perceptions of them. For gender-based hiring, several trends are evident in the research findings concerning its undesirable consequences for women's own sense of worth and others' perceptions of their worth.

(1) Gender-based hiring may have adverse consequences for *some* females. The observed adverse effects include negative perceptions and lowered evaluations of own abilities, competence and future work-orientation (e.g., choosing less demanding tasks or assignments) (e.g., Chacko, 1982; Heilman, Simon, & Repper, 1987; Heilman, Lucas, & Kalow, 1990; Heilman, Rivero, & Brett, 1991; Nacoste, 1985, 1987, 1989; Nacoste & Lehman, 1987). It appears that those females, who have lower self-confidence or who perceive gender-based hiring as unfair in the first place, are more likely to suffer from these negative consequences.

(2) When people thought that the reason for women being appointed to their positions was due to preferential treatment rather than merit, they devalued the position and the women's competence in performance (Heilman & Herlihy, 1984; Jacobson & Koch, 1977; Northcraft & Martin, 1982; Summers, 1991).

(3) Diversity hiring programs may reinforce stereotypical attitudes or prejudicial beliefs about minorities (e.g., Banks, 1984; Crosby & Clayton, 1990; Dovidio, Mann, & Gaertner, 1989; Fernandez, 1982; Jencks, 1985; Kantrowitz & Springen, 1988; Pettigrew & Martin, 1987).

Several studies on ethnicity-based hiring also reported negative consequences for the minority appointee. Garcia (1989) reported that for African American women, diversity hiring has exposed them further to the public's attention and as a result, many of them experienced increased feelings of vulnerability, uncertainty and stress.

However, there is also evidence suggesting that diversity hiring may have positive effects on the sense of self worth among its beneficiaries. These data come primarily from individual case studies or interviews rather than experimental or laboratory research (e.g., Ayers, 1992; Hayashi, 1991-1992). These positive effects include feeling more respected by others, feeling others becoming more genuinely interested in them, and feeling more accepted by others as a person. Diversity hiring may also help raise the level of minorities' educational or career aspirations (e.g., Cullen, Nakamura, & Nakamura, 1988; Davis & Watson, 1982; Pettigrew & Martin, 1987).

A Weakness in the Empirical Literature on the Utility, Rights and Justice of Selection Practices

The application of the normative framework to the evaluation of selection practices requires that thorough consideration be given to all three moral standards. However, taking the entire empirical literature on selection practices as a whole, it becomes clear that there is a predominant research emphasis on justice over other teleological and deontological notions. It is particularly evident from the literature of organisational and social justice that the evaluation of the diversity-based practice has been undertaken overwhelmingly from a justice perspective, and by comparison, a very limited emphasis has been directed to issues of utility or rights. The predominant focus on justice presumably reflects the commonly made claim that the fairness and perceived fairness of the programme determine whether it can achieve its intended goals (e.g., Clayton & Tangri, 1989; Crosby & Clayton, 1990; Optow, 1992).

Given the imbalance in empirical research on the utility, rights and justice of the selection practices, an issue of concern inevitably arises when results of fairness research are deployed as the justifications for the overall desirability of a specific selection practice. To avoid this, it is argued that an evaluation of any significant social and organisational practice needs to be comprehensive in embracing all key constituents of morality (i.e., utility, justice and rights). By implication then, empirical evidence based either solely or largely on a justice analysis is not sufficient to justify the goodness of that practice. Although there exists substantial difficulties in the evaluation of the utility and rights of selection practices, the need for such research is obvious and pressing: it is needed when the normative criteria of goodness are used in a comprehensive and systematic evaluation of the competing practices.

Implications of Findings

Despite the weakness identified in the preceding section, research findings on the utility, justice and rights of diversity hiring can be used in the evaluation of the "perceived goodness" of the practice. Given that the goal of such an evaluation is to help choose between two competing selection practices, the deliberations would need to be made in comparative, rather than absolute, terms. Guided by the philosophical norms for determining goodness, the evaluation has to address these three questions:

(1) the question of justice: " Which selection practice would lead to a distribution of employment opportunities that is perceived as fairer by all concerned?"
(2) the question of individual rights: "Which selection practice would more effectively affirm the rights of all individuals affected by the practice?"
(3) the question of utility: "Which selection practice would result in more beneficial consequences for the society as a whole?"

When the aforementioned research evidence is used to evaluate a hiring practice against each of these questions, it becomes clear that existing research can help illuminate some of the issues with a greater certainty and clarity than others. Specifically, research evidence on fairness perception seems to be consistent in suggesting that selection by merit is generally seen as a fairer means of allocation than diversity-based selection.

Turning to the question of individual rights, merit selection aims to protect the rights of all, regardless of group membership. Yet it has unintentionally resulted in minorities being largely excluded from an "equal share" of a valued societal resource. On the other hand, diversity selection which aims to rectify the position of minorities, has unintentionally created two kinds of undesirable consequences: It has deprived majority job candidates' rights to equal treatment, and it has had adverse effects on minority candidates' sense of self worth and dignity. Taken together, existing empirical evidence on selection practice and individual rights can not help determine with sufficient certainty which of the two practices better affirms the rights of all concerned (i.e., both minority and majority candidates).

Regarding the question of utility, the answer seems to depend on the specific criterion chosen by the research to index "goodness" (or benefits). Different conclusions are likely to be reached when the goodness of a selection practice is measured against a different criterion (e.g., "economic efficiency" versus "intergroup empathy"). The choice of criteria has always been a key problem associated with the evaluation of social programmes at the macro or societal level (e.g., Kendler, 1993; Rosenbloom, 1984). Some researchers argue that the problem is "irresolvable" because it is to do with the political orientation or value commitment of the researchers making the evaluation (Kendler, 1993, p.1015). Regardless of the roots of the problem, the priority of one criterion over the other can be decided upon either through philosophical reflection or the empirical process of majority consensus. However, given the unavoidable disagreement among researchers over these alternative processes in determining appropriate criteria, different and sometimes contradictory conclusions about utility evaluation will inevitably result.

So far, the evaluation of the competing selection practices has examined the three questions of justice, rights and utility individually. One question remains: what is the relative importance of justice, rights and utility in the evaluation? As Velasquez (1982) points out, using the three moral standards to evaluate the goodness of a practice would require that "one keeps in mind how they relate to each other". Considering that no normative rule yet exists in assigning relative weights to the three standards, one may seek guidance from the empirical process of consensus. Here, results of the empirical studies reported in Chapter 5 may be of help. The studies reveal that in judging the goodness of work-related behaviour, people typically place the greatest weight on considerations of utility in terms of community or public good, followed by considerations of rights and then, justice. Given that selection practices are a work-related behaviour, their evaluation could logically involve the assigning of weights in that order of community utility, rights and justice.

To apply empirical findings this way is consistent with Kendler's (1993) idea of a partial reliance on the "democratic process" (majority consensus) in determining the relative virtue of competing social policies: this is because results of empirical studies represent the typical opinion held by the majority of those surveyed. However, in a postmodern climate of moral dissensus, such a process of majority consensus needs to be preceded, and complemented, by rational dialogues between the parties holding opposing views. Here, the process of the dialogue can best be guided by Haan's (1982, 1983) approach to moral disputes and Rossouw's (1994) principle of rational interaction. The former emphasises equality of status for each party in the dialogue, and the latter stresses moral sensitivity each party has for the other.

In conclusion, using the normative framework in the evaluation of empirical evidence on the two selection practices can help shed light on people's typical reactions to and judgements of the selection practice. Despite the fact that such an analysis by itself cannot help settle the dispute concerning the relative virtue or goodness of the competing social programs, the analysis has at least three merits: (1) it represents the most comprehensive and systematic means of evaluating the public's thoughts on key issues surrounding the dispute (after all, the public are the recipients of any social policies), (2) it creates a dialogue between normative and empirical ethicists, which enhances each party's understanding of the other's expertise on the issue, and (3) it can contribute to a pragmatic resolution of the dispute, with the aid of thoughtful philosophical reflection, the exercise of moral sensitivity, and the democratic process of majority consensus.

Acknowledgement:
   Parts of this chapter originally appeared in Singer, M. (1993) *Diversity-based hiring: An introduction from legal, ethical and psychological perspectives.* Aldershot: Avebury. Permission to use the material has been granted by the publisher.

Chapter 7   Ethics and Justice in Leadership

Leadership is vital to social groups. Business organisations, as a special case of social groups, take on a particularly pivotal role in contemporary free market economies. Leadership in organisations thus has two parallel and far-reaching consequences: those at the organisational level pertaining to employee empowerment and efficiency, as well as those at the societal level concerning resource productivity and distribution. The key question confronting leadership is how to ensure that such significant consequences are positive and beneficial to all concerned. This question has been pursued in three different literatures. In the traditional organisational psychology literature, effective leadership is the core of numerous theories of leadership adopting a variety of perspectives (e.g., personality, situation, behaviour or their interactions). In the recent empirical literature on organisational justice, the focus is on fair and just procedures in leadership practices. Alongside this empirical approach to justice in leadership, the recent business ethics literature takes a normative approach and places the personal ethics of leaders at the core of "good" and effective leadership.

It was argued in the introductory chapter of this book that the contemporary study of business ethics, while benefiting from empirical research, needs to have its foundation firmly grounded in moral philosophical thoughts. In the previous chapter it was shown how philosophical norms can be used as criteria in the evaluation of empirical evidence on ethical dilemmas, and consequently their resolutions, in modern-day business. In this chapter, it is argued that philosophical thoughts on personal ethics should form the very foundation of leadership and that empirical findings of leadership research, both in the traditional and the organisational justice literatures, can serve as guidance to "good leadership skills".

PERSONAL ETHICS IN LEADERSHIP

Historically, organisational researchers have taken one of four approaches to leadership. The personality approach seeks to identify key personality traits (e.g., need for power) which are associated with effective leadership. The situational approach aims to delineate the situational characteristics (e.g., Follower support) which enhance the effectiveness of leadership. The behavioural approach focuses on the identification of overt leader behaviour typically displayed by effective leaders (e.g., providing intellectual stimulation to followers). The interactional approach explores how the three factors of personality, situation and behaviour interact in achieving an optimal level of effective leadership. While theories and research adopting each of these approaches have made an invaluable and scholarly contribution to the understanding of leadership, they have failed to acknowledge the significant role of personal ethics which constitute the very foundation of leadership.

The term personal ethics is used to refer to an individual's ethical values and moral virtues. The theoretical framework of leadership taking the "personal ethics" perspective is itself grounded in the classical theories of ethics. Central to the Aristotelean ethics is the idea that *a harmonious balance of virtues leads to a good life*. Aristotle identified these traits among the basic moral Virtues: *Justice, Courage, Temperance, Liberality, Honour, Congeniality,* and *Truthfulness*. These virtues are the ideal traits that are necessary for an individual to attain a state of harmony or integrity within him/herself, and to attain such a state in relation to his/her social environment. Individual existence characterised by harmony and integrity is what Aristotle meant by *living a good life*. The possession of these virtues thus entitles a person to the claim of *being good, moral or ethical*.

The beginning of the 1990s saw a significant shift in leadership research from the traditional approaches to one emphasising fundamental values or virtue ethics. This is evident in the recent upsurge of discussion on moral or ethical leadership (e.g., Smith, 1995). Central to this ethical leadership literature is the pivotal emphasis on the role of Aristotelean virtues in leadership, although most theorists do not refer directly to Aristotle's classical works. Fairholm's (1991) philosophical model of values leadership is such an example. He argues that leadership in an organisation involves the leader's adherence to one or more of five founding values in setting the standards of interpersonal relationships, the culture and the vision of the organisation. The five founding values are *liberty, justice, respect for life, unity* and *happiness*. These values clearly reflect Aristotle's moral virtues. However, Jeannot's (1989) definition of "moral leadership as personal character" explicitly places Aristotle's virtues at the core of leadership. While Goodpaster (1991) emphasises the virtue of *respect for persons* as the means to achieve a leader's moral agenda in orienting, institutionalising and sustaining the values of the organisation, Kouzes and Pozner (1993) stress the ethic of *credibility* in moral leadership. Other theorists also consider the moral character of the leader as being pivotal in leadership (e.g., Heifitz, 1994; McCollough, 1991; Sheehy, 1990). Empirical findings also suggest that in groups attempting to resolve moral dilemmas, when a leadership position is occupied by members who are morally more principled, the group's level of moral reasoning is significantly enhanced (e.g., Dukerich, Nichols, Elm, & Vollrath, 1990).

In a comprehensive review of leadership theories, Ciulla (1995) concluded that existing theories are addressing the ultimate question of *"what is good leadership"* and that good leadership is both *morally good* (ethics) and *technically good* (competence). To develop this point further, it is argued that personal ethics are more pivotal and fundamental to good leadership than any learned or formal leadership skills. While technical skills can be conscientiously learned on the job, sound personal ethics, which are inalienable characters of an individual, oversee and ensure that these skills are put to proper use. In the next two sections, it is first shown how existing literatures on leadership and organisational justice can provide a useful guide to technical leadership skills. Second, it is shown why personal ethics should be "foundational" to the overt skills of good leadership.

GOOD LEADERSHIP SKILLS GUIDED BY EXISTING LEADERSHIP THEORIES AND THEORIES OF ORGANISATIONAL JUSTICE

Existing leadership theories in the traditional organisational psychology literature can provide useful and practical guidance on overt leadership skills. Transformational theory guides leaders as to how to behave in a transformational manner. Contingency theory and the Leader Match programme show leaders how to utilise or modify situational constraints in maximising good results. The normative model of decision making prescribes rules for leaders using either the autocratic or group decision process. Both the vertical-dyad or mutual-influence model and the situational model (Hersey & Blanchard, 1982) bring to leaders' attention that good skills mean how to relate to each and every individual employee in optimising leader effectiveness.

Independent of the traditional leadership literature, the recent literature on organisational justice can also provide practical guidance to good leadership skills. Organisational justice research stems from ethical enquiry. From a philosophical point of view, justice is an integral part of ethics. In Classicism, while Plato considered justice as the most essential of all the absolute, unchanging and eternal *Moral Ideas,* Aristotle spoke of justice as *the* basic Virtue. In the deontological school of modernism, justice is also at the core of ethics. Because of its fundamental importance, justice has become an empirical study in its own right, which is increasingly separate from the mainstream ethical enquiry. As a result, a solid body of literature on social and organisational justice has been rapidly taking shape. In that literature justice research gains inspiration from not only the philosophical tradition on distributive justice, but also the legal and judicial tradition on procedural justice.

Justice research pertaining to organisational practices is directly relevant to good leadership. Why is this the case? Studies have shown that justice is a central concern of human beings and that in allocation decisions, people are typically more concerned with the fairness of the procedures used in deriving the final decision than with the fairness of the final outcome. When people are assured of the fairness of these procedures, they tend to see a negative outcome (e.g. not getting a promotion) as less unfair. Employee perceptions of the fairness of organisational procedures have significant consequences for the organisation. These consequences include accident and compensation costs (Sashkin & Williams, 1990), employee affective reaction and commitment to the organisation (Dubinsky & Levy, 1989; Moorman, Nichoff, & Oran, 1993; Tansky, 1993), employee altruistic behaviour towards the organisation (Greenberg, 1993) as well as worker decisions concerning litigation against the organisation (Bies & Tyler, 1993). Considering that employees are fundamentally concerned with fairness, and that the fairness of organisational procedures can have pervasive and even dire consequences, it becomes both a humane and strategically-sound pursuit for the leaders of an organisation to ensure the fairness of their practices.

Some of the justice research bears directly on good leadership skills. For instance, studies of interactional justice have identified several key criteria for fair treatment in leader-employee interactions. Employees typically consider themselves as being treated fairly provided that the following criteria characterise the leader: *"sincerity"* (Bies, 1987), *"not harming people"* (Sheppard & Lewicki, 1987), and *"not bullying people"* (Karambayya & Brett, 1989).

Sinclair (1988) explored justice issues in leadership by asking this question: *What are the the key factors that make a leader fair?* The police personnel were the respondents for this research. The design of the study followed that of Greenberg (1986), and consisted of using individual interviews to generate factors which are considered important in fair leadership. These factors were then given to 390 police constables, who were asked to rate the importance of each as a determinant of fair leadership.

The importance ratings were factor-analysed. Respondents considered these five factors as the most important determinants of fair leadership: *trustworthiness* , *honesty, approachability, good knowledge of job*, and *consistency* (in order of perceived importance). The first three are personal characteristics which correspond closely to the Aristotelean moral virtues of *truthfulness, honour* , and *congeniality*. These results suggest that a leader's personal ethics are also the key necessary criteria of fair or just leadership.

Other organisational justice research, although not directly addressing the leadership issue, can also provide practical guidelines for fair leadership in various organisational practices (see Singer, 1993 for a review). The procedural justice theories (e.g., Leventhal, 1980; Lind & Tyler, 1988) have prescribed general rules for fair organisational procedures: *consistency* in applying the same decision or process rules; *impartiality* of the decision maker, *accuracy* of information used in the deliberation, allowing for *voice* (i.e., *representation*) in both decision and process controls, observing principles of *ethicality* , and opportunity of *correctability* of the final decision. The theory was used to analyse the key fairness criteria for the staff recruiting practice in New Zealand. Singer (1990, 1992) asked a sample of managerial professionals to list the most important factors that make a selection practice fair. Using Greenberg's methodology mentioned above, results of the factor analysis show that professionals in New Zealand considered these six factors as the key determinants of a fair selection practice:

1. *Honest communication and Choice of selectors*
   (Original statements relating to this factor include:
   Honesty of company in discussing its weaknesses and future plans for change,
   Detailed feedback to know selection was carefully carried out,
   Employer has not made a decision before interview,
   Equal number of male and female interviewers on selection panel,
   Using impartial and competent interviewers)
2. *Information soliciting*
   (Conduct job analysis to clearly identify criteria,
   A selection panel without the present job incumbent allowing the applicant to express ides for changes,
   Using interviews in gathering information, careful cross-check of references and qualifications,
   Collection of recommendations or references in addition to application forms)
3. *Open objective competition*
   (Use past work experience as a criterion,
   Use quantified method by assigning check points for objective comparisons,
   Advertisement of every position for open competition,
   Use job-related competence as a criterion)
4. *Consistency and Ethicality*
   (Equal opportunity regardless of sex, age, or race,
   Same selection procedure for every applicant)
5. *Bias avoidance*
   (Avoidance of nepotism,
   Chance to let applicant make a case for him/herself in the selection process)
6. *Prior knowledge of future colleagues*
   (Chance to meet the work group to check compatibility before taking the job, Chance to meet the boss or supervisor before taking the job).

A further study (Singer, 1992) shows that successful candidates' perceptions of the fairness of their selection procedure significantly affect their post-entry organisational commitment, work satisfaction and their evaluation of the general effectiveness of that organisation.

Reiley (1994) examined the promotion and appointment procedures used by the Police Department. A content analysis was applied to analyse the statements made in unsuccessful applicants' appeals against the decision. Similar to archival research, written appeal reports provide valuable information regarding applicants' genuine concerns about, and evaluations of, the promotion procedures. Results show that violations of the two procedural fairness rules of *Consistency* and *Accuracy* accounted for 81.8% of all the reasons stated in the reports analysed. Officers' fairness perceptions were also significant predictors of their job-related self-efficacy, commitment and satisfaction.

These results have clear implications for good leadership skills. Given that research is convergent in suggesting that employee motivation is significantly affected by their perceptions of the fairness of organisational practices, leaders should ensure that the procedures they adopt in various organisational practices are not only fair, but also perceived as such.

PERSONAL ETHICS AS FOUNDATION TO GOOD LEADERSHIP SKILLS

While good technical skills are necessary for effective leadership, it is argued that these skills are only secondary to personal ethics. This is by virtue of the fact that leadership characterised by "good skills but unethical means and intentions" would ultimately amount to "bad" leadership. While good skills can be conscientiously learned on the job, sound personal ethics oversee and ensure that these skills are properly applied. History has repeatedly shown that excellent leadership skills, while deployed by leaders who lack moral principles, can have more than dire consequences. In the recent transformation leadership literature, the distinction between ethical and unethical transformational leaders is made; it is the former, but not the latter, who are capable of fostering ethical behaviour among the followers (Howell & Avolio, 1992). In the context of fair leadership, good leadership skills are taught in the literature on procedural justice and "voice". "Voice" research suggests that, in managerial decisions such as promotion or resource allocation, giving employees the opportunities to have a say typically results in their feeling more satisfied with the leader and their work. However, Cohen (1989) warns the potential abuse of such a voice procedure by leaders with less than noble intentions. By giving employees a voice but not honestly taking it into account in making the decision, leaders have intentionally created an "illusion of justice" among employees in that they are led to believe that they have been given some control over the decision. As a result of this intentional "fabrication of justice", injustice which benefits the leader (at the expense of those led) is often maintained. This serves as yet another example of the harmful effect of supposedly "good" leadership skills being practiced by leaders devoid of sound personal ethics.

Sound personal ethics can also deter the potential negative leadership consequences of the disempowering of the led. The literature on power and powerholding has identified many negative "metamorphic effects" of powerholding. One of such effects concerns the desire for the powerholder to intentionally distance him/herself from those led and to actively devaluate their worth so as to maintain a desired "power distance" (Bok, 1993; Kipnis, 1976). When this happens, the effects on those led can range from feelings of inequity and resentment to a general sense of disempowerment. Anecdotal accounts suggest that good versus poor leadership typically boils down to the *enabling* versus the *disempowering* of the led. The idea of enabling is central to the notions of transformational leadership and servant leadership. In his theory of servant leadership, Greenleaf (1977) maintains that good leadership can only be evaluated by the degree to which followers have grown into individuals of greater wisdom, freedom and autonomy as a result of being served by the leader. In a similar vein, the justification for self-leadership given by Osterberg (1993) partly rests on the harmful disempowering effect of those occupying leadership positions upon those led by them.

So how can these negative consequences of disempowerment be overcome and moreover, how can leaders actively engage in the enabling of their followers? The answer may require a return to "basics": This means going back to the very foundation of leadership, that is, personal ethics. The question of why and how rulers should rule is an ancient question which was frequently addressed in the Dialogues between Plato and Socrates. The philosophical thinking is that rulers should rule with the intention and the aim to "serve" those they rule, and should never rule for the sake of personal gains in power or wealth. Leadership with the goal of serving others rather than benefiting self naturally brings about outcomes that are enabling to those led. Leaders with sound personal ethics, who possess moral virtues such as *Justice, Honour, Congeniality,* and *Truthfulness,* are by nature more inclined to interact with others in a manner that is enabling, rather than disempowering.

The foregoing discussion suggests a "deterrent" reason for personal ethics to play a foundational role in leadership. A more important reason however concerns the leader's proactive role in setting the vision and hence the "ethical tone" of an organisation. A great deal has been written about the pivotal role of leadership in shaping organisational culture and climate (e.g., Kouzes & Posner, 1993; Schein, 1990). Consequently, scholars have recently argued that the institutionalising of ethics at the entire organisational level can only be achieved through sound leadership (Carlson & Perrewe, 1995). Jones (1995) also argues that it is only through having leaders of high moral standards with an "ascetic personality" that an increase in ethical awareness and accountability within an organisation can be guaranteed. Therefore, personal ethics, as a foundation to organisational leadership, can proactively bring about a more ethical workplace.

Considering the very basic and foundational nature of personal ethics, it is not enough to place the demand to be virtuous and morally principled solely on leaders. While the debate remains inconclusive as to whether a higher level of personal ethics should be required of those in positions of leadership (e.g., Gahl, 1984), the point advanced here is that it should be a mandated qualification for everyone (not just leaders) in the business, or indeed any other, communities. Cognisant of this, researchers and practitioners have in recent years been actively engaged in business ethics teaching and training programmes. In that context, several scholars have argued for the practice *to live,* rather than *to learn,* ethics (e.g., Davis & Welton, 1991; Solberg, Strong, & McGuire, 1995), precisely by virtue of the fact that personal ethics are inalienable aspects of an individual's character. The purpose of ethics teaching is then, according to Solomon (1992), *"...not to 'teach' ethics...but to remind us all that there are standards and virtues at issue...without which the enterprise will not and does not deserve to survive"* (p.224).

The fundamental importance of personal ethics is well summarised by Acklin and King (1995) in their discussion of the Master Virtues of integrity and compassion, *"...they happen to be foundational to 'highly effective people' in our modern times of increasing complexity and pace of change....And learning how to 'scale them up' to group and organisational levels is increasingly the hallmark of effective firms".* (p.14).

Those who carry out the responsibility to *"remind us all of the standards and virtues at issue"* and to *"scale them up to group and organisational levels"*, in the end, become true leaders.

Acknowledgement:
    Part of this chapter originally appeared in: Singer, M. (1996). Leadership: overt behaviour, covert cognition, and personal ethics. In K. Perry (Ed). *Leadership: Research and Practice.* Australia: Pitman. Permission to use the material has been granted by the Editor.

Chapter 8   Epilogue

This book set out to achieve three goals: (1) to argue that an understanding of the normative philosophical thoughts on ethics and justice is foundational to the contemporary study of applied ethics, (2) to contribute to a dialogue between the normative and the empirical efforts in ethical enquiry in an organisational context, and (3) to argue that social and organisational programmes such as diversity hiring need to be evaluated systematically against the normative criteria of its overall goodness by including considerations of utility, rights and justice.

These three goals are conceptually interconnected. Although it is argued that the very foundation of the contemporary study of applied ethics should be grounded in normative philosophy, at this point in time, the development of sciences has made it possible for the study of applied ethics to derive much inspiration and insight from the results of empirical investigations of ethical issues. This book has demonstrated explicitly how such a combined normative-empirical framework can be applied to an organisation's leadership as well as its recruiting practices.

In the case of leadership, while the classical ethics of personal virtues should be the foundation of good leadership, empirical research helps provide technical guidance to sound leadership skills which are necessary in the "channelling" of such virtues into effective leadership practices.

Turning to recruitment, moral philosophy provides a systematic and comprehensive framework for the evaluation of the overall goodness of competing hiring practices, against the normative criteria of utility, rights and justice. Empirical research furnishes actual data for that evaluation. A pragmatic resolution of the dilemma is only possible through the combined efforts of empiricists' scientific investigation of facts and philosophers' intuitive deliberation over values.

However, this normative framework requires that considerations be given to all three moral standards. Even though justice is considered pivotal in Classical theories of ethics, a singular focus on justice in ethical considerations is inadequate. The argument is that while justice is a necessary criterion in bringing about an ethical outcome, it may not be sufficient by itself to do so (e.g., Hoffman & Moore, 1984). As noted in Chapter 6, in the context of the empirical research on selection practices, a clear predominant emphasis on justice over other teleological (i.e., utility) and deontological (e.g., rights and duties) notions is evident. Because of this, it is argued that a greater attention to empirical research on utility and rights is needed to ensure a "balanced" evaluation. This can only be achieved by focusing rigourous empirical efforts on each and every one of the normative criteria.

On a final note, a normative-empirical dialogue is necessary for a complete understanding of organisational ethics and justice. An analogy is made to a wholistic understanding of all beings which requires the knowledge of the senses and the knowledge of the soul (a view held by the old masters including Pythagoras, Plato, and Plotinus): the former can be acquired through scientific investigations and the latter, intuition and reflection. In a similar vein, to understand the whole meaning of organisational ethics and justice also requires the knowledge of what people's understandings of ethics and justice actually are and the knowledge of what they ought to be: Empirical research supplies the former; philosophical reflection provides the latter.

Readings and References

References for Chapter 1

Bloom, A. (1987). *The closing of the American mind.* New York: Simon and Schuster.

Casti, J. (1989). *Paradigms lost.* London: Abacus Books.

Davis, J.R., & Welton, R.E. (1991). Professional ethic: Business students' perceptions. *Journal of Business Ethics, 10,* 451-463.

Donaldson, T. (1994). When integration fails: The logic of prescription and description in business ethics. *Business Ethics Quarterly, 4(2),* 157-169.

Etzioni, A. (1989). Toward deontological social sciences. *Philosophy of the Social Sciences, 19,* 145-156.

Glenn, J.R. (1992). Can a business and society course affect the ethical judgement of future managers. *Journal of Business Ethics, 11,* 217-223.

Greenberg, J., & Bies, R. (1992). Establishing the role of empirical studies of organizational justice in philosophical inquiries into business ethics. *Journal of Business Ethics, 11,* 433-444.

Solberg, J., Strong, K.C., & McGuire, C. Jr. (1995). Living (Not learning) ethics. *Journal of Business Ethics, 14,* 71-84.

Solomon, R. C. (1992). *Ethics and excellence: Cooperation and integrity in business.* Oxford: Oxford University Press.

Trevino, L.K., & Weaver, G.R. (1994). Business ETHICS/BUSINESS ethics: ONE FIELD OR TWO? *Business Ethics Quarterly, 4(2),* 113-128.

Victor, B., & Stephens, C.U. (1994). Business ethics: A synthesis of normative philosophy and empirical social science. *Business Ethics Quarterly, 4(2),* 145-156.

Waterman, A. (1988). On the uses of psychological theory and research in the process of ethical inquiry. *Psychological Bulletin, 103,* 282-298.

Weaver, G.R., & Trevino, L.K. (1994). Normative and empirical business ethics. *Business Ethics Quarterly, 4(2),* 129-144.

Weber, J. (1990). Measuring the impact of teaching ethics to future managers: A review, assessment, and recommendations. *Journal of Business Ethics, 9,* 183-190.

Werhane, P.H. (1994). The normative/descriptive distinction in methodologies of business ethics. *Business Ethics Quarterly, 4(2),* 175-180.

References for Chapter 2

Ake, C. (1975). Justice as equality. *Philosophy and Public Affairs, 5,* 69-89.

Aristotle (1985). *Nicomachean ethics* (translated by T. Irwin). Indianapolis, IN: Hackett.

Barry, B. (1973). *The liberal theory of justice.* Oxford: Clarendon Press.

Bayles, M.D. (Ed.) (1968). *Contemporary utilitarianism.* New York: Doubleday.

Benjamin, A. (Ed.) (1989). *The Lyotard Reader.* Oxford: Basis Blackwell.

Bentham, J. (1948). *Introduction to principles of morals and legislation.* Oxford: Oxford University Press.

Bierman, A.K. (1980). *Life and morals: An introduction to ethics.* New York: Harcourt Brace Jovanovich.

Binkley, L.J. (1961). *Contemporary ethical theories.* New York: The Citadel Press.

Bowie, N. (1982). *Business ethics.* Englewood Cliffs, NJ: Prentice-Hall.

Brandt, R. (1959). *Ethical theory.* Englewood Cliffs, NJ: Prentice-Hall.

Brandt, R. (Ed.) (1962). *Social justice.* Englewood Cliffs, NJ: Prentice-Hall.

Cohen, M., Nagel, T., & Scanlon, T. (Eds.) (1980). *Marx, justice and history.* Princeton: Princeton University Press.

Derrida, J. (1978). Structure, sign and play in the discourse of the human sciences. In J. Derrida, *Writing and difference.* Chicago: University of Chicago Press.

Donagan, A. (1977). *The theory of morality.* Chicago: Chicago University Press.

Donaldson, T., & Werhane, P.H. (1983). *Ethical issues in business: A philosophical approach* (2nd Ed.). Englewood Cliffs, NJ: Prentice-Hall.

Feinberg, J. (1973). *Social philosophy.* Englewood Cliffs, NJ: Prentice-Hall.

Field, G.C. (1969). *The philosophy of Plato (2nd Ed.).* London: Oxford University Press.

Gadamer, H-G. (1976). *Philosophical Hermeneutics.* Berkeley: University of California Press.

Gellner, E. (1959). *Words and things.* London: Victor Gollancz.

Habermas, J. (1983). *Moral consciousness and communicative action.* Cambridge: The MIT Press.

Hare, R. (1964). *The language of morals.* Oxford: Oxford University Press.

Heidegger, M. (1962). *Being and time.* New York: Harper & Row.

Hobbes, T. (1926). *The Leviathan.* New York: Hafner.

Irwin, T. (1985). Translation of *The works of Aristotle*. Indianapolis: Hackett.

Kant, I. (1964). *Groundwork of the metaphysics* (translated by H.Paton). New York: Harper & Row.

Lee, H.D.P. (1955). Translation of *The Republic*. (the Penguin Classics Series). London: Penguin.

Locke, J. (1963). *Two treatises of government* (Ed., P. Laslett). New York: Cambridge University Press.

Lyons, D. (1965). *Forms and limits of utilitarianism.* Oxford: Oxford University Press.

Lyotard, J-F. (1984). *The postmodern condition: A report on knowledge.* Geoff Bennington and Brian Massumi, translators. Minneapolis: University of Minnesota Press.

Manser, A. (1966). *Satre: A philosophic study.* London: Athlone Press.

Mellema, G. (1991). *Beyond the call of duty.* Albany, NY: State University of New York Press.

McKeon, R. (Ed.) (1941). *The basic works of Aristotle.* New York: Random House.

Mill, J.S. (1957). *Utilitarianism.* Indianapolis: Bobbs-Merrill.

Moore, G.E. (1903). *Principia Ethica.* Cambridge: Cambridge University Press.

Neilsen, R.P. (1993). Varieties of postmodernism as moments in ethics action learning. *Business Ethics Quarterly, 3,* 251-269.

Nietzsche, F. (1887, 1969). *The genealogy of morals.* Translated by Walter Kaufman and R.J. Hollingdale. New York: Random House.

Nozik, R. (1974). *Anarchy, state and utopia.* New York: Basic Books.

Perelman, C. (1963). *The idea of justice and the problem of argument.* New York: Humanities Press Inc.

Rawls, J. (1971). *A theory of justice.* Cambridge, Massachusetts: Harvard University Press.

Rescher, N. (1993). *A system of pragmatic idealism.* Princeton, NJ: Princeton University Press.

Rorty, R. (1979). *Philosophy and the mirror of nature.* Princeton: Princeton University Press.

Rorty, A. (Ed.) (1982). *Essays on Aristotle's ethics.* Berkeley: University of California Press.

Rorty, R. (1982). *Consequences of pragmatism.* Minneapolis: University of Minnesota Press.

Ross, W.D. (1939). *Foundations of ethics.* Oxford: Oxford University Press.

Rossouw, G.J. (1994). Rational interaction for moral sensitivity: A postmodern approach to moral decision-making in business. *Journal of Business Ethics, 13,* 11-20.

Russell, B. (1959). *My philosophical development.* London: Allen and Unwin.

Schilpp, P.A. (Ed.) (1942). *The philosophy of G.E. Moore.* Evanston: Northwestern University Press.

Sidgwick, H. (1962). *Methods of ethics.* Chicago: Chicago University Press.

Smart, J.J.C., & Williams, B. (1973). *Utilitarianism: For and against.* London: Cambridge University Press.

Smith, A. (1976). *An inquiry into the nature and causes of the wealth of nations.* Oxford: Clarendon.

Solomon, R.C. (1990). A passion for justice. Reading, Mass.: Addison-Wesley.

Solomon, R.C. (1992).*Ethics and excellence: Cooperation and integrity in business.* Oxford: Oxford University Press.

Stevenson, L. (1974). *Seven Theories of human nature.* New York: Oxford University Press.

Urmson, J.O. (1956). *Philosophical analysis.* Oxford: Clarendon.

Velasquez, M.G. (1982). *Business ethics: Concepts and Cases.* Englewood Cliffs, NJ: Prentice-Hall.

Walton, C.C. (1993). Business ethics and postmodernism: A dangerous dalliance. *Business Ethics Quarterly, 3,* 285-305.

Werhane, P. (1991). *Adam Smith and his legacy for modern capitalism.* New York: Oxford University Press.

Wolff, J.L., & Smith, K.S. (1983). Normative ethics of two categories of offenders. *Psychological Reports, 53,* 443-446.

References for Chapter 3

Adams, J.S. (1965). Inequity in social exchange. In L. Berkowitz (Ed.), *Advances in experimental social psychology,* (Vol.2, pp.267-299). New York: Academic Press.

Alexander, R. (1987). The biology of moral system. New York: Adline de Gruyter.

Alexander, R. (1993). Biological considerations in the analysis of morality. In M.H. Nitecki & D.V. Nitecki (Eds). *Evolutionary ethics.* New York: State University of New York Press.

Ayala, F.J. (1987). The biological roots of morality. *Biology and Philosophy, 2,* 235-252.

Ayers, L.R. (1992). Perceptions of affirmative action among its beneficiaries. *Social Justice Research, 5,* 223-238.

Axelrod, R. (1984). The evolution of cooperation. New York: Basic Books.

Axelrod, R., & Hamilton, W. (1981). The evolution of cooperation. *Science, 211,* 1390-1396.

Barnes Nacoste, R. (1993). Procedural justice and preferential treatment: A brief review and comment. *Current Psychology: Research and Reviews, 12,* 230-235.

Barnett, T., Bass, K., & Brown, G. (1994). Ethical ideology and ethical judgement regarding ethical issues in business. *Journal of Business Ethics, 13,* 469-480.

Barrett-Howard, E., & Tyler, T.R (1986). Procedural justice as a criterion in allocation decisions. *Journal of Personality and Social Psychology 50*, 296-304.

Battistich, V., Waston, M., Solomon, D., Schaps, E., & Solomon, J. (1991). The child development project: A comprehensive program for the development of prosocial character. In W. Kurtines & J.L. Gewirtz (Eds.), *Handbook of moral behavior and development (Vol. 3: Application)*, Hillsdale, NJ: Lawrence Erlbaum.

Berger, J., Zeiditch, M., Anderson, B., & Cohen, B.P. (1972). Structural aspects of distributive justice: A status-value formulation. In J.Berger, M. Zelditch & B. Anderson (Eds.) *Sociological theories in progress* (Vol. 2, pp. 21-45). Boston: Houghton Mifflin.

Bies, R.J. (1987). Beyond voice: The influence of decision-maker justification and sincerity on procedural fairness judgements. *Representative Research in Social Psychology, 17*, 3-14.

Bies, R.J., & Moag, J.S. (1986). Interactional justice: Communication criteria of fairness. In R.J. Lewicki, B.H. Sheppard, & M.H. Bazerman (Eds.), *Research on negotiation in organisations*. Greenwich, CT: JAI Press.

Bies, R.J., & Shapiro, D.L. (1988). Voice and justification: Their influence on procedural fairness judgements. *Academy of Management Journal, 31*, 676-685.

Blasi, A. (1980). Bridging moral cognition and moral action: A critical review of the literature. *Psychological Bulletin, 88*, 1-45.

Blasi, A. (1990). Connected, unconnected, disconnected: A response to Linn and Gilligan. *New Ideas in Psychology, 8*, 209-213.

Bora, A. (1995). Procedural Justice as a contested concept: Sociological remarks on the group value model. *Social Justice Research, 8(2)*, 175-196.

Boudon, R. (1992). Sentiments of justice. *Social Justice Research, 5(2)*, 13-136.

Boyce W.D., & Jensen, L.C. (1978). Moral reasoning: A psychological-philosophical integration. Lincoln: University of Nebraska Press.

Brockner, J. (1990). Scope of justice in the workplace: How survivors react to co-worker layoffs. *Journal of Social Issues, 46*, 95-106.

Brockner, J. (1994). Perceived fairness and survivors' reactions to layoffs, or how downsizing organizations can do well by doing good. *Social Justice Research, 7(4)*, 345-364.

Brockner, J., DeWitt, R., Grover, S., & Reed, T. (1990). When it is especially important to explain why: Factors affecting the relationship between managers' explanations of a layoff and survivors' reactions to the layoff. *Journal of Experimintal Social Psychology, 26*, 389-407.

Brockner, J., Konovsky, M., Cooper-Schneider, R., Folger, R., Martin, C., & Bies, R. (1994). Interactive effects of procedural justice and outcome negativity on victims and survivors of job loss. *Academy of Management Journal, 37*, 397-409.

Bruins, J., Platow, M.J., & Ng, S.H. (1995). Distributive and procedural justice in interpersonal and intergroup situations: Issues, solutions and extensions. *Social Justice Research, 8,* 103-121.

Charles, E.M., & Carver, C.S. (1979). Effects of person salience versus role salience on reward allocation in the dyad. *Journal of Personality and Social Psychology, 37,* 2071-2080.

Chusmir, L.H., & Mills , J. (1989). Gender differences in conflict resolution styles of managers: At work and at home. *Sex Roles, 20,U 149-163.*

Clayton, S.D., & Crosby, F.J. (1992). *Justice, gender and affirmative action.* Ann Arbor: The University of Michigan Press.

Colby, A., & Kohlberg, L. (1987). *The measurement of moral judgement: Theoretical foundations and research validations* (Vol.1). Cambridge, MA: Cambridge University Press.

Cropanzano, R., & Folger, R. (1989). Referent cognitions and task decision autonomy: Beyond equity theory. *Journal of Applied Psychology, 74,* 293-299.

Cropanzano, R., & Randall, M.L. (1995). Advance notice as a means of reducing relative deprivation. *Social Justice Research, 8(2),* 217-238.

Crosby, F. (1976). A model of egoistic relative deprivation. *Psychological Review, 83,* 85-113

Crosby, F. (1982). *Relative deprivation and working women.* New York: Oxford University Press.

Davies, J. (1959). A formal interpretation of the theory of relative deprivation. *Sociometry, 22,* 280-296.

Dawkins, R. (1976). The selfish gene. Oxford: Oxford University Press.

deCarufel, A. (1986). Pay secrecy, social comparison and relative deprivation in organizations. In J.M. Olson, C.P. Herman & M.P. Zanna (Eds.), *Relative deprivation and social comparison: The Ontario Symposium* (Vol. 4), pp. 181-199.

Dennett, D.C. (1995). *Darwin's dangerous idea.* London: Alen Lane.

Derrida, J. (1978). Structure, sign and play in the discourse of the human sciences. In J. Derrida, *Writing and difference.* Chicago: University of Chicago Press.

Derry, R. (1987). Moral reasoning in work-related conflicts. In W.C. Frederick (Ed.), *Research in corporate social performance and policy: Empirical studies of business ethics and values* (Vol.9), Greenwich, CT: JAI Press.

Deutsch, M. (1985). *Distributive justice.* New Haven, CT: Yale University Press.

Dornstein, M. (1989). The fairness judgements of received pay and their determinants. *Journal of Occupational Psychology, 62,* 287-299.

Dugan, D.O. (1987). Masculine and feminine voices: Making ethical decisions in the care of the dying. *Journal of Medical Humanities and Bioethics, 8,* 129-140.

Elm, D.R. & Weber, J. (1994). Measuring moral judgement: The Moral Judgement Interview or the Defining Issues Test? *Journal of Business Ethics, 13,* 341-355.

Flax, J. (1993). The play of justice: Justice as a transitional space. *Political Psychology, 14(2)*, 331-346,

Folger, R. (1986a). Rethinking equity theory: A referent cognitions model. In H.W. Bierhoff, R.L. Cohen & J. Greenberg (Eds.), *Justice in social relations.* (pp. 145-162). New York: Plenum.

Folger, R. (1986b). A referent cognitions theory of relative deprivation. In J.M. Olson, C. P. Herman & M.P. Zanna (Eds.), *Social comparison and relative deprivation: The Ontario Symposium* (Vol. 4, pp. 33-55). Hillsdale, N.J.: Erlbaum.

Folger, R., & Konovsky, M.A. (1989). Effects of procedural and distributive justice on reactions to pay raise decisions. *Academy of Management Journal, 32*, 115-130.

Folger, R., Rosenfield, D., & Robinson, T. (1983). Relative deprivation and procedural justifications. *Journal of Personality and Social Psychology, 45*, 268-273.

Folger, R. (1994). Workplace justice and employee worth. *Social Justice Research, 7(3)*, 225-240.

Forsyth, D.R. (1980). A taxonomy of ethical ideologies. *Journal of Personality and Social Psychology, 39*, 175-184.

Forsyth D.R. (1981). Moral judgement: The influence of ethical ideology. *Personality and Social Psychology Bulletin, 7*, 218-223.

Forsyth, D.R. (1985). Individual differences in information integration during moral judgement. *Journal of Personality and Social Psychology, 49*, 264-272.

Forsyth, D.R. (1992). Judging the morality of business practices: The influence of personal moral philosophies. *Journal of Business Ethics, 11*, 461-470.

Forsyth, D.R., & Berger, R.E. (1982). The effects of ethical ideology on moral behavior. *Journal of Social Psychology, 117*, 53-56.

Forsyth, D.R., & Matney, L. (1990). *The emotional consequences of selfish and selfless actions.* Paper presented at the Second Annual Convention of the American Psychological Association, Dallas, TX.

Forsyth, D.R., & Nye, J.L. (1990). Personal moral philosophies and moral choice. *Journal of Research in Personality, 24*, 398-414.

Forsyth, D.R., & Pope, W.R. (1984). Ethical ideology and judgements of social psychological research. *Journal of Personality and Social Psychology, 46*, 1365-1375.

Fry, W.R., & Cheney, G. (1981). *Perceptions of procedural fairness as a function of distributive preference.* Paper presented at the meeting of the Midwestern Psychological Association, Detroit.

Fryxell, G.E., & Gordon, M.E. (1989). Workplace justice and job satisfaction as predictors of satisfaction with union and management. *Academy of Management Journal, 32*, 851-866.

Gadamer, H-G. (1976). *Philosophical Hermeneutics.* Berkeley: University of California Pres.

Gatens, M. (1991). *Feminism and philosophy: Perspectives on difference and equality.* Cambridge, UK: Polity Press.

Giacalone, R.A., Fricker, S., & Beard, J.W. (1995). The impact of ethical ideology on modifiers of ethical decisions and suggested punishment for ethical infractions. *Journal of Business Ethics, 14,* 497-510.

Gilligan, C. (1982). *In a different voice: Psychological theory and women's development.* Cambridge, Massachusetts: Harvard University Press.

Gilligan, C. (1986). Exit-voice dilemmas in adolescent development. In A. Foxley, M. McPherson, & G. O'Donnell (Eds.), *Development, democracy, and the art of trespassing: Essays in honour of Albert O. Hirschman.* Notre Dame, IN: University of Notre Dame Press.

Gilligan, C., & Pollak, S. (1988). The vulnerable and invulnerable physician. In C. Gilligan, J.V. Ward, & J.M. Taylor (Eds.), *Mapping the moral domain.* Cambridge, Massachusetts: Harvard University Press.

Gilligan, C., & Wiggins, G. (1988). The origins of morality in early childhood relationships. In C. Gilligan, J.V. Ward, & J.M. Taylor (Eds.), *Mapping the moral domain.* Cambridge, Massachusetts: Harvard University Press.

Gilligan, C., Ward, J.V., & Taylor, J.M. (1988). *Mapping the moral domain.* Cambridge, Massachusetts: Harvard University Press.

Gould, S.J. (1991). Explanation: A crucial tool for an evolutionary psychology. *Journal of Social Issues, 47,* 43-65.

Greenberg, J. (1982). Approaching equity and avoiding inequity in groups and organizations. In J. Greenberg & R.L. Cohen (Eds.), *Equity and justice in social behavior* (pp. 389-435). New York: Academic Press.

Greenberg, J. (1986a) Determinants of perceived fairness of performance evaluations. *Journal of Applied Psychology, 71,* 340-342.

Greenberg, J. (1986b). Organizational performance appraisal procedures: What makes them fair? In R.J. Lewicki, B.H. Sheppard, & M. Bazerman (Eds.), *Research on negotiation in organizations.* (vol. 1, pp. 25-41). Greenwich, CT: JAI Press.

Greenberg, J. (1987). A taxonomy of organizational justice theories. *Academy of Management Review, 12,* 9-22.

Greenberg, J. (1990). Organizational justice: Yesterday, today and tomorrow. *Journal of Management, 16,* 399-432.

Greenberg, J. (1993). Stealing in the name of justice: Informational and interpersonal moderators of theft reactions to underpayment inequity. *Organisational Behavior and Human Decision Processes, 54,* 81-103.

Greenberg, J., & Cohen, R.L. (1982). Why justice? Normative and instrumental interpretations. In J. Greenberg & R.L. Cohen (Eds.), *Equity and justice in social behavior* (pp. 437-469). New York: Academic Press.

Gurr, T.R. (1970). *Why men rebel.* Princeton, N.J.: Princeton University Press.

Haan, N. (1977). Coping and defending: Processes of self-environment organization. New York: Academic Press.

Haan, N. (1978). Two moralities in action contexts: Relationships to thought, ego regulation and development. *Journal of Personality and Social Psychology, 36,* 286-305.

Haan, N. (1982). Can research on morality be "scientific"? *American Psychologist, 37,* 1096-1104.

Haan, N. (1983). An interactional morality of everyday life. In N. Haan, R.N. Bellah, P. Rabinow, & W.M. Sullivan (Eds.), *Social science as moral inquiry.* New York: Columbia University Press.

Hamilton, W. (1964). The genetical evolution of social behavior. *Journal of Theoretical Biology, 7,* 1-52.

Hartnett, J., & Shumate, M. (1980). Ethical attitudes and moral maturity among prison inmates. *Journal of Psychology, 106,* 147-149.

Hasse, L. (1987). Legalizing gender-specific values. In E.F. Kittay & D.T. Meyers (Eds.), *Women and moral theory.* Totowa, NJ: Rowman and Littlefield.

Heider, F. (1958). *The psychology of interpersonal relations.* New York: Wiley.

Higgins, A., Power, C., & Kohlberg, L. (1984). The relationships of moral atmosphere to judgements of responsibility. In W. Kurtines & J. Gewirtz (Eds.), *Morality, moral behavior and moral development.* New York: Wiley.

Hogan, R. (1970). A dimension of moral judgement. *Journal of Consulting and Clinical Psychology, 35,* 205-212.

Hogan, R. (1973). Moral conduct and moral character: A psychological perspective. *Psychological Bulletin, 79,* 217-232.

Hogan, R. (1974). Dialectical aspects of moral development. *Human Development, 17,* 107-117.

Jack, D., & Jack, R. (1988). Women lawyers: Archetype and alternatives. In C. Gilligan, J.V Ward, & J.M. Taylor (Eds.), *Mapping the moral domain.* Cambridge, Massachusetts: Harvard University Press.

Jackson, L.A. (1989). Relative deprivation and the gender wage gap. *Journal of Social Issues, 45,* 117-133.

Kagan, J. (1984). *The nature of the child.* New York: Basic Books.

Kanfer, R., Sawyer, J., Earley, P.C., & Lind, E.A. (1987). Participation in task evaluation procedures: The effect of influential opinion expression and knowledge of evaluation criteria on attitudes and performance. *Social Justice Research, 1,* 235-249.

Karambayya, R., & Brett, J.M. (1989). Managers handling disputes: Third party roles and perceptions of fairness. *Academy of Management Journal, 33,* 687-704.

Kitcher, P. (1993). The evolution of human altruism. *Journal of Philosophy, 90,* 497-516.

Kitwood, T. (1990). *Concern for others: A new psychology of conscience and morality.* London: Routledge.

Klaas, B.S. (1989). Determinants of grievance activity and the grievance system's impact on employee behaviour: An integrative perspective. *Academy of Management Review, 32,* 705-717.

Kohlberg, L. (1969). Stage and sequence: The cognitive-developmental approach to socialization. In D.A. Goslin (Ed.), *Handbook of socialization theory and research* (pp.347-480). Chicago, IL: Tand McNally.

Kohlberg, L. (1976). Moral stages and moralization: The cognitive-developmental approach. In T. Lickona (Ed.), *Moral development and behavior: Therapy, research and social issues.* New York: Holt, Rinehart & Winston.

Konovsky, M.A., & Cropanzano, R. (1991). Perceived fairness of employee drug testing as a predictor of employee attitudes and job performance. *Journal of Applied Psychology, 76,* 698-707.

Konovsky, M.A., & Folger, R. (1991). The effects of procedures, social accounts and benefits level on victim's layoff reactions. *Journal of Applied Social Psychology, 21,* 630-650.

Koper, G., & Vermunt, R. (1988). The effects of procedural aspects and outcome salience on procedural fairness judgements. *Social Justice Research, 2,* 289-301.

Koper, G., Van Knippenberg, D., Bouhuijs, F., Vermunt, R., & Wilke, H. (1993). Procedural fairness and self-esteem. *European Journal of Social Psychoogy, 23,* 313-325.

Kulik, C.T., & Campbell Clark, S. (1993). Frustration effects in procedural justice research: The case of drug-testing legislation. *Social Justice Research, 6(3),* 287-300.

Landy, F.J., Barnes, J.L., & Murphy, K.R. (1978). Correlates of perceived fairness and accuracy of performance evaluation. *Journal of Applied Psychology, 63,* 751-754.

Lansberg, I. (1989). Social categorization, entitlement and justice in organizations: Contextual determinants and cognitive underpinnings. *Human Relations, 41,* 871-899.

Leary, M.R., Knight, P.D., & Barnes, B.D. (1986). Ethical ideologies of the machiavellian. *Personality and Social Psychology Bulletin, 12,* 75-80.

Lehning, P.B. (1990). Liberalism and capabilities: Theories of justice and the neutral state. *Social Justice Research, 4,* 187-213.

Lehning, P.B. (1994). Justice for women! *Social Justice Research, 7,* 155-165.

Lerner, M.J. (1977). The justice motive: Some hypotheses as to its origins and forms. *Journal of Personality, 45,* 1-52.

Lerner, M.J. (1980). The belief in a just world: A fundamental delusion. New York: Plenum Press.

Lerner, M.J. (1982). The justice motive in human relations and the economic model of man: A radical analysis of facts and fictions. In V. Derlega & J. Grezlak (Eds.), *Cooperation and helping behavior: Theory and Research* (pp. 121-145). New York: Academic Press.

Lerner, M.J., & Lerner, S.C. (Eds.), (1981). *The justice motive in social behavior: Adopting to times of scarcity and change.* New York: Plenum.

Leventhal, G.S. (1976). The distribution of rewards and resources in groups and organizations. In L.Berkowitz & E. Walster (Eds.), *Advances in experimental social psychology,* (Vol.9, pp. 91-131) New York: Academic Press.

Leventhal, G.S. (1980). What should be done with equity theory? In K.J. Gergen, M.S. Greenberg, & R.H. Willis (Eds.), *Social exchange: Advances in theory and research* (pp. 27-55). New York: Plenum.

Leventhal, G.S., Karuza, J., & Fry, W.R. (1980). Beyond fairness: A theory of allocation preferences. In G. Mikula (Ed.), *Justice and social interaction* (pp. 167-218). New York: Springer-Verlag.

Lickona, T. (1991). Moral development in elementary school classroom. In W. Kurtines & J.L. Gewirtz (Eds.), *Handbook of moral behavior and development (Vol. 3: Application),* Hillsdale, NJ: Lawrence Erlbaum.

Lind, E.A., & Tyler, T.R. (1988). *The social psychology of procedural justice.* New York: Plenum Press.

Lipkus, I.M. (1992). A heuristic model to explain perceptions of unjust events. *Social Justice Research, 5(4),* 359-384.

Lyotard, J-F. (1984). *The postmodern condition: A report on knowledge.* Geoff Bennington and Brian Massumi, translators. Minneapolis: University of Minnesota Press.

Mackie, J.L. (1978). The law of the jungle. *Philosophy, 53,* 553-573.

Martin, W., & Shaw, B. (1993). White, Gilligan and the voices of business ethics. *Business Ethics Quarterly, 3,* 437-443.

Maynard Smith, J. (1978). *The evolution of sex.* Cambridge: Cambridge University Press.

McEnrue, M.P. (1989). The perceived fairness of managerial promotion practices. *Human Relations, 42,* 815-827.

Moore, D. (1991a). Discrimination and deprivation: The effects of social comparisons, *Social Justice Research, 4,* 49-64.

Moore, D. (1991b). Entitlement and justice evaluation: Who should get more and why. *Social Psychology Quarterly, 54,* 208-223.

Nitecki M.H., & Nitecki D.V. (Eds.) (1993). *Evolutionary ethics.* New York: State University of New York Press.

Nowak, M., & Simund, K. (1993). A strategy of win-stay, lose-shift that outperforms tit-for-tat in the Prisoner's Dilemma game. *Nature, 364,* 56-58.

Nozik, R. (1974). *Anarchy, state and utopia.* New York: Basic Books.

Nye, J., & Forsyth, D.R. (1984). *The impact of ethical ideology on moral behavior.* Paper presented at the meeting of the Eastern Psychological Association, Baltimore.

Organ, D.W., & Moorman, R.H. (1993). Fairness and organizational citizenship behaviour: What are the connections? *Social Justice Research, 6(1),* 5-18.

Pavlak, T.J., Clark, P.F., & Gallagher, D.G. (1992). Measuring attitudes toward grievance systems: A procedural justice perspective applied to the workforce. *Social Justice Research, 5,* 173-194.

Petrinovich, L., O'Neill, P., & Jorgensen, M. (1993). An empirical study of moral intuitions: Toward an evolutionary ethics. *Journal of Personality and Social Psychology, 64,* 467-478.

Pettigrew, T. (1967). Social evaluation theory. In D. Levine (Ed.), *Nebraska symposium on motivation* (vol. 15). Lincoln: University of Nebraska Press.

Piaget, J. (1932, 1965). *The moral judgement of the child.* New York: the Free Press.

Pratt, M.W., Diessner, R., Hunsberger, B., Pancer, S.M., & Savoy, K. (1991). Four pathways in the analysis of adult development and aging: Comparing analyses of reasoning about personal-life dilemmas. *Psychology and Aging, 6,* 666-675.

Putnam, H. (1990). *Realism with a human face.* Cambridge, MA: Harvard University Press.

Puka, B. (1991). Interpretative experiments: Probing the care-justice debate in moral development. *Human Development, 34,* 61-80.

Rawls, J. (1993). *Political liberalism.* New York: Columbia University Press.

Reiley, J., & Singer, M. (1996). Perceived fairness of promotion procedures: Identification of justice rules and consequences for job attitudes. *International Journal of Selection and Assessment, 4,* 129-138.

Rest, J.R. (1979). *Development in judging moral issues.* Minneapolis: University of Minnesota Press.

Rest, J.R., Barnett, R., Beveau, M., Deemer, D., Getz, I., Moon, Y., Spickelmier, J., Thoma, S., & Volker, J. (1986). *Moral development: Advances in research and theory.* New York: Praeger.

Rettig, K.D., & Dahl, C.M. (1991). The unlikely possibility of justice in divorce settlements. Proceedings, Theory Construction and Research Methodology Workshop, National Council on Family Relations. Denver, Co.

Rettig, K.D., & Dahl, C.M. (1993). Impact of procedural factors on perceived justice in divorce settlements. *Social Justice Research, 6,* 301-321.

Rorty, R. (1979). *Philosophy and the mirror of nature.* Princeton: Princeton University Press.

Rorty, R. (1982). *Consequences of pragmatism.* Minneapolis: University of Minnesota Press.

Rorty, R. (1989). *Contingency, irony and solidarity.* Cambridge: Cambridge University Press.

Rossouw, G.J. (1994). Rational interaction for moral sensitivity: A postmodern approach to moral decision-making in business. *Journal of Business Ethics, 13,* 11-20.

Rottschaefer, W.A., & Martinsen, D. (1990). Really taking Darwin seriousy: An alternative to Michael Ruse's Darwinian metaethics. *Biology and Philosophy, 5,* 149-173.

Runciman, W.G. (1966). *Relative deprivation and social justice: A study of attitudes to social inequality in twentieth-century England.* Berkeley, CA: University of California Press.

Ruse, M. (1979). *Sociobiology: Sense or nonsense?* Dordrecht: Reidel.

Ruse, M. (1993). The new evolutionary ethics. In M.H. Nitecki & D.V. Nitecki (Eds.), *Evolutionary ethics.* New York: State University of New York Press.

Ruse, M. (Ed.), (1989). *Philosophy of biology.* London: Macmillan.

Ruse, M. , & Wilson, E.O. (1985). The evolution of ethics. *New Scientist, 17,* 50-52.

Rutte, C.G., & Messick, D.M. (1995). An integrated model of perceived unfairness in organizations. *Social Justice Research, 8(3),* 239-262.

Sampson, E.E. (1994). Justice and the neutral state: A postmodern, feminist critique of Lehning's account of justice. *Social Justice Research,7(2),* 145-155.

Sandel, M.J. (1982). *Liberalism and the limits of justice.* Cambridge, UK: Cambridge University Press.

Sheppard, B.H., & Lewicki, R.J. (1987). Towards general principles of managerial fairness. *Social Justice Research, 1,* 161-176.

Sheppard, B.H., Lewicki, R.J. & Minton, J.W. (1992). *Organisational justice: The search for fairness in the workplace.* New York: Lexington Books.

Skitka, L.J., & Tetlock, P.E. (1992). Allocating scarce resources: A contingency model of distributive justice. *Journal of Experimental Social Psychology, 28,* 491-522.

Skoe, E.E., & Diessner, R. (1994). Ethic of care, justice, identity and gender: An extension and replication. *Merrill-Palmer Quarterly, 4,* 272-289.

Singer, M.S. (1990). Preferential selection and outcome justice: Effects of justification and merit discrepancy. *Social Justice Research, 4,* 285-305.

Singer, M.S. (1992b). The application of relative deprivation theory to justice perception of preferential selection. *Current Psychology: Research and Reviews, 11,* 128-144.

Singer, M.S. (1993). Gender-based preferential selection: Perceptions of injustice and empathy of deprivation. *International Journal of Selection and Assessment, 1,* 184-202.

Singh, B., & Forsyth, D.R. (1989). Sexual attitudes and moral values: The importance of idealism and relativism. *Bulletin of the Psychonomic Society, 27,* 160-162.

Stouffer, S.A., Suchman, E.A., DeVinney, L.C., Star, S.A., & Williams, R.M. Jr. (1949). *The American soldier: Adjustment during army life.* Princeton: Princeton University Press.

Sugawara, I., & Huo, Y.J. (1994). Disputes in Japan: A cross-cultural test of the procedural justice model. *Social Justice Research, 7(2),* 129-144.

Sweeney, P.D., & McFarlin, D.B. (1993). Workers' evaluations of the "ends" and the "means": An examination of four models of distributive and procedural justice. *Organistional Behavior and Human Decision Processes, 55,* 23-40.

Sweeney, P.D., McFarlin, D.B., & Inderrieden, E.J. (1990). Using relative deprivation theory to explain satisfaction with income and pay level: A multistudy examination. *Academy of Management Journal, 33,* 423-436.

Syroit, J. (1991). Interpersonal and intergroup injustice: Some theoretical considerations. In H. Steensma & R. Vermunt (Eds.), *Social justice in human relations: Societal and psychological consequences of justice and injustice.* (Vol.1). New York: Plenum Press.

Syroit, J., Lodewijkx, H., Franssen, E., & Gerstel, I. (1993). Organizational commitment and satisfaction with work among transferred employees: An application of referent cognitions theory. *Social Justice Research, 6(2),* 219-234.

Tajfel, H., & Turner, (1979). An integrative theory of intergroup conflict. In W.G. Austin & S. Worchel (Eds.), *The social psychology of intergroup relations.* Monterey, CA: Brooks/Cole.

Thibaut, J., & Walker, L. (1978). A theory of procedure. *California Law Review, 66,* 541-566.

Tougas, F.L., & Veilleux, F. (1989). Who likes affirmative action: Attitudinal processes among men and women. In F.A. Blanchard & F.C. Crosby (Eds.), *Affirmative action in perspective.* (pp. 111-124). New York: Springer-Verlag.

Trevino, L.K. (1992). Moral reasoning and business ethics: Implications for research, education and management. *Journal of Business Ethics, 11,* 445-459.

Tyler, T.R., & Lind, E.A. (1990). Intrinsic versus community-based justice models: When does group membership matter. *Journal of Social Issues, 46,* 83-94.

Tyler, T.R., & Lind, E.A. (1992). A relational model of authority. *Advances in Experimental Social Psychology, 25,*115-191.

Veilleux, F., & Tougas, F. (1989). Male acceptance of affirmative action programs for women: The results of altruistic or egoistical motives. *International Journal of Psychology, 24,* 485-496.

Vermunt, R., Van der Kloot, W.A., & Van der Meer, J. (1993). The effect of procedural and interactional criteria on procedural fairness judgements. *Social Justice Research, 6(2),* 183-194.

Walster, E., Walster, G.W., & Berscheid, E. (1978). *Equity: Theory and research.* Boston: Allyn & Bacon.

Wegener, B. (1990). Equity, relative deprivation and the value consensus paradox. *Social Justice Research, 4 ,* 65-86.

White, T. (1992). Business, ethics, and Carol Gilligan's "Two voices". *Business Ethics Quarterly, 2,* 51-61.

Williams, M., Vaughn, R., & Savia, A. (1976). Moral judgement philosophies in three offender categories. *Criminology, 14,* 283-286.

Wilson, E.O. (1975). *Sociobiology: The new synthesis.* Cambridge, Mass: Harvard University Press.

Wilson, E.O. (1978). *On human nature.* Cambridge, Mass: Harvard Univesity Press.

Wolff, J.L., & Smith, K.S. (1983). Normative ethics of two categories of offenders. *Psychological Reports, 53,* 443-446.

Wood, J.T. (1986). Different voices in relationship crises: An extension of Gilligan's theory. *American Behavioural Scientist, 29,* 273-301.

References for Chapter 4

Ajzen, I., & Fishbein, M. (1980). *Understanding attitudes and predicting social behaviour.* Englewood Cliffs, NJ: Prentice-Hall.

Akaah, I.P., & Lund, D. (1994). The influence of personal and organistional values on professionals' ethical behavior. *Journal of Business Ethics, 13,* 417-430.

Baron, M. (1987). Kantian ethics and supererogation. *Journal of Philosophy, 84,* 237-262.

Berenbeim, R.E. (1988). *Corporate ethics: Research Report No. 900.* New York: The Conference Board.

Bishop, J.D. (1995). Adam Smith's invisible hand argument. *Journal of Business Ethics, 14,* 165-180.

Boatright, J.R. (1995). Aristotle meets Wall Street: The case for virtue ethics in business. *Business Ethics Quarterly, 5,* 351-359.

Business Ethics Quarterly, (1995). *Special Issue on The Environment, 5.*

Cannon, T. (1994). *Corporate responsibility.* London: Pitman.

Carlson, D.S., & Perrewe, P.L. (1995). Institutionalization of organizational ethics through transformational leadership. *Journal of Business Ethics, 14,* 829-838.

Carr, A.Z. (1968). "Is business bluffing ethical?" *Harvard Business Review,* 143-153.

Coker, E.W. (1990). Adam Smith's concept of the social system. *Journal of Business Ethics, 9,* 139-142.

Centre for Business Ethics (1986). Are corporations institutionalising ethics? *Journal of Business Ethics, 5,* 85-91.

Crosthwaite, J. (1995). Moral expertise: A problem in the professional ethics of professional ethicists. *Bioethics, 9,* 361-379.

Davis, J.R., & Welton, R.E. (1991). Professional ethics: Business students' preceptions. *Journal of Business Ethics, 10,* 451-463.

Dubinsky, A.J., & Loken, B. (1989). Analysing ethical decision making in marketing. *Journal of Business Research, 19(2),* 83-107.

Elm, D.R., & Weber, J. (1994). Measuring moral judgement: The moral judgement interview or the defining issues test? *Journal of Business Ethics, 13,* 341-355.

Ewin, R.E. (1995). The virtues appropriate to business. *Business Ethics Quarterly,* *5,* 833-842.

Ferrell, O.C., & Gresham, L.G. (1985). A contingency framework for understanding ethical decision making in marketing. *Journal of Marketing,* (Summer), 87-96.

Ferrell, O.C., Gresham, L.G., & Fraedrich, J. (1989). A synthesis of ethical decision models for marketing. *Journal of Macromarketing, 9(2),* 55-64.

Finegan, J. (1994). The impact of personal values on judgements of ethical behavior in the workplace. *Journal of Business Ethics, 13,* 747-755.

Fleming, D. (1970). Social Darwinism. In A. Jr. Schlesinger & M. White (Eds.), *Paths of American thoughts.* Boston: Houghton Mifflin.

Fletcher, J. (1966). *Situation ethics: The new morality.* Philadelphia: Westminster Press.

Fraedrich, J., Thorne, D.M., & Ferrell, O.C. (1994). Assessing the application of cognitive moral development. *Journal of Business Ethics, 13,* 829-838.

Frederick, W. (Ed.), (1992). The empirical quest for normative meaning: Empirical methodologies for the study of business ethics. *Business Ethics Quarterly,* *2(2),* 91-246.

French, P.A. (1979). The corporation as a moral person. *American Philosophical Quarterly, July,* p. 207.

French, P.A. (1984). The principle of responsive adjustment in corporate moral responsibility: The crash on Mount Erebus. *Journal of Business Ethics, 3,* 101-111.

Friedman, M. (1962). *Capitalism and freedom.* Chicago: University of Chicago Press.

Fritzsche, D.J. (1995). Personal values: Potential inluences on ethical decision making. *Journal of Business Ethics, 14,* 909-922.

Gilliland, S.W. (1993). The perceived fairness of selection systems: An organisational justice perspective. *Academy of Management Review, 18(4),* 694-734.

Grace, D., & Cohen, S. (1995). *Business ethics.* Melbourne: Oxford University Press.

Goodpaster, K.E., & Mathews, Jr. J.B. (1982). Can a corporation have a conscience? *Harvard Business Review, (Feb.),* 132-141.

Harrington, S.J. (1991). What corporate America is teaching about ethics. *Academy of Management Executive, 5(1),* 21-30.

Horvath, C.M. (1995). Excellence v. effectiveness: MacIntyre's critique of business. *Business Ethics Quarterly, 5,* 499-532.

Hunt, S.D., & Vitell, S. (1986). A general theory of marketing ethics. *Journal of Macromarketing, 6(1),* 5-16.

Jones, H.B. Jr. (1995). The ethical leader: An ascetic construct. *Journal of Business Ethics, 14,* 867-874.

Jones, T.M. (1991). Ethical decision making by individuals in organizations: An issue-contingent model. *Academy of Management Review, 16(2)*, 366-395.

Kahn, W.A. (1990). Toward an agenda for business ethics rsearch. *Academy of Management Review, 15,* 311-328.

Koehn, D. (1992). Toward an ethic of exchange. *Business Ethics Quarterly, 2,* 341-355.

Kohlberg, L. (1969). Stage and sequence. The cognitive-developmental approach to socialization. In D. Goslin (Ed.), *Handbook of Socialization Theory and Research.* Chicago: Rand McNally.

Kolnai, A. (1973). Forgiveness. *Aristotelian Society Proceedings, 84,* 91-106.

Kuhn, J. W. (1992). Ethics in business: What managers practice that economists ignore. *Business Ethics Quarterly, 2(3)*, 305-315.

Ladd, J. (1970). Morality and the ideal of rationality in formal organisations. *Monist, 54,* 488-516.

Lux, K. (1990). Adam Smith's mistake: How a moral philosopher invented economics and ended morality. Boston: Shambhala.

McCracken, J., & Shaw, B. (1995). Virtue ethics and contractarianism. *Business Ethics Quarterly, 5(2)*, 297-312.

MacIntyre, A. (1984). *After virtue* (2nd ed.). Notre Dame, IN: Notre Dame Press.

Malloy, D.C., & Lang, D.L. (1993). An Aristotelian approach to case study analysis. *Journal of Business Ethics, 12*, 511-516.

Mellema, G. (1991). *Beyond the call of duty.* Albany, NY: State University of New York Press.

Mellema, G. (1994). Business ethics and doing what one ought to do. *Journal of Business Ethics, 13,* 149-153.

Molz, R. (1995). The theory of pluralism in corporal governance: A conceptual framework and empirical test. *Journal of Business Ethics, 14,* 789-804.

Montada, L., & Kals, E. (1995). Perceived justice of ecological policy and proenvironmental commitments. *Social Justice Research, 8,* 305-327.

Morris, S.A., & McDonald, R.A. (1995). The role of moral intensity in moral judgements: An empirical investigation. *Journal of Business Ethics, 14,* 715-726.

Nagel, T. (1978). Ruthless in public life. In S. Hamshire, *Public and private morality.* New York: Cambridge University Press.

Nesteruk, J. (1995). Law and the virtues: Developing a legal theory for business ethics. *Business Ethics Quarterly, 5,* 361-369.

Newton, L. (1992). Virtue and role: Reflections on the social nature of morality. *Business Ethics Quarterly, 2,* 357-365.

Olson, S. (1995). Old guards, young turks, and the $64,000 question. *Business Ethics Quarterly, 5(2)*, 371-380.

Rest, J.R. (1979). *Development in judging moral issues.* Minneapolis: University of Minnesota Press.

Rest, J.R. (1983). Morality. In P. Mussen (Ed.), *Manual of Child Psychology* (4th ed., Vol. 3, 556-629). New York: Wiley.

Rest, J. R. (1986). *Moral development: Advances in reserch and theory.* New York: Praeger.

Rest, J.R. (1989). Why does college promote development in moral judgement. *Journal of Moral Education, 17,* 183-194.

Rest, J.R., Deemer, D., Barnett, R., Spickelmier, J., & Volker, T. (1986). Life experiences and developmental pathways. In J. Rest (Ed.), *Moral development: Advances in research and theory.* (pp.28-58). New York: Praeger.

Rossouw, G.J. (1994). Rational interaction for moral sensitivity: A postmodern approach to moral decision-making in business. *Journal of Business Ethics, 13,* 11-20.

Sagoff, M. (1988). *The economy of the earth.* Cambridge: Cambridge University Press.

Shaw, B. (1995). Virtues for a postmodern world. *Business Ethics Quarterly, 5(2),* 843-864.

Sherwin, D.S. (1989). The ethical roots of the business system. In K. R. Andrews (Ed), Ethics in practice: *Managing the moral corporation.* Boston: Harvard Business School Press.

Singer, A.E. (1994). Strategy as moral philosophy. *Strategic Management Journal, 15,* 191-213.

Singer, M. (1993). *Fairness in personnel selection: An organisational justice perspective.* Aldershot: Avebury.

Singer, M. (1996). The role of moral intensity and fairness perception in judgements of ethicality: A comparison of managerial professionals and the general public. *Journal of Business Ethics, 15,* 469-474.

Singer, M., & Singer, A.E. (in press). Observer judgements about moral agents' ethical decisions: The role of scope of justice and moral intensity. *Journal of Business Ethics.*

Singer, M., Mitchell, S., & Turner, J. (in press). Consideration of moral intensity in ethicality judgements: Its relationship with whistle-blowing and need-for-cognition. *Journal of Business Ethics.*

Singhapakdi, A., & Vitell, S.J. (1993). Personal and professional values underlying the ethical judgements. *Journal of Business Ethics, 12,* 525-533.

Smith, A. (1976). *An inquiry into the nature and causes of the wealth of nations.* Oxford: Clarendon.

Social Justice Research (1996). *Special Issue on Psychological contributions to business ethics, 9.*

Solberg, J., Strong, K.C., & McGuire, C. Jr. (1995). Living (not learning) ethics. *Journal of Business Ethics, 14,* 71-84.

Solomon, R. C. (1992). *Ethics and excellence.* Oxford: Oxford University Press.

Starkey, K. (Ed.) (1995). Special Issue on corprate governance and control. *Human Relations, 48.*

Trevino, L.K. (1986). Ethical decision making in organisations: A person-situation interactionalist model. *Academy of Management Review, 11(3)*, 601-617.

Trevino, L.K. (1992). Moral reasoning and business ethics: Implications for research, education and management. *Journal of Business Ethics, 11*, 445-459.

Trevino,L.K., & Youngblood, S.A. (1990). Bad apples in bad barrels: A causal analysis of ethical decision-making behavior. *Journal of Applied Psychology, 75*, 378-385.

Varian, H.R. (1975). Distributive justice, welfare economics, and the theory of justice. *Journal of Philosophy and Public Affairs, 4*, 223-247.

Velasquez, M.G. (1982). *Business ethics*. Englewood Cliffs, NJ: Prentice-Hall.

Victor, B., & Cullen, J.B. (1988). The organisational bases of ethical work climates. *Administrative Science Quarterly, 33*, 101-125.

Wasserstrom, R.A. (1971). *Morality and the criminal law*. Belmont, California: Wadsworth.

Weber, J. (1993). Institutionalising ethics into business organisations: A model and research agenda. *Business Ethics Quarterly, 3(4)*, 419-436.

Werhane, P. (1991). *Ethics and economics: The legacy of Adam Smith for modern capitalism*. Oxford: Oxford University Press.

Westra, L. (1994). *An environmental proposal for ethics: The principle of integrity*. Lanham, MD: Rowman & Littlefield.

Wilson, K.L., Rest, J.R., Boldizar, J.P., & Deemer, D.K. (1992). Moral judgement development: The effects of education and occupation. *Social Justice research, 5*, 31-48.

Wilson, R.J. (1967). *Darwinism and the American intellectual*. Homewood, Il: Dorsey.

Zajac, E.E. (1995). *Political economy of fairness*. Cambridge: MIT Press.

References for Chapter 5

Baron, M. (1987). Kantian ethics and supererogation. *Journal of Philosophy, 84*, 237-262.

Bies, R.J., & Moag, J.S. (1986). Interactional justice: Communication criteria of fairness. In R.J. Lewicki, B.H. Sheppard, & M.H. Bazerman (Eds.), *Research on negotiation in organisations*. Greenwich, CT: JAI Press.

Bond, D., & Park, J-C. (1991). An empirical test of Rawls' theory of justice: A second approach, in Korea and the United States. *Simulation and Gaming, 22*, 443-462.

Boulding, K.E. (1962). Social justice in social dynamics. In R.B. Brandt (Ed.), *Social Justice*. Englewood Cliffs, NJ: Prentice Hall.

Brickman, P. (1977). Preference for inequality. *Sociometry, 40*, 303-310.

Buchanan, A.E. (1983). Marx on democracy and the obsolescence of rights. *South African Journal of Philosophy, 2*, 130-135.

Buchanan, A.E., & Mathieu, D. (1986). Philosophy and Justice. In R.L. Cohen (Ed.), *Justice: Views from the Social Sciences.* New York: Plenum Press.

Curtis, R.C. (1979). Effects of knowledge of self-interest and social relationship upon the use of equity, utilitarian, and Rawlsian principles of allocation. *European Journal of Social Psychology, 9*, 165-175.

Elm, D.R., & Weber, J. (1994). Measuring moral judgement: The moral judgement interview or the defining issues test? *Journal of Business Ethics, 13*, 341-355.

Donaldson, T. (1994). When integration fails: The logic of prescription and description in business ethics. *Business Ethics Quarterly, 4(2)*, 157-169.

Etzioni, A. (1989). Toward Deontological Social Sciences. *Philosophy of the Social Sciences, 19*, 145-156.

Fisk, M. (1975). History and reason in Rawls' moral theory. In N. Daniels (Ed.), *Reading Rawls: Critical studies on Rawls' A theory of Justice.* Oxford: Basil Blackwell.

Flanagan, O.J. Jr. (1982). Virtue, sex and gender: Some philosophical reflections on the moral psychology debate. *Ethics, 92*, 499-512.

Folger, R. (1988). *Justice as dignity.* Paper presented at American Psychological Association meeting, Atlanta.

Forsyth, D.R. (1980). A taxonomy of ethical ideologies. *Journal of Personality and Social Psychology, 39*, 175-184.

Forsyth, D.R. (1992). Judging the morality of business practices: The influence of personal moral philosophies. *Journal of Business Ethics, 11*, 461-470.

Frederick, W. (Ed.), (1992). The empirical quest for normative meaning: Empirical methodologies for the study of business ethics. *Business Ethics Quarterly, 2(2)*, 91-246.

Fredrickson, J.W. (1986). An exploratory approach to measuring perceptions of strategic decision process constructs. *Strategic Management Journal, 7*, 473-483.

Frohlich, N., Oppenheimer, J., & Eavey, C.L. (1987a). Laboratory results on Rawls' distributive justice. *British Journal of Political Science, 17*, 1-21.

Frohlich, N., Oppenheimer, J., & Eavey, C.L. (1987b). Choices of principles of distributive justice in experimental groups. *American Journal of Political Science, 31*, 606-636.

Gilligan, C. (1982). *In a Different Voice.* Cambridge, M.A: Harvard University Press.

Gilligan, C. (1986). Exit-voice dilemmas in adolescent development. In A. Foxley, M. McPherson, & G. O'Donnell, (Eds.), *Development, democracy, and the art of trespassing: Essays in honour of Albert O. Hirschman.* Notre Dame, Ind: University of Notre Dame Press.

Goodpaster, K. E. (1983). The concept of corporate responsibility. *Journal of Business Ethics, 2*, 1-22.

Goodpaster, K.E. (1985). Ethical frameworks for management. In J.B. Mattews, K.E. Goodpaster, & L.L. Nash, *Policies and persons* (pp. 507-522). New York: McGraw-Hill.

Greenberg, J., & Bies, R. (1992). Establishing the role of empirical studies of organizational justice in philosophical inquiries into business ethics. *Journal of Business Ethics, 11*, 433-444.

Haan, N. (1982). Can research on morality be "scientific"? *American Psychologist, 37*, 1096-1104.

Haan, N., Bellan, R.N., Rabinow, P., & Sullivan, W.M. (Eds.) (1983). *Social sciences as moral inquiry.* New York: Columbia University Press.

Jones, T.M. (1991). Ethical decision making by individuals in organizations: An issue-contingent model. *Academy of Management Review, 16*, 366-395.

Kagan, J. (1984). *The nature of the child.* New York: Basic Books

Kahn, W.A. (1990). Towards an agenda for business ethics research. *Academy of Management Review, 15*, 311-328.

Kitwood, T. (1990). *Concern for others: A new psychology of conscience and morality.* London: Routledge.

Kohlberg, L. (1976). Moral stages and moralization: The cognitive-developmental approach. In T. Lickona (Ed.), *Moral Development and behavior: Therapy, research and social issues.* New York: Holt, Rinehart & Winston.

Kohlberg, L. (1982). A reply to Owen Flanagan and some comments on the Puka-Goodpaster exchange. *Ethics, 92*, 513-528.

Kolnai, A. (1973). Forgiveness. *Aristotelian Society Proceedings, 84*, 91-106.

Kurtines, W.M., Azmitia, M., & Alvarez, M. (1990). Science and morality: The role of values in science and the scientific study of moral phenomena. *Psychological Bulletin, 107(3)*, 283-295.

Lane, R.E. (1988). Book review of Lind and Tyler, The social psychology of procedural justice. *Social Justice Research, 2*, 309-317.

Lerner, M.J. (1977). The justice motive: Some hypotheses as to its origins and forms. *Journal of Personality, 45*, 1-52.

Lerner, M.J. (1982). The justice motive in human relations and the economic model of a man: A radical analysis of facts and fictions. In V. Derlega & J. Grezlak (Eds.), *Cooperation and helping behaviour: Theory and research.* New York: Academic Press.

Lind, E.A., & Tyler, T.R. (1988). *The social psychology of procedural justice.* New York: Plenum.

Lissowski, G., Tyszka, T., & Okrasa, W. (1988). *Principles of distributive justice: Preferences of Polish and American students.* Unpublished manuscript.

Mellema, G. (1994). Business ethics and doing what one ought to do. *Journal of Business Ethics, 13*, 149-153.

Mitchell, G., Tetlock, P.E., Mellers, B.A., & Ordonez, L.D. (1993). Judgements of social justice: Compromises between equality and efficiency. *Journal of Personality and Social Psychology, 65(4)*, 629-639.

Piaget, J. (1965). *The moral Judgement of the Child.* New York: The Free Press.

Rachels, J. (1986). *The elements of moral philosophy.* New York: McGraw-Hill.

Rawls, J. (1971). *A Theory of Justice.* Cambridge, MA: Harvard University Press.

Rossouw, G.J. (1994). Rational interaction for moral sensitivity: A post-modern approach to moral decision-making in business. *Journal of Business Ethics, 13,* 11-20.

Simpson, E.L. (1974). Moral development research: A case study of scientific cultural bias. *Human Development, 17,* 81-106.

Singer, M. (1993). *Fairness in personnel selection: An organisational justice perspective.* Aldershot: Avebury.

Singer, M. (1996). The role of moral intensity and fairness perception in judgements of ethicality: A comparison of managerial professionals and the general public. *Journal of Business Ethics,* in press.

Stevenson, C.L. (1963). *Facts and values,* New Haven, CT: Yale University Press.

Trevino, L.K., & Weaver, G.R. (1994). Business ETHICS/BUSINESS ethics: ONE FIELD OR TWO? *Business Ethics Quarterly, 4(2),* 113-128.

Velasquez, M.G. (1982). *Business ethics: Concepts and cases.* Englewood Cliffs, N.J.: Prentice-Hall.

Velasquez, M.G. (1996). Business ethics, the social sciences, and moral philosophy. *Social Justice Research, 9,* 97-107.

Victor, B., & Stephens, C.U. (1994). Business ethics: A synthesis of normative philosophy and empirical social science. *Business Ethics Quarterly, 4(2),* 145-156.

Waterman, A. (1988). On the uses of psychological theory and research in the process of ethical inquiry. *Psychological Bulletin, 103,* 282-298.

Weaver, G.R., & Trevino, L.K. (1994). Normative and empirical business ethics. *Business Ethics Quarterly, 4(2),* 129-144.

Weber, J. (1992). Scenarios in business ethics research: Review, critical assessment and recommendations. *Business Ethics Quarterly, 2,* 137-159.

Werhane, P.H. (1994). The normative/descriptive distinction in methodologies of business ethics. *Business Ethics Quarterly, 4(2),* 175-180.

References for Chapter 6

America, R.F. (1986). Affirmative action and redistributive ethics. *Journal of Business Ethics, 5,* 73-77.

Anderson , S.B., & Muchinsky, P.M. (1991). An examination of the robustness of the general utility function. *Educational and Psychological Measurement, 51,* 49-65.

Ayers, L.R. (1992). Perceptions of affirmative action among its beneficiaries. *Social Justice Research, 5,* 223-238.

Banks, W.M. (1984). Afro-American scholars in the university. *American Behavioral Scientists, 27*, 325-338.

Bantel, K.A., & Jackson, S.E. (1989). Top management and innovations in banking: Does the composition of the top team make a difference? *Strategic Management Journal, 10*, 107-124.

Barnes Nacoste, R. (1990). Sources of stigma: Analysing the psychology of affirmative action. *Law Policy, 12*, 175-195.

Barnes Nacoste, R. (1992). Towards a psychological ecology of affirmative action. *Social Justice Research, 5*, 269-289.

Barnes Nacoste, R., & Powell, T.E. (1991). Quotas as procedure: Affirmative action and its discontents. Paper presented at the 98th annual convention of the American Psychological Association, Boston.

Becker, G.S. (1971). *The economics of discrimination*, (2nd ed.). Chicago: The University of Chicago Press.

Bell, D. (1989). The effects of affirmative action on male-female relationships among African Americans. *Sex Roles, 21*, 13-24.

Benokraitis, N.V., & Gilbert, M.K. (1989). Women in federal government employment. In F.A. Blanchard & F.L. Crosby (Eds.), *Affirmative action in perspective*. New York: Springer-Verlag.

Bies, R.J. (1987a). The predicament of injustice: The management of moral outrage. In L.L. Cummings & B.M. Staw (Eds.), *Research in organizational behavior*. (Vol.9, pp.289-319). Greenwich, CT: JAI Press.

Bies, R.J. (1987b). Beyond voice: The influence of decision-maker justification and sincerity on procedural fairness judgements. *Representative Research in Social Psychology, 17*, 3-14.

Bies, R.J., & Shapiro, D.L. (1988). Voice and justification: Their influence on procedural fairness judgements. *Academy of Management Journal, 31*, 676-685.

Block, C.J., Robertson, L., & Neuger, D.A. (1995). White racial identify theory: A framework for understanding reactions toward interracial situations in organizations. *Journal of Vocational Behaviour, 46*, 71-88.

Bok, D. (1985). Admitting success. *The New Republic*, (Feb 4), 15.

Boxill, B.R. (1984). *Blacks and social justice*. Totawa, NJ: Rowman & Allanheld.

Brockner, J. (1990). Scope of justice in the workplace: How survivors react to co-worker layoffs. *Journal of Social Issues, 46*, 95-106.

Bronstein, P., & Pfennig, J.L. (1989). Beliefs versus realities: Response to Elliott. *American Psychologist, 44*, 1550.

Broxhill, B. (1972). The morality of reparations. *Social Theory and Practice, 2*, 113-122.

Bruner, J. (1986). *Actual minds, possible worlds*. Cambridge, MA: Harvard University Press.

Carter, S. (1991). *Reflections of an affirmative action baby*. New York: Basic Books.

Cascio, W.F. (1981). Fair personnel decision making. In C.J. Brotherton (Ed.), *Towards fairness in selection and placement process*. London: Wiley.

Cascio, W. (1982). Scientific, operational and legal imperatives of workable performance appraisal systems. *Public Personnel Management Journal*, 11, 367-375.

Cascio, W. (1989). *Managing human resources*. New York: McGraw-Hill.

Cascio, W. (1991). *Applied psychology in personnel management* (4th ed.). Englewood Cliffs, NJ.: Prentice-Hall.

Chacko, T.I. (1982). Women and equal employment opportunity: Some unintended effects. *Journal of Applied Psychology*, 67, 119-123.

Clayton, S.D. (1992). Remedies for discrimination: Race, sex and affirmative action. *Behavior, Science and Law*, 10, 245-257.

Clayton, S.D., & Tangri, S.S. (1989). The justice of affirmative action, In F.A. Blanchard & F.L. Crosby (Eds.), *Affirmative action in perspective* (pp.177-192). New York: Springer-Verlag.

Cohen, C. (1975). Race and constitution. *The Nation*, 8 February.

Cronbach, L.J., & Schaeffer, G.A. (1981). *Extensions of personnel selection theory to aspects of minority hiring* (Project Report No. 81-A2). Palo Alto, CA: Stanford University.

Cronbach, L.J., Yalow, E., & Schaeffer, G.A. (1980). A mathematical structure for analyzing fairness in selection. *Personnel Psychology*, 33, 693-704.

Crosby, F.J., Allen, B., & Opotow, S. (1992). Changing patterns of income among blacks and whites before and after executive order 11246. *Social Justice Research*, 5(3), 335-341.

Crosby, F., & Clayton, S. (1990). Affirmative action and the issue of expectancies. *Journal of Social Issues*, 46, 61-79.

Cullen, D., Nakamura, A., & Nakamura, M. (1988). Occupational sex segregation in Canada and the United States: Does affirmative action make a difference? In S. Rose & L. Larwood (Eds.), *Women's careers: Pathways and pitfalls* (pp.163-177). New York: Praeger.

Daniels, N. (1978). Merit and meritocracy. *Philosophy and Public Affairs*, 7, 208-219.

Davies, J. (1959). A formal interpretation of the theory of relative deprivation. *Sociometry*, 22, 280-296.

Davis, G., & Watson, G. (1982). *Black life in corporate America: Swimming in the mainstream*. Garden City, NY: Anchor Press/Doubleday.

Decter, M. (1980). Benign victimization. *Policy Review*, 13, 65-72.

Dovidio, J., Mann, J., & Gaertner, S. (1989). Resistance to affirmative action: The implications of aversive racism. In F. Blanchard & F. Crosby (Eds.), *Affirmative action in perspective* (pp. 83-102). New York: Springer-Verlag.

Eastland, T., & Bennett, W.J. (1979). *Counting by race: Equality from the founding fathers to Bakke and Weber*. New York: Basic Books.

Feather, N.T. (Ed.) (1982). *Expectations and actions: Expectancy-value models in psychology.* Hillsdale, NJ: Erlbaum.

Fernandez, J.P. (1982). *Racism and sexism in corporate life: Changing values in American business.* Lexington, MA: Heath.

Finkelstein, M.J. (1984). The status of academic women: An assessment of five competing explanations. *Review of Higher Education, 7,* 223-246.

Finkelstein, S., & Hambrick, D.C. (1990). Top-management-team tenure and organizational outcomes: The moderating role of managerial decision. *Administrative Science Quarterly, 35,* 484-503.

Fishkin, J.S. (1983). *Justice, equal opportunity and the family.* New Haven, CT: Yale University Press.

Fiss, O.M. (1976). Groups and the equal protection clause. *Philosophy and Public Affairs, 5,* 150-151.

Folger, R., & Bies, R.J. (1989). Managing responsibilities and procedural justice. *Employee Responsibilities and Rights Journal, 2,* 79-90.

Gallup Poll (1984). *Gallup Report, 28.*

Garcia, S.A. (1989). My sister's keeper: Negative effects of social welfare and affirmative action programs on black women. *Sex Roles, 21,* 25-43.

Gelman, D., Springer, K., Brailsford, K., & Miller, M. (1988). Black and white in America. *Newsweek,* (March 7), 18-23.

Goldman, A.H. (1976). Affirmative action. *Philosophy and Public Affairs, 5,* 187.

Goldsmith, N., Cordova, D., Dwyer, K., Langlois, B., & Crosby, F.J. (1989). Reactions to affirmative action: A case study. In F.A. Blanchard & F.L. Crosby (Eds.), *Affirmative action in perspective* (pp.139-146). New York: Springer-Verlag.

Goodpaster, K.E. (1985). Ethical frameworks for management. In J.B. Mattews, K.E. Goodpaster, & L.L. Nash, *Policies and persons* (pp. 507-522). New York: McGraw-Hill.

Goodpaster, K.E. (1995). Ethical frameworks for management. In J.B. Matthews, K.E. Goodpaster, & L.L. Nash (Eds). *Policies and persons: A casebook in business ethics.* New York: McGraw-Hill.

Greenberg, J. (1987). A taxonomy of organizational justice theories. *Academy of Management Review, 12,* 9-22.

Greenberg, J. (1990a). Organizational justice: Yesterday, today and tomorrow. *Journal of Management, 16,* 399-432.

Greenberg, J. (1990b). Employee theft as a reaction to underpayment inequity: Hidden cost of pay cuts. *Journal of Applied Psychology, 75,* 561-568.

Griswold, A.W. (1934). Three Puritans on prosperity. *The New England Quarterly, 7,* 475-487.

Gross, A.L., & Su, W. (1975). Defining a "fair" or "unbiased" selection model: A question of utility. *Journal of Applied Psychology, 60,* 345-351.

Gurr, T.R. (1970).*Why men rebel.* Princeton, NJ: Princeton University Press.

Haan, N. (1982). Can research on morality be "scientific"? *American Psychologist,* *37,* 1096-1104.

Haan, N. (1983). An interactional morality of everyday life. In N. Haan, R.N. Bellah, P. Rabinow, & W.M. Sullivan (Eds.), *Social science as moral inquiry.* New York: Columbia University Press.

Hartigan, J.A., & Wigdor, A.K. (1989). *Fairness in employment testing.* Washington, DC: National Academy Press.

Hayashi, P. (1991-1992). Affirmative action: A personal view. *The College Board Review, 162,* 18-32.

Heckman, J.J. (1989). The impact of government on the economic status of Black Americans. In S. Shulman & W. Darity (Eds.), *The question of discrimination: Racial inequality in the US labor market.* Middletown, CT: Wesleyan University Press.

Heilman, M.E., & Herlihy, J.M. (1984). Affirmative action, negative reaction? Some moderating conditions. *Organisational Behaviour and Human Performance, 33,* 204-213.

Heilman, M.E., Lucas, J., & Kaplow, S. (1990). 'Self-derogating consequences of sex-based preferential selection: The moderating role of initial self-confidence'. *Organizational Behavior and Human Decision Processes, 46,* 202-216.

Heilman, M.E., Rivero, J.C., & Brett, J.F. (1991). Skirting the competence issue: Effects of sex-based preferential selection on task choices of women and men. *Journal of Applied Psychology, 76,* 99-105.

Heilman, M.E., Simon, M.C., & Repper, D.P. (1987). Intentionally favored, unintentionally harmed? Impact of sex-based preferential selection on self-perceptions and self-evaluations. *Journal of Applied Psychology, 72,* 62-68.

Horne, P. (1979). Police women—2000 AD. *Law and Order, 27,* 48-61.

Howard, J., & Hammond, R. (1985). Rumors of inferiority: The hidden obstacles to black success. *The New Republic (*Sep. 9), 17-21.

Hunter, J.E., & Hunter, R. (1984). Validity and utility of alternative predictors. *Psychological Bulletin, 96,* 72-98.

Hunter, J.E., Schmidt, F.L., & Coggin, T.D. (1988). Problems and pitfalls in using capital budgeting and financial accounting techniques in assessing the utility of personnel programs. *Journal of Applied Psychology, 73,* 522-528.

Hunter, J.E., Schmidt, F.L., & Rauschenberger, J.M. (1977). Fairness of psychological tests: Implications of four definitions for selection utility and minority hiring. *Journal of Applied Psychology, 62,* 245-260.

Irons, E.D., & Moore, G.W. (1985). *Black managers: The case of the banking industry.* New York: Praeger.

Jackson, S.E., Stone, V.K., & Alvarez, E.B. (1992). Socialization amidst diversity: The impact of demographics on work team oldtimers and newcomers. *Research in Organizational Behaviour, 15,* 45-109.

Jacobson, M.B., & Koch, W. (1977). Women as leaders: Performance evaluation as a function of method of leader selection. *Organisational Behaviour and Human Performance, 20,* 149-157.

Jencks, C. (1985). Affirmative action for blacks: Past, present and future. *American Behavioral Scientist, 28,* 731-760.

Kantrowitz, B., & Springen, K. (1988). A tenuous bond from 9 to 5. *Newsweek,* March 8, 24-25.

Kendler, H.H. (1993). Psychology and the ethics of social policy. *American Psychologist, 48,* 1046-1053.

Kinder, D.R., & Sanders, L.M. (1990). Mimicking political debate with survey questions: The case of white opinion on affirmative action for blacks. *Social Cognition, 8,* 73-103.

Kluegel, J.R., & Smith, E.R. (1986). *Beliefs about inequality: American's views of what is and what ought to be.* New York: Aldine de Gruyter.

Kroeck, K.G., Barrett, G.V., & Alexander, R.A. (1983). Imposed quotas and personnel selection: A computer simulation study. *Journal of Applied Psychology, 68,* 123-136.

LaMond, A.M. (1977). Economic theories of employment discrimination. In P.A. Wallace & A.M. LaMond (Eds.), *Women, minorities, and employment discrimination.* Lexington, MA: D.C. Heath & Co.

Leventhal, G.S., Karuza, J., & Fry, W.R. (1980). Beyond fairness: A theory of allocation preferences. In G. Mikula (Ed.), *Justice and social interaction* (pp.167-218). New York: Springer-Verlag.

Lind, E.A. & Tyler, T.R. (1988). *The social psychology of procedural justice.* New York: Plenum Press.

Lipset, S.M., & Schneider, W. (1978). The Bakke case: How would it be decided at the bar of public opinion? *Public Opinion, 1,* 38-44.

Loury, G. (1986). Beyond civil rights. In J.D. Williams (Ed.), *The state of black America-1986* (pp.163-174). New York: National Urban League.

Lovrich, N.P., & Steel, B.S. (1983). Affirmative action and productivity in law enforcement agencies. *Review of Public Personnel Administration, 4,* 55-66.

Lovrich, N.P., Steel, B.S., & Hood, D. (1986). Equity versus productivity: Affirmative action and municipal police services. *Public Productivity Review, 39,* 61-72.

McCombs, H.G. (1989). The dynamics and impact of affirmative action processes on higher education, the curriculum and Black women. *Sex Roles, 21,* 127-143.

Minas, A.C. (1977). How reverse discrimination compensates women. *Ethics, 88,* 74-79.

Minsky, M. (1975). A framework for representing knowledge. In P.H. Wilson (Ed.), *The psychology of computer vision.* New York: McGraw-Hill.

Morrison, A.M., & Von Glinow, M.A. (1990). Women and minorities in management. *American Psychologist, 45,* 200-208.

Murphy, K.P. (1984). Cost-benefit considerations in choosing among cross-validation methods. *Personnel Psychology, 37*, 15-22.

Murray, A.J. (1989). Top management group heterogeneity and firm performance. *Strategic Management Journal, 10*, 125-142.

Murrell, A.J., Dietz-Uhler, B.L., Dovidio, J.F., Gaertner, S.L., & Drout, C. (1994). Aversive racism and resistance to affirmative action: Perceptions of justice are not necessarily color blind. *Basic and Applied Social Psychology, 15*, 71-86.

Nacoste, R.W. (1985). Selection procedure and responses to affirmative action: The case of favorable treatment. *Law and Human Behavior, 9*, 225-242.

Nacoste, R.W. (1987). But do they care abut fairness?: The dynamics of preferential treatment and minority interest. *Basic and Applied Social Psychology, 8*, 177-185.

Nacoste, R.W. (1989). Affirmative action and self-evaluation. In F.A. Blanchard & F.L. Crosby (Eds.), *Affirmative action in perspective* (pp.103-109). New York: Springer-Verlag.

Nacoste, R.W., & Lehman, D. (1987). Procedural stigma. *Representative Research in Social Psychology, 17*, 25-38.

Nagel, T. (1973). Equal treatment and compensatory discrimination. *Philosophy and Public Affairs, 2*, 348-363.

Newton, L.H. (1973). Reverse discrimination as unjustified. *Ethics, 83*, 308-312.

Nickel, J.W. (1974). Preferential policies in hiring and admissions: A jurisprudential approach. *Columbia Law Review, 75*, 534-558.

Northcraft, G.B., & Martin, J. (1982). Double jeopardy: Resistance to affirmative action from potential beneficiaries. In B.A. Gutek (Ed.), *Sex role stereotyping and affirmative action policy* (pp.81-130), UCLA: Institute of Industrial Relations

Norvell, N., & Worchel, S. (1981). A re-examination of the relation between equal status contact and intergroup attraction. *Journal of Personality and Social psychology, 41*, 902-908.

Nozick, R. (1974). *Anarchy, state and utopia*. New York: Basic Books.

Optow, S. (1992). Affirmative action and social justice: Introduction. *Social Justice Research, 5*, 219-222.

Overlaet, B. (1991). Merit criteria as justification for differences in earnings. *Journal of Economic Psychology, 12*, 689-706.

Pettigrew, T.F. (1967). Social evaluation theory. In D. Levine (Ed.), *Nebraska symposium on motivation* (Vol.15). Lincoln: University of Nebraska Press.

Pettigrew, T.F., & Martin, J. (1987). Shaping the organizational context for Black American inclusion. *Journal of Social Issues, 43*, 41-78.

Reid, P.T., & Clayton, S. (1992). Racism and sexism at work. *Social Justice Research, 5*, 249-268.

Rescher, N. (1966). *Distributive justice*. New York: Bobbs-Merrill.

Roberts, L.W. (1981). Understanding affirmative action. In W.E. Block & M.A. Walker (Eds.), *Discrimination, affirmative action and equal opportunity* (pp.147-182). Vancouver, B.C.: The Fraser Institute.

Rodgers, D.T. (1978). *The work ethic in industrial America.* Chicago: University of Chicago Press.

Rosenbloom, D.H. (1984). What have policy studies told us about affirmative action and where can we go from here? *Policy Studies Review, 4,* 43-48.

Rossouw, G.J. (1994). Rational interaction for moral sensitivity: A post-modern approach to moral decision-making in business. *Journal of Business Ethics, 13,* 11-20.

Runciman, W.G. (1966). *Relative deprivation and social justice: A study of attitudes to social inequality in twentieth-century England.* Berkeley, CA: University of California Press.

Runciman, W.G. (1968). Problems of research on relative deprivation. In H.H. Hyman & E. Singer (Eds.), *Readings in reference group theory and research.* New York: Free Press.

Ryan, J.A. (1941). *Distributive justice.* New York: MacMillan.

Schmidt, F.L., Hunter, J.E., McKenzie, R.C., & Muldrow, T.W. (1979). Impact of valid selection procedures on work-force productivity. *Journal of Applied Psychology,* 64, 609-626.

Schmidt, F.L., Mack, M.J., & Hunter, J.E. (1984). Selection utility in the occupation of US Park Ranger for three modes of test use. *Journal of Applied Psychology, 69,* 490-497.

Schmidt, F.L., Ones, D.S., & Hunter, J.E. (1992). Personnel selection. *Annual Review of Psychology,* 43, 627-670.

Schmitt, N. (1989). Fairness in employment selection. In M. Smith & I. Robertson (Eds.), *Advances in personnel selection and assessment* (p.133-152). Chichester: Wiley.

Schmitt, N., & Noe, R.A. (1986). Personnel selection and equal employment opportunity. In C. L. Cooper & I.T. Robertson (Eds.), *International review of industrial and organizational psychology.* New York: Wiley.

Schmitt, N., & Robertson, I. (1990). Personnel selection. *Annual Review of Psychology, 41,* 289-319.

Schuman, H., Steeh, C., & Bobo, L. (1985). *Racial attitudes in America: Trends and interpretations.* Cambridge, MA: Harvard University Press.

Scott, K.D., & Little, B.L. (1991). Affirmative action: New interpretations and realities. *Human Resources Planning, 14,* 177-182.

Seltzer, R., & Thompson, E. (1985). *Attitudes towards discrimination and affirmative action for minorities and women.* Mimeograph. Institute for Urban Affairs and Research, Howard University, Washington, DC.

Shaw, B. (1988). Affirmative action: An ethical evaluation. *Journal of Business Ethics, 7,* 763-770.

Sher, G. (1975). Justifying reverse discrimination in employment. *Philosophy and Public Affairs, 4*, 159-170.

Sichel, J., Friedman, L., Quint, J., & Smith, M. (1978). *Women on patrol: A pilot study of police performance in New York City*. Washington, DC: National Institute of Law Enforcement and Criminal Justice.

Singer, M.S. (1990). Preferential selection and outcome justice: Effects of justification and merit discrepancy. *Social Justice Research, 4*, 285-305.

Singer, M.S. (1992). The application of relative deprivation theory to justice perception of preferential selection. *Current Psychology: Research and Reviews, 11*, 128-144.

Singer, M.S. (1993a). *Diversity-based hiring: An introduction from legal, ethical and psychological perspectives*: Aldershot: Avebury.

Singer, M.S. (1993b). The effect of information frame and informant gender on judgements of merit vs. gender-based employment selection. *International Journal of Selection and Assessment, 1(3)*, 143-152.

Singer, M.S. (1993c). Gender based preferential selection: Perceptions of injustice and empathy of deprivation. *International Journal of Selection and Assessment, 1(4)*, 184-202.

Singer, M.S. (1994). Mental framing by consequence thinking: Its effect on judgements of gender-based employment selection. *Journal of Economic Psychology, 15*, 149-172.

Singer, M.S. (1996). Merit, preferential or diversity based selection: Effect of information frame and informant gender on the public's views on preferential treatment in selection. *International Journal of Selection and Assessment, 4(1)*, 1-11.

Singer, M.S., & Lang, C. (1994). Preferential hiring: A managerial viewpoint. *Journal of Managerial Psychology, 9(1)*, 17-21.

Smith, E.R., & Kluegel, J.R. (1984). Beliefs and attitudes about women's opportunity: Comparisons with beliefs about Blacks and a general perspective. *Social Psychology Quarterly, 47*, 81-95.

Sniderman, P.M., & Hagen, M.G. (1985). *Race and inequality: A study in American values*. Chatham, NJ: Chatham House.

Sowell, T. (1978). Are quotas good for blacks? *Commentary, 65*, 39-43.

Sowell, T. (1990). *Preferential policies: An international perspective*. New York: William Murrow.

Steel, B.S., & Lovrich, N.P. (1987). Equality and efficiency tradeoffs on affirmative action—real or imagined? The case of women in policing. *Social Science Journal, 24*, 53-70.

Steele, S. (1990). *The content of our character*. New York: St. Martin's Press.

Steffy, B. D., & Ledvinka, J. (1989). The long-range impact of definitions of "fair" employee selection on black employment and employee productivity. *Organizational Behavior and Human Decision Process, 44*, 297-324.

Summers, R.J. (1991). The influence of Affirmative action on perceptions of a beneficiary's qualifications. *Journal of Applied Social Psychology, 21*, 1265-1276.

Taylor, P.W. (1973). Reverse discrimination and compensatory justice. *Analysis, 33*, 177-182.

Thomas, R.R. (1990). From affirmative action to affirming diversity. *Harvard Business Review*, (March-April), 107.

Thomson, J.J. (1973). Preferential hiring. *Philosophy and Public Affairs, 2*, 381.

Tickamyer, A., Scollay, S., Bokemeier, J., & Wood, T. (1989). Administrators' perceptions of affirmative action in higher education. In F.A. Blanchard & F.L. Crosby (Eds.), *Affirmative action in perspective.* (pp. 125-138). New York: Springer-Verlag.

Tougas, F., & Beaton, A.M. (1992). Women's views on affirmative action: A new look at preferential treatment. *Social Justice Research*, 5, 239-248.

Tougas, F., Beaton, A.M., & Veilleux, F. (1991). Why women approve of affirmative action: The study of a predictive model. *International Journal of Psychology, 26*, 761-776.

Tougas, F., Dube, L., & Veilleux, F. (1987). Privation relative et programmes d'action positive. *Revue Canadienne des Sciences du Comportement, 19*, 167-176.

Tougas, F.L., & Veilleux, F. (1988). The influence of identification, collective relative deprivation and procedure of implementation on women's responses to affirmative action: A causal modeling approach. *Canadian Journal of Behavioral Sciences, 20*, 16-29.

Tougas, F.L., & Veilleux, F. (1989). Who likes affirmative action. In F.A. Blanchard & F.L. Crosby (Eds.), *Affirmative action in perspective.* New York: Springer-Verlag.

Tsui, A.S., Egan, T.D., & O'Reilly, C.A. (1992). Being different: Relational demographic and organizational achievement. *Administrative Science Quarterly, 37*, 549-579.

Tversky, A., & Kahneman, D. (1981). The Framing of decisions and the psychology of choice. *Science, 211*, 453-458.

Tyler, T.R., & Bies, R.J. (1990). Beyond formal procedures: The interpersonal context of procedural justice. In J. Carroll (Ed.), *Applied social psychology in organizational settings* (pp. 77-98). Hillsdale, NJ: Erlbaum.

U.S. Department of Labor (1984). *Employment patterns of minorities in federal contractor and noncontractor establishments 1974-1980.* Washington, DC: Office of Federal Contract Compliance.

Veilleux, F., & Tougas, F.L. (1989). Male acceptance of affirmative action programs for women: The results of altruistic or egotistical motives. *International Journal of Psychology, 24*, 485-496.

Velasquez, M.G. (1982). *Business ethics: Concepts and cases.* Englewood Cliffs, N.J.: Prentice-Hall.

Vroom, V.H. (1964). *Work and motivation.* New York: Wiley.

Walker, S. (1983). Employment of Black and Hispanic police officers. *Academy of Criminal Justice,* (November), 1-10.

Warner, R.L., & Steele, B.S. (1989). Affirmative action in times of fiscal stress and changing value priorities: A case of women in policing. *Public Personnel Management Journal, 18,* 291-309.

Wigdor, A.K., & Hartigan, J.A. (1988). *Interim Report: Within-group scoring of the GATB.* Committee on the GATB, Commission on Behavioral and Social Sciences and Education, National Research Council, Washington, DC: National Academy Press.

Wilson, W.J. (1987). *The truly disadvantaged: The inner city, the underclass, and public policy.* Chicago: University of Chicago Press.

Witt, S.L. (1990). *The pursuit of race and gender equity in American academe.* New York: Praeger.

Woody, B. (1989). Black women in the emerging services economy. *Sex Roles, 21,* 45-67.

References for Chapter 7 and 8

Acklin, D., & King, J. (1995). Creating common ground: A lesson from the past. *Journal of Business Ethics, 14,* 1-16.

Bies, R.J. (1987). Beyond voice: The influence of decision-maker justification and sincerity on procedural fairness judgements. *Representative Research in Social Psychology, 17,* 3-14.

Bies, R.J., & Tyler, T.R. (1993). The 'litigation mentality' in organisations: A test of alternative psychological explanations. *Organisational Science, 4,* 352-366.

Bok, D. (1993). *The cost of talent.* New York: Free Press.

Carlson, D.S., & Perrew, P.L. (1995). *Journal of Business Ethics, 14,* 829-838.

Ciulla, J.B. (1995). Leadership ethics: Mapping the territory. *Business Ethics Quarterly, 5,* 5-28.

Cohen, R.L. (1989). Fabrications of justice. *Social Justice Research, 3,* 31-46.

Davis, J.R., & Welton, R.E. (1991). Professional ethic: Business students' perceptions. *Journal of Business Ethics, 10,* 451-463.

Dubinsky, A.J., & Levy, M. (1989). Influence of organisational fairness on work outcomes of retail salespeople. *Journal of Retailing, 65,* 221-252.

Dukerich, J.M., Nichols, M.L., Elm, D.R., & Vollrath, D.A. (1990). Moral reasoning in groups: Leaders make a difference. *Human Relations, 43,* 473-493.

Fairholm, G.W. (1991). *Values leadership: Towards a new philosophy of leadership.* New York: Praeger.

Gahl, L.L. (1984). "Moral courage: The essence of leadership". *Presidential Studies Quarterly, 14,* 43-52.

Goodpaster, K.E. (1991). Ethical imperatives and corporate leadership. In Freeman, R.D. (Ed.), *Business ethics* (pp. 89-110). New York: Oxford University Press.

Greenberg, J. (1986). Determinants of perceived fairness of performance evaluations. *Journal of Applied Psychology, 71,* 340-342.

Greenberg, J. (1993). Justice and organizational citizenship: A commentary on the state of the science. *Employee Responsibility and Rights Journal, 6,* 249-256.

Greenleaf, R.K. (1977). *Servant leadership.* New York: Paulist Press.

Heifitz, R. (1994). *A leadership without easy answers.* Cambridge, MA: Harvard University Press.

Hersey, P., & Blanchard, K. (1982). *Management of organizational behaviour* (4th ed.). Englewood Cliffs, NJ: Prentice Hall.

Hoffman, W.M., & Moore, J.M. (1984). *Business ethics: Readings and cases in corporate morality.* New York: McGraw-Hill.

Howell, J.M., & Avolio, B.J. (1992). The ethics of charismatic leadership: Submission of liberation? *Academy of Management Executives, 6,* 43-54.

Jeannot, T.M. (1989). Moral leadership and practical wisdom. *International Journal of Social Economics, 16,* 14-38.

Jones, H.B., Jr. (1995). The ethical leader: An ascetic construct. *Journal of Business Ethics, 14,* 867-874.

Karambayya, R., & Brett, J.M. (1989). Managers handling disputes: Third party roles and perceptions of fairness. *Academy of Management Journal, 32,* 687-704.

Kipnis, D. (1976). *The powerholders.* Chicago: University of Chicago Press.

Kouzes, J.M., & Posner, B.Z. (1993). *Credibility: How leaders gain and lose it and why people demand it.* San Francisco: Josey-Bass.

Leventhal, G.S. (1980). What should be done with equity theory? New approaches to the study of fairness in social relationships. In K.Gergen, M. Greenerg, & R.Willis (Eds.), *Social exchange: Advances in theory and research.* New York: Plenum.

Lind, E.A., & Tyler, T.R. (1988). *The social psychology of procedural justice.* New York: Plenum.

McCollough, T.E. (1991). *The moral imagination and public life.* New Jersey: Chatham House Publishers.

Moorman, R.H., Nichoff, B.P., & Oran, D.W. (1993). Treating employees fairly and organisational citizenship behaviour: Sorting the effects of job satisfaction, organisational commitment and procedural justice. *Employee Responsibility and Rights Journal, 6,* 209-225.

Osterberg, R. (1993). *Corporate renaissance.* Mill Valley, CA: Nataraj Publishing.

Reiley, J. (1994). Performance appraisal in the Police: An organisational justice perspective. Unpublished M.A. thesis, University of Canterbury.

Sashkin, M., & Williams, R.I. (1990). Does fairness make a difference? *Organisational Dynamics, 19,* 56-71.

Schein, E.H. (1990). Organisational culture. *American Psychologist, 45(2)*, 109-119.

Sheehy, G. (1990). *Character: America's search or leadership.* New York: Bantam Books.

Sheppard, B.H., & Lewicki, R.J. (1987). Towards general principles of managerial fairness. *Social Justice Research, 1*, 161-176.

Sinclair, N., (1988). Justice in leadership: An integration. Unpublished M.A. thesis, University of Canterbury.

Singer, M. (1990). Determinants of perceived fairness in selection practices: An organisational justice perspective. *Genetic, General and Social Psychology Monographs, 116*, 475-494.

Singer, M. (1992). Procedural justice in managerial selection: Identification of fairness determinants and consequences of fairness perceptions. *Social Justice Research, 5*, 47-69.

Singer, M. (1993). *Fairness in personnel selection: An organisational justice perspective.* Aldershot: Avebury.

Smith, D.C. (1995) (Ed.). Ethics and leadership: The 1990s. *Business Ethics Quarterly, 5* (Special Issue).

Solberg, J., Strong, K.C., & McGuire, C. Jr. (1995). Living (Not learning) ethics. *Journal of Business Ethics, 14*, 71-84.

Solomon, R. C. (1992). *Ethics and excellence: Cooperation and integrity in business.* Oxford: Oxford University Press.

Tansky, J.W. (1993). Justice and organizational citizenship behaviour: What is the relationship. *Employee Responsibility and Rights Journal, 6*, 195-207.

Index

Absolutism, 28, 31, 32
Accommodation v assimilation, 39
Adversary system, 52, 53
Affirmation of dignity, 118, 141
Affirmative action, 6, 72, 121-145
Applied ethics, 4, 5, 155
    (see Ethical decision making
        theories)
Burdens of society, 29-30
Business ethics, 5, 63-94
Care-based morality, 41-42, 117
Categorical Imperative, 3, 17-18,
    28, 102, 108
Classicism, 2, 9, 10, 11-14, 149, 153
    Plato, 3, 4, 11-13, 149, 153
    Aristotle, 3, 4, 13-14, 106-107,
        149, 150, 153
Common good, 4, 15, 27, 119
Compensatory justice, 25
Comte's positivism, 10, 22-23, 31, 33
Contractarianism, 3, 18-20, 21, 65
Corporate governance, 5, 72-73
Corporate responsibility, 68-69
Decision control, 52
Deontological theories, 3, 10,
    17-20, 28-30
    Kant, 3, 17-18, 28, 108
    Rawls, 3, 18-20, 29-30, 98,
        104-106
    Satre, 3, 20
Dirty hands, 70-71
Distributive Justice, 4, 24, 29-30
    44-51
    Contingency theory of

        distributive justice,
        4, 51
Distributive justice judgement
    theory, 4, 45
Equity theories, 4, 44-45
Justice motive theory, 4,
    45-46
Referent cognition theory, 4,
    47-49
Relative deprivation theory,
    4, 46-47, 138
Social categorisation theory of
    entitlement, 4, 49-50
Diversity-based selection, 123-126,
    127-131, 132-145
Duties, 3, 17-18, 21
Economic fairness, 68, 71, 75
Egalitarianism, 29
Egocentrism, 36
Emotivism, 3, 10, 22
Empirical theories of ethics, 3, 4
    (see Moral psychology)
Enabling v. disempowering, 153
Environmental or ecological
    restoration, 5, 72
Envy-free theory, 68
Ethical culture, climate, 79, 81-82, 153-
    154
Ethical decision making, 5, 61, 75-91
(see also Moral psychology)
    Analytic model of marketing
        decision making,
        89-90
    Contingency model, 5, 86-87

Index

Four component model, 5,
        77-78
Theory of marketing ethics,
        5, 87-88
Moral intensity model, 5,
        79-80, 110-114,
Multi-component model of
        institutionalising
        ethics, 5, 84-86
Person-situation interactionist
        model, 5, 78-79
Principle of responsive
        adjustment, 5, 77
Reasoned action model, 6
Situational model, 5, 75-76
Solomon's model, 80-83
Synthesis model, 5, 88-89
Nature-based business value
        theory, 5, 83-84
Ethics of personal conscience, 39
Ethics of social responsibility, 39
Ethos, 13
Evolutionary ethics, 4, 34, 60-61
Existentialism, 3, 20
Experimental pragmatism, 31, 42
Extraptation, 60
Fabrication of justice, 152
Fact v. value, 21, 32, 100, 101
Fair leadership, 149-152
Fair selection practice, 151
(see also merit-based selection)
Fairness, 2-3, 17-18, 110-114, 114-119,
        138-139
Feminist perspective
        on ethics, 58-60, 73
        on justice, 4, 58-60
Final Cause, 10, 14
Form, 13
Framing, 141
Free-market ideology, 4, 5, 64-66,
        67-68, 71
Free will, 12, 17-18
Game-ethics, 69-70
Grand narratives, 31, 59
Happiness, 13-14
Happiness calculus, 16
Harmony, 12,-13, 14, 17
Ideal state, 12
Ideal utilitarianism, 21
Ideas, 11-12, 13
Inclusive fitness, 60, 61

Individualism, 29
Inquisitorial system, 52, 53
Intentionality, 39
Interactional justice, 57-58, 118, 150
Intergroup justice, 58
Interpersonal morality, 43
Intuitionism, 3, 10, 20-22
Invisible hand, 65-66
Issues of debate in philosophy of
        ethics and justice, 32-34
Justice, 2, 12, 18-20, 24-30, 30-34
        Homer, 3, 26
        Plato, 4, 26-27
        Aristotle,4, 26-27
        Kant, 4, 28, 30, 104, 108
        Rawls, 4, 18-20, 29-30, 104-106
        (see Psychology of Justice)
Justification, 139
Language of morals, 23
Leader Match programme, 149
Leadership, 6, 147-154, 155
        good leadership skills,
                149-152, 155
        leader personal ethics,
                148-149, 152-154, 155
Libertarianism, 30, 58, 68, 98
Logical positivism, 3, 10, 22, 33
Maximin principle, 19, 104-106
Maxims, 18
Merits, 29, 67, 106, 107, 121
Merit-based selection, 120-127,
                127-131, 132, 139, 140, 144
Metaethics, 103
Modernity, 3, 10, 14-23, 27-30
        Deontology, 3, 17-20, 28-30
        Teleology, 3, 15-17, 27
        Intuitionism, 3, 20-22
        Logical Positivism, 3, 22-23
Moral balance, 42
Moral dissensus, 43, 90
Moral expertise, 91
Moral *Ideas*, 10, 11, 13, 149
Moral intensity, 5, 79-80, 110-114
Moral norms, 9, 31, 33
Moral psychology, 4, 35-43
        Taxonomic theories, 4, 36-38,
                100, 111
        Dialectical theories, 4, 38-39,
                111

Cognitive developmental
theories, 4, 39-42,
100, 111
Interactional theories, 4, 42-43,
111, 145
Moral sensitivity, 43, 64, 90, 145
Mutual influence model, 149
Native endowments, 104, 106
Natural law, 9-10, 14
Natural rights, 65
Naturalisitc fallacy, 20, 60, 100
Naturalisitc theories, 9-10, 20, 32
Nature-based values, 83-84
Neutrality, 59
Nicomachean Ethics, 14
Noncognitivism, 22, 100
Normative model of decision
making. 149
Normative theories of ethics, 3, 9-34, 101
Normative v. empirical approaches,
2, 95, 96-104
Normative-empirical dialogue,
2-3, 5, 95-96, 104-119, 122-123,
123-131, 132, 155-156
Original position, 19, 104, 118
Organisational justice, 2, 138-139
149-152
ought v. is, 21, 95, 100, 101
Pareto optimality, 67
Personal ethics, 4, 6, 36-37, 73-74,
81-82, 148-149, 152-154
Postmodern perspective, 4, 9, 11, 30-32,
34
on ethics, 4, 9, 30-32, 61
on justice, 4, 9, 30-32, 58-60
on ethical decision making, 5,
42-43, 90-91
Practice of "good" ethics, 5, 74, 117
Prescriptivism, 10, 23
Prima facie duties, 21-22
Principle of difference, 19, 104-106
Principle of equal liberty, 19
Principle of fair equality of
opportunity, 19
Prisoner' dilemma game, 60-61
Problem of scope, 100
Procedural justice theories, 4, 43-44,
52-57
Allocation preference theory,
4, 54
Group value model, 56-57

Informed self-interest model, 56
Theory of procedural justice,
4, 52-53
Process control, 52, 56
Profit-making, 14, 30, 72
Prudence, 3, 17
Psychology of Justice, 4, 43-57
Distributive theories, 4, 43, 44-
51
Procedural theories, 4, 43-44,
52-57
Public v. private ethics, 70
Punishment, 24-25, 28, 107
Rational Benevolence, 3, 17
Rational interaction, 43, 64, 90-91, 145
Rationality, 33-34, 58
Reason, 10, 12, 13, 28, 33-34
Recruiting, selection, 121-145
Relational justice, 4, 58
Relationship between moral standards
between teleology and
deontology, 102
between ethics and justice,
5, 9, 33, 110-114,
149
between Judgement of ethicality
and fairness, 5-6, 110-
114
between utility, rights and
justice, 109, 115-119,
143-144, 155-156
Relativism, 11, 32, 33, 36
Retributive justice, 24-25
Reversibility, 18, 41
Rights, 3, 16, 17-18, 30, 118-119,
143-145
Self-interest, 15, 17, 34, 38, 56-65
81, 107, 119
Senses, 11, 13
Situational ethics, 75-76
Social community, 11, 12-13, 13-14, 15,
18-19, 73, 82-83
Social consensus, 79-80, 110-111,
113-114
Social contract, 15, 27, 40
Social v. business goals, 71-73
Social Darwinism, 60-61, 66
Social dialogue, 4, 42-43
Socialism, 29-30
Subjectivistic, 32-33, 36
Superfairness theory, 68

Index

Supererogatory acts, 5, 74, 117
Symbiotic approach, 2, 103
Teleological theories, 3, 10, 15-16,
         27
         Egoism,3, 15, 27
         Act-utilitarianism, 3, 15-16, 27
         Rule-utilitarianism, 3, 15-16, 27
         Dualism, 3, 17
Telos, 14, 15
the *Republic*,, 11-13
Theoretical integration, 103-104
to *live*, v. to *learn*, ethics, 2, 74, 154
Transformational leadership, 149, 152
Universalisability, 18, 33, 41
Utility analysis, 132-134
Veil of ignorance, 19, 101
Vertical-dyad model, 149
Virtue ethics, 5, 31, 73, 80-83, 148
Virtues, 1, 2, 3, 13-14, 34, 73, 80, 81,
         148-149, 153
Voice, 152